PRESERVING LINKS IN THE PANDEMIC

Policies to Maintain Worker-Firm Attachment in the OECD

Essays by

Roel Beetsma ▪ Jeff Borland ▪ Russell Cooper
Miles Corak ▪ Jonathan Cribb ▪ Raymond Gradus
Jennifer Hunt ▪ Xavier Jaravel ▪ Juan F. Jimeno
Paul Johnson ▪ Tom Krebs ▪ Ricardo Reis
Ian M. Schmutte ▪ Immo Schott
Michael R. Strain ▪ Stan Veuger

Edited by

Michael R. Strain and Stan Veuger

AEI

AMERICAN ENTERPRISE INSTITUTE

Distributed by arrangement with the Rowman & Littlefield Publishing Group, 4501 Forbes Boulevard, Suite 200, Lanham, Maryland 20706. To order, call toll-free 1-800-462-6420 or 1-717-794-3800. For all other inquiries, please contact AEI Press, 1789 Massachusetts Avenue, NW, Washington, DC 20036, or call 1-202-862-5800.

ISNB-13: 978-0-8447-5048-4 Hardback
ISNB-13: 978-0-8447-5049-1 Paperback
ISNB-13: 978-0-8447-5050-7 eBook

American Enterprise Institute
1789 Massachusetts Avenue, NW
Washington, DC 20036
www.aei.org

Contents

Introduction: Preserving Employer-Employee Links in the COVID-19 Era 1
Michael R. Strain and Stan Veuger

1. The Value of Job Matches 9
Ian M. Schmutte

2. Did the Australian JobKeeper Program Save Jobs by Subsidizing Temporary Layoffs? 32
Jeff Borland and Jennifer Hunt

3. The Canada Emergency Wage Subsidy as an Employer-Based Response to the Pandemic: First Steps, Missteps, and Next Steps 66
Miles Corak

4. Whatever It Takes: Subsidizing Short-Time Work During the COVID-19 Pandemic in France 90
Xavier Jaravel

5. German Labor Market Policy During and After the COVID-19 Recession 115
Tom Krebs

6. COVID-19: The Italian Job 136
Russell Cooper and Immo Schott

7. The Dutch Experience with Job-Preserving Policy During the Coronavirus Pandemic 174
Roel Beetsma and Raymond Gradus

8. **Labor Hoarding and Employment Protection During the COVID-19 Crisis in a Dual Labor Market: Spain** 198
Juan F. Jimeno

9. **Policies to Preserve Worker-Firm Links During the Pandemic: Lessons from the UK's Coronavirus Job Retention Scheme** 224
Jonathan Cribb and Paul Johnson

10. **How Was the US Government Able to Borrow So Much During the COVID-19 Pandemic?** 246
Ricardo Reis

About the Authors 264

Introduction: Preserving Employer-Employee Links in the COVID-19 Era

MICHAEL R. STRAIN AND STAN VEUGER

In a typical recession, there are economic benefits to business closure. While often disruptive and damaging to owners and employees, closure allows for a reallocation of labor and capital resources away from firms that can't generate profits during the new economic environment. This process ultimately benefits the overall economy, including workers overall.

The economic crisis triggered by the COVID-19 pandemic was different than a typical recession. Governments had intentionally restricted activity in significant parts of the economy to reduce the in-person interactions that might spread the virus. As a consequence, businesses that were productive and profitable in February 2020 were in grave danger of bankruptcy just weeks later, in March 2020.

The threat of business closure, then, did not reflect an inability of at-risk firms to compete in the market or survive a period of depressed aggregate demand. Instead, the threat came from forced reductions in business activity of unknown duration and severe intensity.

This unique circumstance created the possibility of liquidations. For many businesses, the "black box" of production—consisting of organizational knowledge, robust customer and supplier networks, and, importantly, worker-firm links and the firm-specific human capital held by workers—was at risk of being shattered. These liquidations would have been wasteful because they did not result from market forces or factors. This logic was especially compelling in the spring of 2020, when the lockdowns were expected to be relatively short.

Recognizing this, governments in advanced economies provided various types of support to aid business continuity and preserve worker-firm links.

These programs were often expensive, and some had complex rules. Even seemingly secondary aspects of the design of these programs involved allocating significant amounts of resources and could affect economic outcomes for years to come.

In this volume, we present preliminary evidence on the efficacy and efficiency of a number of these design choices. We do so through a comparative lens, by studying the different decisions reached by policymakers in eight Organisation for Economic Co-operation and Development (OECD) member states: Australia, Canada, France, Germany, Italy, Spain, the Netherlands, and the United Kingdom.[1]

While policymakers in these countries faced similar trade-offs—between preserving existing ties between firms and workers and facilitating the process of creative destruction that is so central to a dynamic economy and between providing social insurance and incentivizing innovation and adjustment—they responded to them in different ways.

In the first chapter of the volume, Ian M. Schmutte of the University of Georgia sets the stage by addressing fundamental questions: When are employer-employee matches valuable? Under which conditions are they worth preserving, and when are they not? After outlining the conceptual considerations at play, Schmutte outlines a number of significant challenges associated with measuring the value of matches empirically.

He then turns to an overview of the evidence economists have started to collect. Perhaps the most easily measured component of match value is the value of a match to employees: Sudden firm death or downscaling generates quasi-experimental variation that researchers can exploit. Similar efforts are now underway from the firm's perspective, but it remains difficult to map the value of continuity for an individual firm or worker to society as a whole.

The latter is crucial if we want to evaluate policies that preserve matches, as preserved matches typically come at the expense of reduced reallocation of workers, jobs, and capital across occupations, firms, and industries. The significant general-equilibrium effects involved are precisely why the comparative lens applied in the later chapters is an essential complement to the microeconomic evidence typically adduced by labor economists.

Existing assessments of the two main labor market programs in the United States illustrate the limitations of microeconomic evidence. Take research by David Autor et al. and R. Glenn Hubbard and Michael R. Strain, for example, three papers that analyze aspects of the Paycheck Protection Program (PPP).[2] They analyze in detail the effects of funds spent on the PPP on important outcomes and its role in preserving employment at firms that were at the margin of eligibility for PPP funds. While this evidence is valuable, it is entirely unclear what it tells us about a counterfactual world where the US implemented a wage-subsidy scheme, as did Australia and Canada, or relied much more heavily on short-time work, as France and Germany did. Or consider research from Harry J. Holzer, Hubbard, and Strain, who study the employment effects of the early expirations of additional pandemic-era unemployment benefits in certain states.[3] How does one compare those additional benefits to the kind of restrictions on layoffs implemented by Italy or Spain?

Comparing how different countries fared is a first step toward understanding the pros and cons of such large policy differences, differences that are difficult to observe in one country, even one as large and decentralized as the United States.

This volume seeks to provide precisely this. In this way, the chapters in this volume—and the volume as a whole—will help economists understand better the microeconomic evaluations of country-specific programs by placing them in a comparative context. It will also allow policymakers to understand various options should a situation similar to the spring of 2020 arise again.

Summary of Country-Specific Chapters

Jeff Borland of the University of Melbourne and Jennifer Hunt of Rutgers University study Australia's JobKeeper program. This program, which was rolled out in response to the pandemic, provided a wage subsidy to employers with significant revenue losses. As we will see in other cases, a key idea behind the wage subsidy was to make it attractive for both workers and firms to preserve employment ties instead of relying on unemployment benefits. Borland and Hunt argue that while the program preserved employment ties early in the pandemic, it did not help the recovery much: Firms relied more on new hires than on reactivating incumbent workers.

Miles Corak of the City University of New York's Graduate Center also studies a wage-subsidy program, the Canada Emergency Wage Subsidy. His assessment is perhaps even more negative: He highlights policymakers' triple failure "to (1) address the factors that influence a firm's decision to shut down, (2) recognize that the legal incidence of a subsidy is not necessarily its economic incidence, and (3) target policy at the margin." And yet, he is ultimately not sure whether better alternatives were feasible at the time: As in the American case, program design was severely hampered by the feasibility of program delivery.

France used a different type of labor market policy. The London School of Economics and Political Science's Xavier Jaravel analyzes the short-time work scheme introduced in France in response to the pandemic. He draws a clear distinction between micro- and macroeconomic effects of the program. At the micro level, he claims, the key trade-off is between reaching firms and individuals in need versus inefficiently supporting "zombie firms" and matches that are not valuable. On the macro level, he argues that the program raised consumer confidence while reducing uncertainty for businesses. While that helped produce a swift recovery, it produced a perhaps overly tight labor market and created a risk of large numbers of delayed bankruptcies.

While France's short-time work program was a central component of its crisis response, Germany is probably the country most closely associated with this kind of policy. Tom Krebs of the University of Mannheim studies Germany's use of this policy in response to the COVID-19 crisis as it unfolded there. He comes to three main findings. First, the short-time work program prevented a large increase in unemployment. Second, he argues that the program probably did not slow the pace of recovery by reducing hours per employee. And third, he is optimistic that the program—by not disrupting the process of worker reallocation too much while preserving (firm-specific) human capital—set the stage for faster postcrisis productivity growth than we would have witnessed otherwise.

The chapter on Italy, by Russell Cooper of the European University Institute and Immo Schott of the University of Montreal, analyzes a short-time work scheme as well, but one that was introduced in conjunction with firing restrictions. This drastic measure was in place throughout most of the second quarter of 2020 and remained in place in select industries afterward. The authors find that the restrictions on firing were particularly crucial in explaining developments in the Italian labor market. While employment was reduced during the first two quarters of 2020—due to job losses among the self-employed and temp workers—the unemployment rate actually went down. But it is not all good news: Based on simulation, Cooper and Schott argue that the Italian government's intervention had a detrimental impact on productivity by making it difficult for the most productive firms to find workers.

Juan F. Jimeno of the Bank of Spain analyzes a program similar in spirit to the short-time work programs we have seen so far. Unlike some short-time work programs, the Spanish job-retention scheme allowed for temporary layoffs and, during the crisis, incorporated financial incentives for employers to reactivate workers.

To provide the reader with context, Jimeno emphasizes that the Spanish labor market has a dual structure: Three-quarters of workers have permanent contracts with high levels of employment protection, while the rest are employed on a temporary basis. Unsurprisingly, the overwhelming majority of new hires (and layoffs) during a given period fall into the latter category. While Jimeno believes it is too early for a comprehensive assessment, he expresses concern that a generously funded job-retention scheme in this context would mostly protect relatively low-value matches. An ominous sign on that front is the limited training that appears to have taken place for workers on reduced or zero hours.

The labor market policy response in the United Kingdom emphasized temporary layoffs, or furloughs, even more strongly. As Jonathan Cribb and Paul Johnson of the Institute for Fiscal Studies explain in their contribution, at its peak the furlough scheme supported the incomes of 30 percent of UK employees. While the furlough program allowed for short-time work after the initial COVID-19 wave, it was overwhelmingly used for full-fledged temporary layoffs. As in the other countries studied, the unemployment rate did not escalate—certainly not to the extent one might expect based on the reduction in economic activity. Based on that fact, the relatively high reactivation rate of furloughed workers, and the income smoothing facilitated by the program, Cribb and Johnson deliver a positive assessment of the furlough scheme.

The final country chapter in the volume, by Roel Beetsma of the University of Amsterdam and Raymond Gradus of Vrije Universiteit Amsterdam, provides an overview of the COVID-19 economic policy response in the Netherlands. More than previous chapters, it emphasizes the consequences policymaking during the crisis will have for the future. The authors highlight three challenges in particular. First, the crisis response significantly increased the government's role in the economy, including through outright equity stakes in some industries. Second, as hinted at in a number of previous chapters, processes of dynamic reallocation were disrupted by some of the measures taken. And finally, the dramatic scale of the interventions has exacerbated existing budgetary challenges by contributing to debt levels and creating expectations of future largesse.

The latter challenge is the central concern of the volume's concluding chapter, by Ricardo Reis of the London School of Economics and Political Science. He takes us back to the United States for a detailed look at the implications of the crisis for fiscal sustainability. He provides a brief sketch of the past few decades of increasing public debt in the United States and other advanced economics before analyzing why the federal government accumulated and was capable of accumulating so much additional debt during the pandemic response. Reis concludes his chapter and the book with a sobering look at the limits on continued accumulation of debt by the US federal government.

Conclusion

Were these programs successful? Even in a microeconomic sense, that question is hard to answer because policymakers were often "building the car while driving it"—adapting and modifying the program as the pandemic and associated social-distancing restrictions changed. In many cases, programs that were designed to offer a bridge of a few months ended up lasting many times that length.

These programs also had more goals than is typically the case. Determining eligibility was difficult in the fog-of-war atmosphere of the spring of 2020. And, unusually, these programs were racing against the clock, attempting to get money to recipients rapidly. Hubbard and Strain make this argument with respect to the PPP:

> PPP is a novel program, and many standard intuitions about fiscal policy do not apply to it. It was not a stimulus program in the sense that its purpose was not to stimulate the economy; that is, it is not a program calling for a measure of the multiplier. Instead, its purpose was to preserve the productive capacity of the small business sector and to shorten the transition to a new, post-pandemic equilibrium by supporting labor demand over the medium term, allowing for a more rapid economic recovery. It was not a jobs program in the sense that its goal was not exclusively to preserve employment. Instead, its goals were to maintain worker-firm attachments, particularly during the shutdown, and to ensure small business continuity. It intentionally did not attempt to exclude inframarginal recipients because the unique circumstances under which it was enacted made this impractical. In the early days of the shutdown, how could the government have known which firms were inframarginal? And given the numerous goals of the program, it's not clear how *marginal* would be defined in this context.[4]

Were these programs successful? The various authors in this volume have different perspectives on this answer. We hope that reading their chapters—and taking the volume as a whole—will inform your answer to this question.

Notes

1. For evaluations of the United States' Paycheck Protection Program, see David Autor et al., "An Evaluation of the Paycheck Protection Program Using Administrative Payroll Microdata" (working paper, National Bureau of Economic Research, Cambridge, MA, April 2022), https://www.nber.org/papers/w29972; David Autor et al., "The $800 Billion Paycheck Protection Program: Where Did the Money Go and Why Did It Go There?" (working paper, National Bureau of Economic Research, Cambridge,

MA, January 2022), https://www.nber.org/papers/w29669; and R. Glenn Hubbard and Michael R. Strain, "Has the Paycheck Protection Program Succeeded?," Brookings Institution, September 23, 2020, https://www.brookings.edu/bpea-articles/has-the-paycheck-protection-program-succeeded.

2. Autor et al., "An Evaluation of the Paycheck Protection Program Using Administrative Payroll Microdata"; Autor et al., "The $800 Billion Paycheck Protection Program"; and Hubbard and Strain, "Has the Paycheck Protection Program Succeeded?"

3. Harry J. Holzer, R. Glenn Hubbard, and Michael R. Strain, "Did Pandemic Unemployment Benefits Reduce Employment? Evidence from Early State-Level Expirations in June 2021" (working paper, National Bureau of Economic Research, Cambridge, MA, December 2021), https://www.nber.org/papers/w29575.

4. Hubbard and Strain, "Has the Paycheck Protection Program Succeeded?," 336–37.

1

The Value of Job Matches

IAN M. SCHMUTTE

The coronavirus pandemic hit the global economy like a natural disaster, disrupting lives and livelihoods and causing widespread damage. Unlike most natural disasters, the damage to the economy was not primarily through the destruction of physical capital. Rather, the pandemic simply severed what had been productive economic relationships. People either could not or would not continue patronizing certain types of businesses, and workers could not or would not perform certain types of jobs. Unlike in other recessions, which are triggered by changes in economic fundamentals or macroeconomic policy, in the absence of the pandemic, all the relationships that were cut off by the public health crisis were still valuable. Had the pandemic been short enough and all those economic relationships frozen in place, the economy might have been able to pick up where it left off in March 2020.

These observations motivate a broader question about the value inherent in specific employer-employee relationships. Finding the right person for any job can be hard. Even in jobs that do not require specialized skills that are hard to acquire, employers need to find workers who are reliable and can fit in with an organization's working culture. It is costly to find such workers and replace them if they depart.

Moreover, the longer a job lasts, the more a worker learns about the operations of a particular firm, and the more the employer learns about the worker's capabilities. All these factors can give a match value in excess of the other opportunities available to the worker in a new job or the employer with a new hire. At any point in time, all the job matches in the economy have some amount of this relationship-specific value embedded in them.

In this chapter, I make three arguments about the value in job matches. First, there is evidence of a substantial amount of match-specific value in many of the jobs in the US labor market. Second, match value is not limited to occupations with specialized skills or employers with high average productivity. Finally, in recessions, active labor market policies should balance the benefits of preserving the value in job matches against the costs of preventing labor from reallocating to higher-valued uses. For the purposes of developing and implementing such policies, there is insufficient empirical evidence on the value of job matches. Therefore, at the end of the chapter, I consider future directions for research.

Economists describe the value of job matches in general terms, often referring to match-specific "rents" or "surplus." The core idea is to conceive of the excess value that each party to the match—in this case, a worker and their employer—gets relative to their next-best option. For workers, their next-best option is usually another job, though it could also be pursuing an education, retiring, or engaging in childcare or eldercare. For workers, the value in a job match need not be entirely in earnings or pecuniary benefits. From a worker's perspective, a match can have high value because they find it satisfying or enjoy the conditions of work. For the employer, their next-best option is generally to find another employee to perform the job.

It should be clear from these descriptions that match value is impossible to measure in almost all circumstances. It depends on inherently unknowable information about the options that workers and firms are not taking. Even in the rare cases in which we can directly measure the value of output attributable to a specific worker in a specific job, we cannot measure the full set of other opportunities available. Direct measurement of match value thus depends on good data and strong assumptions about how output is produced and the value of outside options. In this chapter, I focus on indirect evidence that points to the existence of match-specific value without measuring it directly.

The concept of job-match value that I consider in this chapter should not be confused with the related, but distinct, concept of the value of a job. A firm's decisions about whether to hire or retain a particular worker in a given job are different from its decisions about whether to create a new position or destroy an existing position. As the structure of the economy changes, some firms grow and others contract in a process of job reallocation. Even without job reallocation, we can still see worker reallocation as workers and employers try to find the best matches across a fixed set of jobs.

Policies that attempt to preserve worker-employer matches by stifling worker reallocation may also obstruct potentially beneficial job reallocation. This became a concern in the pandemic-induced recession as, over time, the demand for labor shifted away from in-person services and toward "essential jobs." By preserving job matches in anticipation of a "post-pandemic" economy that looks essentially like the pre-pandemic economy, might we hinder the real structural changes the pandemic has wrought? While answering such a question is beyond the scope of this chapter, the question makes clear the motivation for focusing on understanding the nature of job matches and their value.

Defining the Value of a Job Match

The main question of this chapter can be framed as a simple thought experiment: If a job is destroyed today, but nothing else changed, how much total value is lost? This sort of thing happens all the time. At any time, a perfectly productive worker might suddenly announce that they must resign because their spouse has found a new job in a different part of the country. Even more dramatically, a firm might be hit with the unexpected death of an extremely good employee.[1]

We want to understand how costly these events are in general and the circumstances under which the costs are low or high.

To begin with an obvious but important point, the value of a job match is directly related to the next best option—that is, how difficult it is to replace. Clearly, if the departing worker has an exact clone endowed with exactly the same skills and experience, and that person is immediately available to hire, then the departure was costless, and there was no excess value in the match. The value in job matches thus arises from characteristics that make the relationship unique and hard to replace.

An immediate consequence is that there are, broadly speaking, two kinds of surplus in a match: productive surplus and unproductive surplus.[2] A worker and employer might be particularly productive when matched together so that even in the presence of many other potential workers and job opportunities, they are most productive where they are. Alternatively, job-match value can arise simply because one side or the other has limited outside options. For example, if a firm can costlessly replace a worker with no loss of productivity but workers have no other employment opportunities, then job match carries surplus arising entirely from the worker's lack of outside options.[3]

Match value arising from especially productive relationships seems clearly good, while match value arising from limited options seems bad. Changes that could facilitate productive surplus while reducing unproductive surplus would be desirable. Be that as it may, whether match surplus is productive or unproductive, if the match is exogenously destroyed, at least one of the parties to the match will be worse off.

Surplus Value and Efficient Job Destruction. Some basic notation may help formalize these ideas. The economy comprises a set of firms that offer jobs, j, to a pool of workers, i. I refer to the outside option for jobs as 0 and the outside option for workers as b. Denote the expected net revenue received by a firm from job j when matched with worker i by $V(j, i)$.

Similarly, $V(j, 0)$ denotes the expected net revenue when the job is matched with its next-best option. The value of the match for the firm is then defined as

$$V_{ij} = V(j, i) - V(j, 0).$$

Similarly, if $U_i(j)$ represents the worker's expected utility from the match with job j and $U_i(b)$ the expected utility from their next-best option, then the value for the worker is defined as

$$U_{ij} = U_i(j) - U_i(0).$$

The total surplus, or value, from the match is the sum of the firm's and the worker's valuations:

$$S_{ij} = V_{ij} + U_{ij}$$

It is economically efficient to preserve matches whenever $S_{ij} > 0$.[4] Clearly, the worker will walk away from the match if $U_i(j) < U_i(0)$, and the firm will walk away if $V(j, i) < V(j, 0)$. When the surplus is positive, the parties can strike a deal that makes both of them better off by splitting the surplus according to some formula. If λ is the worker's share of the surplus, they receive a payment $W = \lambda S_{ij}$, and the firm receives $(1 - \lambda)S_{ij}$.

It is easy to verify that splitting the surplus will make both the worker and the firm better off. Under this framework, separations happen when one of the parties becomes unhappy with the match. If the surplus turns negative, then there is no way that the match can continue, and it will end. Such a separation is efficient in the sense that it is better to allocate the worker and the job to alternative uses.[5]

There are many realistic contexts in which inefficient separations can occur. The main case of interest is one in which the outside option for one party or the other has changed. For example, a worker may learn about a new employment opportunity paying a higher wage, or a firm may suddenly experience a decrease in the demand for its output. Either will shrink the available surplus but need not turn it negative. In the case of a worker getting a better outside wage offer, as long as the firm has sufficient surplus in the match, the parties can, in principle, renegotiate to pay the worker a higher wage.

In reality, such precise renegotiation may be difficult. If the firm does not react to an outside wage offer, the worker will leave, even though both parties could still be better off in the match. This is what it means to say that a job separation is inefficient.

Establishing whether the destruction of a particular job is inefficient is hard to establish empirically. It requires knowing the outside options for both parties and the value they derive from the match. There is some evidence that inefficient separations are not unusual. Pierre Cahuc, Fabien Postel-Vinay, and Jean-Marc Robin developed and estimated a model in which job matches have different values that depend on the worker's skill and the productive characteristics of the firm.[6] Using data from France, they find evidence that the competition between firms—and resulting renegotiations—are highly significant in determining wages and the duration of employment relationships.

In a recent paper, Simon Jäger, Benjamin Schoefer, and Josef Zweimüller show evidence that Austrian firms do not seem to select low surplus matches when choosing which employment relationships to terminate.[7] A key distinction is the presence of strong wage rigidities in the particular sector in the Austrian study. While these findings apply to specific situations and countries outside the United States, they indicate that match surplus is important to firms and that inefficient separations may not be unusual.

From a policy perspective, we can reason about this framework in light of the COVID-19 shock.

Early on it seemed plausible that a full shutdown could halt the pandemic. If it had, the economic fundamentals before and after the shutdown presumably would have been more or less the same.

On that view, COVID-19 was a temporary shock to the firm's revenue from the match. Under the model, any match that was in progress just before the shutdown had positive surplus and would have positive surplus after the shutdown. Policy designed to preserve matches through the shutdowns would clearly make sense (subject to distortions introduced by the needed taxes and transfers). Short-time work—in which firms are subsidized to keep workers on payroll with reduced hours—is one such policy that was expanded aggressively throughout Europe.

In a study of short-time work, Pierre Cahuc, Francis Kramarz, and Sandra Nevoux point out that without verifiable claims, short-time work may not be well targeted and will distort the total hours each employee works. Putting these significant details of implementation to the side, policies to help firms keep workers on board are sensible in the face of a temporary demand shortfall that is not tied to any change in the fundamental structure of the economy, like a natural disaster. José María Barrero, Nicholas Bloom, and Steven J. Davis rightly argue that the COVID-19 shock did ultimately change the structure of the economy in ways that require the reallocation of workers across different sectors of the economy.[8] In particular, once COVID-19 started spreading out of control, keeping workers tied to their employers would have affected the reallocation of workers into the health care sector or into shipping, where they were suddenly in high demand.

I return to the trade-off between preserving job matches and facilitating worker reallocation later. First, I want to explore the factors that contribute to the value of job matches.

What Makes a Job Match Valuable? Clearly many factors can contribute to making an employment relationship special and difficult to replace. There is no match-specific value in the simple textbook model of a frictionless labor market that matches firms with identical and interchangeable workers. Once we move away from that model, employment relationships become miniature monopolies in which each party has something to lose from exit.

Studies by Henry S. Farber[9] and Paul Oyer and Scott Schaefer[10] enumerate several sources of match value. Employers may need workers to invest in job-specific skills that have no value in the external market. Once an employee has acquired those skills, it is costly to the firm for them to leave, as it would require them to hire and train a replacement. More generally, some jobs require a particular combination of skills. Recruiting and screening to find someone with those skills takes time and money. Thus, once a firm has found the right worker, there is surplus in the match simply because the firm's only outside option involves repeating a difficult screening process.

Alternatively, it may be difficult for firms to determine whether workers are a good match for the job. They need to see them in action for a while, through a probationary period, before deciding whether to retain them long-term. This notion is formalized in Boyan Jovanovic's classic model, which establishes the existence of an informational rent that accrues as a firm and worker become more certain about the quality of the match between them.

Evidence on the Value of Employer-Employee Matches

Many different kinds of evidence support the claim that most employment relationships embed match-specific capital. As noted in the introduction, match surplus is generally impossible to measure, so researchers have found other ways to infer the presence and, in some cases, relative magnitudes of match value. I review updated descriptive statistics on job tenure and job mobility that suggest not only that match is value substantial but also that it is not restricted to highly educated skilled workers and jobs. I also review evidence from the US and other countries on hiring, job displacement, and rent sharing that paint a similar picture.

Job Tenure and Employment Flows. Under our simple conceptual framework, if a job match remains intact, it must be providing match value for both the firm and the worker. As Farber argues,[11] the existence of

Figure 1. The Share of Workers Between Age 35 and 65 with Job Tenure Above 10 Years

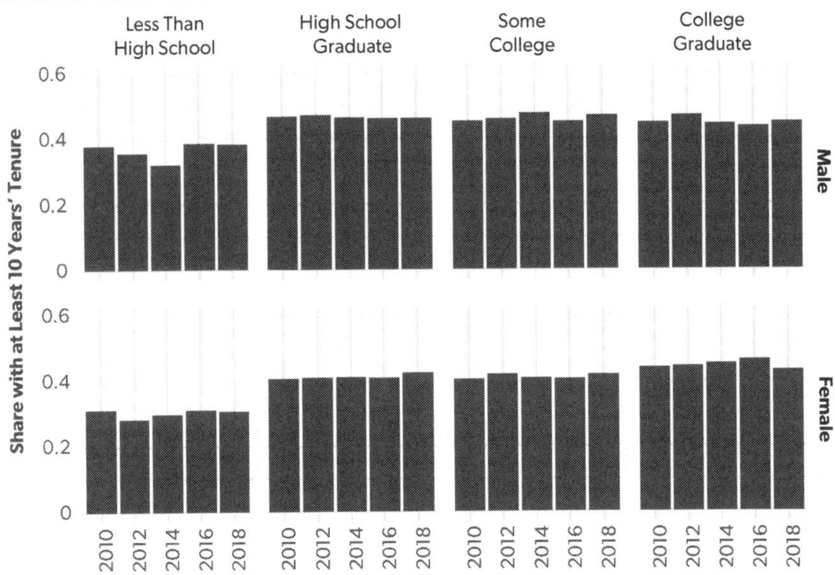

Source: See US Census Bureau, "Supplemental Surveys," October 8, 2021, https://www.census.gov/programs-surveys/cps/about/supplemental-surveys.html.

match surplus predicts the existence of jobs with long tenure. Figures 1 and 2 show the share of workers with job tenure above 10 years and 20 years, respectively. The data are for individuals between age 35 and 65 included in the Current Population Survey Job Tenure Supplement.[12] I plot the share of workers with high tenure separately by education and gender in 2010, 2012, 2014, 2016, and 2018—the years in which the supplement was administered.

Notwithstanding popular views that job security has declined in the 21st century, the data show rates of long-tenure jobs comparable to those reported by Farber. Around 40 percent of male workers have job tenure over 10 years, and just under 20 percent have tenure greater than 20 years. The share of long-tenure jobs is only slightly lower for female workers.

Perhaps more surprisingly, long tenure is equally likely for workers with only a high school diploma and those with a college degree. Workers with

Figure 2. The Share of Workers Between Age 35 and 65 with Job Tenure Above 20 Years

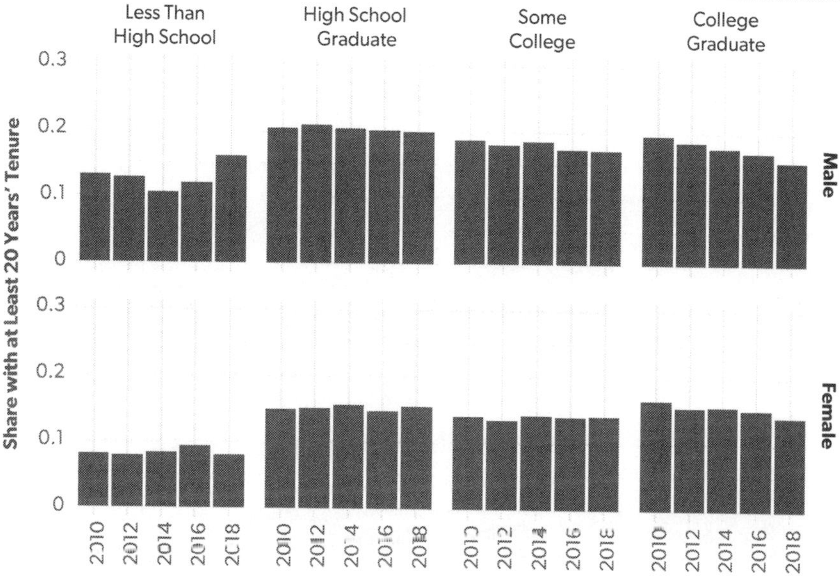

Source: See US Census Bureau, "Supplemental Surveys," October 8, 2021, https://www.census.gov/programs-surveys/cps/about/supplemental-surveys.html.

less than a high school education have a notably lower share of long-tenure jobs. But, focusing on males, I still find that nearly 40 percent of such workers are in jobs with more than 10 years of tenure, and over 10 percent are in jobs with more than 20 years of tenure. The patterns are similar for female workers. Finally, these shares are quite stable over time, with some evidence of decline in jobs with more than 20 years' tenure for college graduates.

While the presence of long-tenure jobs suggests that workers and employers prefer to keep their existing relationships, it leaves open the question of how those relationships form in the first place. Many jobs have long tenure, but at the same time, most new jobs end early.[13] This is not because the jobs themselves become economically unviable (job destruction) but because workers turn over and their labor must be replaced. Studies have recognized this churning of workers through jobs as evidence

Figure 3. Excess Churn Measures the Difference Between Hires and Separations Net of Total Job Growth (Education)

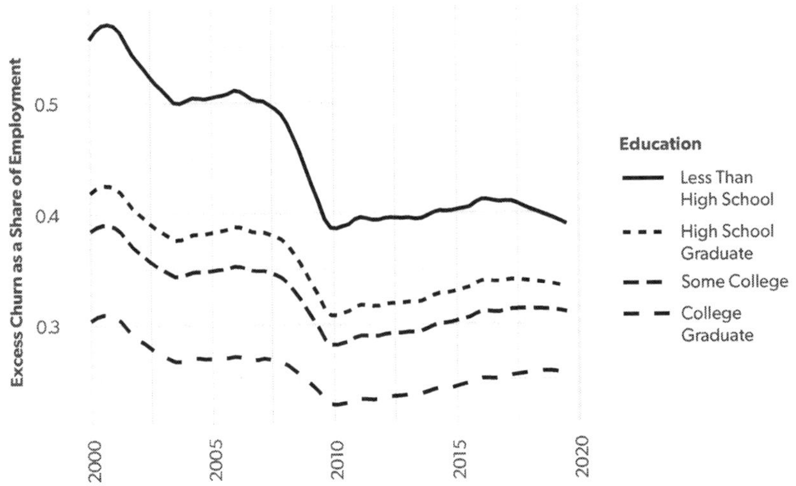

Note: The raw data exhibit strong seasonality, and the plot is smoothed to emphasize trend changes.
Source: See US Census Bureau, "Data—Longitudinal Employer-Household Dynamics," https://lehd.ces.census.gov/data/#qwi.

of—and instrumental to—the process by which workers and firms find better matches.[14]

Figure 3 provides evidence on the extent of match-improving worker reallocation in the US economy, using data from the National Quarterly Workforce Indicators. Specifically, it plots excess churn, which is derived from the accounting identity:[15]

$$\textit{Hires} + \textit{Separations} = \textit{Job Creation} + \textit{Job Destruction} - 2 \times \textit{Churn}$$

Intuitively, excess churn measures the movements of workers into alternative employment relationships above and beyond the number that would be required to account for the creation of new jobs and the destruction of old jobs. Education categories are reported in Quarterly Workforce Indicators only for workers age 25 or older, limiting the cases for which completed educational attainment does not measure total educational attainment.[16]

Several features stand out: First, levels of churn are generally high. The lowest churn rate in the graph, just about 0.10, implies that even

Figure 4. Excess Churn Measures the Difference Between Hires and Separations Net of Total Job Growth (Age)

Note: The raw data exhibit strong seasonality, and the plot is smoothed to emphasize trend changes.
Source: See US Census Bureau, "Data—Longitudinal Employer-Household Dynamics," https://lehd.ces.census.gov/data/#qwi.

in the depths of the Great Recession, around 10 percent of jobs held by college-age workers turned over. Second, rates of churn are decreasing in educational attainment of the workforce. Finally, as noted elsewhere,[17] there has been a steady decline in churn triggered during recessions, resulting in a "stairstep" pattern in which churn falls during recessions and then remains stable at a new lower level.

Figure 4 plots excess churn by age group. Churn is declining with age. While we see the same stairstep pattern of declining churn with each recession, for younger workers, churn actually recovers considerably after recessions. These facts are not entirely conclusive regarding the production of valuable matches, but they are certainly consistent with a model in which workers experience different jobs while younger and gravitate over time toward matches that are more valuable.

Finally, the high rates of churn for all workers but especially for younger and less-educated workers implies that, on one hand, many such workers find themselves in matches that are revealed to have low value. On

Figure 5. Transitions to Persistent Nonemployment

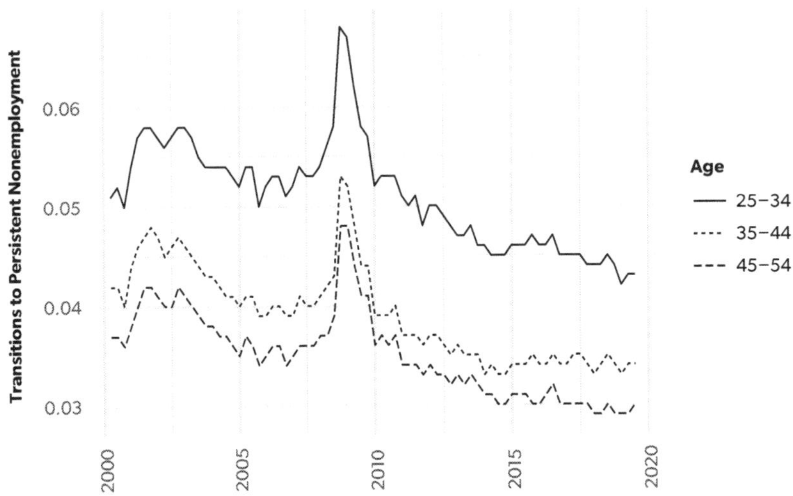

Source: US Census Bureau, "Data—Longitudinal Employer-Household Dynamics," https://lehd.ces.census.gov/data.

the other hand, it also suggests that such workers are moving toward higher-valued matches in the future.

Declining churn might indicate that workers find themselves in high-value matches more quickly but could also indicate that workers' outside options are deteriorating. To better understand the forces driving declining worker flow, Figures 5 and 6 plot transitions of workers to persistent nonemployment and from job to job, using the Longitudinal Employer-Household Dynamics program's Job-to-Job Flows statistics.[18] In light of our conceptual framework, a transition to permanent nonemployment for prime-age workers would indicate an employer-initiated separation, possibly reflecting a discovery that the worker is a poor match. In an environment with limited outside options, many such discoveries would result in nonemployment, possibly inefficiently if wages are unable to adjust.

Figure 5 clearly shows that rates of transition to permanent nonemployment are steadily declining, particularly for workers age 24 to 34. More strikingly, Figure 6 shows that separations in which workers move to new jobs have been sharply rising, particularly for younger workers. In fact, job-to-job movements have recovered to their pre–Great Recession levels

Figure 6. Transitions from Job to Job

Source: US Census Bureau, "Data—Longitudinal Employer-Household Dynamics," https://lehd.ces.census.gov/data.

for all age groups. Workers of all ages appear to increasingly be able to find better matches.

Without further evidence, it is hard to know whether these movements are efficient or inefficient, but apparently firms are decreasingly willing or able to retain workers. One interpretation is that there is a growing number of jobs for which there is marginal surplus but also for which workers and firms perceive there are better opportunities elsewhere.

Sudden Worker Deaths and Departures. Recall the value of a job match is what the firm would lose if the match were suddenly to dissolve without any other changes to the economic environment. Some recent work has used this idea to infer the nature of job matches by studying firm behavior in response to the sudden departure of a worker. A report I coauthored with Meghan M. Skira argues that when the factors that support match surplus are low, firms can be expected to turn to external markets to replace workers who suddenly exit.[19]

Using data from Brazil, we study how firm hiring changes in the months surrounding the start of sick leave or maternity leave. First, we show that leave spells are not timed to correspond to firm-specific hiring trends—that is, workers don't tend to take leave when the firm is shrinking or expanding anyway (relative to the market in which they operate). Next, we find that external hiring increases in the month the leave spell starts, but only by a small amount. The implication is that firms do not turn to external markets to replace the labor of their departing workers. The hiring responses are stronger for jobs for which match surplus is likely to be low—jobs in less technical occupations and more dynamic labor markets. Overall, the fact that firms find their jobs difficult to quickly replace indicates that they provided a nontrivial surplus.

In their study of worker deaths, Simon Jäger and Jörg Heining find similar results examining firm responses to unexpected deaths in small firms, which are arguably harder for firm managers to anticipate.[20] They also find muted hiring responses and evidence that firms turn instead to internal labor markets, leaning on their incumbent workers more when workers suddenly depart.

Morten Bennedsen, Francisco Pérez-González, and Daniel Wolfenzon have the most direct evidence of match value.[21] They find that the sudden death of a CEO or firm owner has a large negative effect on the firm's value. While CEO deaths have profound effects on firm value, both Jäger and Heining's study and mine with Skira find that hiring responses are muted when workers depart, even when those workers have less education or are employed in less-skill-intensive occupations. It therefore seems that match value is not limited to managerial positions or jobs in which measured skills or education are scarce.

There is a much more well-developed literature that considers the consequences of sudden match destruction from the worker's perspective. In a classic study, Louis S. Jacobson, Robert J. LaLonde, and Daniel G. Sullivan examine what happens to workers' earnings when their employer suddenly shuts down or radically reduces its scale of operation.[22] They find large losses for displaced workers of around 25 percent of pre-displacement earnings. The size of the loss increases with worker tenure, as would be expected if workers with long tenure had been in valuable matches from which they could extract a large part of the surplus.

Marta Lachowska, Alexandre Mas, and Stephen A. Woodbury have reexamined the earnings losses of displaced workers much more recently using data from Washington state.[23] Decomposing earnings losses into firm-specific and match-specific factors (following the method of John A. Abowd, Kramarz, and David N. Margolis[24]), they show that the loss of match-specific value explains more than half of total earnings losses. The rest of the loss is because workers are displaced from firms that pay higher earnings and find new jobs in lower-paying firms.

An older and longer literature attempts to measure job value directly by measuring quasi-rents: the difference between a firm's value added and the replacement cost of its inputs.[25] This literature shows that quasi-rents may be substantial and in particular that a large part of worker wages actually arise from rent sharing. In a comprehensive review, David Card et al. relate evidence of rent sharing to a growing body of evidence on the existence of firm-specific wage premia.[26]

However, this literature does not speak as much to the match-specific value enjoyed by the firm from employing specific workers as it does to the manner in which job-specific rents are or are not shared with workers. It must also face the difficult issue of evaluating the outside options facing firms and workers. Some studies assume that the cost of replacing a worker is just the value of the minimum wage or the average wage in an industry or region. While these approximations are useful, they may miss important sources of heterogeneity in the kinds of labor to which particular firms have access. Moreover, they also do not account for match-specific productivity, the value of accumulated job-specific skills, or informational rents enjoyed because the firm has had time to get to know its employees' strengths.

Policies That Preserve Match Value

Several policies that seek to preserve match value were widely used during the pandemic recession and the Great Recession. Unemployment insurance (UI) programs provide workers with an income after a layoff. While UI programs do not explicitly tie workers to their pre-layoff employers, they are designed to help workers endure temporary furloughs while waiting to be recalled to their jobs in sectors in which temporary demand disruptions are common.

Short-time work programs focus more directly on preserving worker-employer matches by subsidizing firms that keep workers on payroll during a temporary slowdown. The idea is that firms, rather than laying off some workers, will move all workers onto reduced hours, with the government compensating firms for part of their payroll and workers for a portion of their lost earnings.[27]

A third policy, which is a sort of mixture of the first two, subsidizes firms that put workers on furlough during slack demand and operates like a UI program in which payments are made through the firm. The US Coronavirus Aid, Relief, and Economic Security Act had elements of this latter system, and Denmark implemented such a program in the early stages of the pandemic, which helped keep workers tied to their employers.[28] All three policies share a common concern that they inhibit reallocation of workers to more productive jobs, and this is particularly the case for short-time work, since it explicitly ties workers to firms.

In a standard business cycle downturn, active labor market programs may prevent unproductive matches from dissolving and obstruct the reallocation of employment toward more productive uses. In the early phases of the pandemic, such concerns were plainly less relevant, as the economic shock was unrelated to productivity or other market fundamentals. Further, the public health benefits provide a clear rationale for borrowing against the future to preserve job matches while providing people uninterrupted payments to facilitate compliance with stay-at-home orders.

Even with a conventional recession, short-time work programs can still be efficient. Recall that job separations can be inefficient if it is difficult for firms and workers to renegotiate over match surplus. In a recession, firms may face demand shortfalls or be unable to make payroll due to problems in financial markets. Workers may not be able to accept temporary wage cuts, and firms may not be able to credibly commit to returning wages to normal. In circumstances where we expect most business activity to return to normal but wage contracts are not flexible, job destruction may be inefficient, warranting either short-time work or financial interventions.[29]

However, determining whether, and when, preserving matches is efficient or inefficient is not straightforward. Some creative research has begun building a base of evidence, but it is far from complete. Overall, the research suggests policies that preserve matches are successful but face cost concerns arising from moral hazard from employers that take up the programs unnecessarily. Studying variation in the use and take-up of short-time work in France during the Great Recession, Cahuc, Kramarz, and Nevoux show that the policy did indeed save jobs among firms that experienced particularly severe shocks.[30] However, they find that the policy also inadvertently provided a windfall to healthy firms, which used it to cut hours for workers on jobs they would have preserved anyway.

In an evaluation of the Danish government's response to the labor market effects of the pandemic, Bennedsen et al. find strong evidence of match-specific value but also that furlough aid may have generated windfall effects for some firms.[31] The Danish policy response had three main arms: The government provided subsidies to firms to furlough workers, direct aid to offset other fixed costs, and deferral of tax payments. We find that the Danish policy prevented 81,000 layoffs but also induced 285,000 furloughs. That the number of induced furloughs exceeded the number of layoffs prevented by more than two to one suggests that some firms took up the aid that did not strictly need it to prevent layoffs.

Regarding match quality, Danish firms had considerable skin in the game with the furlough policy. Specifically, they were required to pay 25 percent of the salary cost for their furloughed workers. That payment reflects a floor on how much firms would have been willing to pay to preserve the match value in their existing employment relationships. Even accounting for expected severance costs, Bennedsen et al. find that for 36 percent of furloughs, firms were willing to pay to maintain workers in their jobs. This was true for workers in both full-time and part-time jobs. Our results also suggest that the adoption of furlough aid significantly hastened the country's return to its pre-pandemic level of unemployment.

Suggestions for Research

Many different empirical approaches have shed light on the existence and nature of match value. However, with few exceptions,[32] most of this literature is not directly focused on measuring match quality, its determinants, and its distribution within and between groups of firms and workers. Alongside continuing evaluations of short-time work and related policies, primary research that sheds light on match quality can be an important input to labor market and policy research.

First, empirical research could attempt to directly measure match quality using the approach taken to measure quasi-rents in the literature on rent sharing. That literature has the advantage of making direct measurements of labor productivity, though not necessarily match-specific productivity. Using theoretically motivated assessments of determinants of match value and outside options, this literature could characterize the overall magnitude of match value and its distribution across different types of workers and jobs.

Second, structural models of assortative matching could be used to estimate the distribution of job-match value and the consequences of destroying or preserving matches under different policies. This approach has the advantage that, by making strong assumptions about sources of match value, it is possible to draw strong conclusions about match value. The disadvantage is that the results may be sensitive to particular modeling assumptions. Research that focuses primarily on the value of job matches can evaluate how various conclusions change based on modeling assumptions. New methods that combine revealed-preference empirical strategies (i.e., paying attention to the kinds of jobs people take and what they choose when leaving a job) reduce the dependence in earlier studies on strict modeling assumptions.

A related approach might combine structural analysis of wage and job-mobility patterns to infer match surplus. Two classic works argue that as much as half of the variation in wages in France could be explained by firms shifting match surplus toward workers to help counter outside offers.[33] Their analysis notably suggested that match value was particularly high for workers in jobs that do not require specialized skills. However, in the context of their model, all match surplus arises from a surfeit of outside options. More recent work that combines assortative matching and frictional job search could provide a useful platform for measuring the distribution and nature of match value.[34]

Third, moving away from structural models, it would also be useful to have more work along the lines of the aforementioned Jäger, Schoefer, and Zweimüller and Cahuc, Kramarz, and Nevoux reports, which evaluate labor market policies in light of their effects on match quality. While both papers are based on models that provide a clear interpretive framework, their results do not depend as heavily on model assumptions as the structural literature discussed previously.[35]

A segment of the literature on UI has long focused on whether generous benefits trade off longer searches against better matches, with somewhat ambiguous findings.[36] It would also be interesting to know whether UI programs successfully keep workers in productive employment relationships through periods of temporary hardship, focusing on the rates at which workers are recalled to their previous jobs. When workers are not recalled, what is the reason?

As a complement to all the model-focused research described in the preceding paragraphs, it would be tremendously useful to learn what employers say about how difficult it would be to replace their existing workers and why. Indeed, there is scope for surveys that directly probe workers and employers about the value of different job matches. A number of high-profile studies have used contingent valuation surveys to make progress on tough labor market questions where observational data are inherently limited, particularly workers' valuation of working conditions.[37] Similar methods might be used in employer or manager surveys to infer the sources of match value.

Discussion

This chapter focuses on match value in a thought experiment that asks: What is lost when job matches are exogenously destroyed, and how difficult is it to re-create that value? In March 2020, it seemed like the pandemic could end quickly if the US just put the economy on hold, locked down, flattened the curve, and opened back up. That is not how things ultimately played out. The pandemic and the associated recession are still with the US and have triggered what are probably permanent changes in preferences and the organization of work. At this point, while it may make sense to continue subsidizing consumption, the rationale for using policy to preserve job matches is far less clear.

From this perspective, what matters for policy is not so much how much time has passed or how close we are to the "end" of the pandemic, but whether the structural changes wrought by the pandemic now require the reallocation of workers into different jobs than they held previously. There may still be jobs where, if employers could preserve their value for a few more months, the economy would be better off than if the matches ended and had to re-form later. However, it may be more efficient to subsidize consumption but refrain from tying workers to their employers. A full evaluation of policies for preserving job matches is beyond the scope of this chapter, but policies clearly must trade off the prevention of inefficient job destruction against the flexible reallocation of labor.

While the direct evidence on match value is limited, at any point in time, the sum of the value in specific job matches is probably quite high. It is also apparent that workers need to churn through a number of different jobs to find good matches. Because matches can end inefficiently, there is likely a role for policy, particularly in recessions when match value temporarily dips and is expected to recover.

It is also clear that match value is substantial for all kinds of jobs and workers. Changes that increase the outside options for workers may reduce the value in specific matches but in ways that would generally be advantageous, at least from workers' perspectives. Progress in understanding how labor markets function and the role of policy requires better information on the size, distribution, and origins of match value.

Notes

1. Several studies consider the ramifications of unexpected worker deaths for firm outcomes and behavior, which I consider in more detail in this chapter. See Matthew Smith et al., "Capitalists in the Twenty-First Century," *Quarterly Journal of Economics* 134, no. 4 (November 2019): 1675–745, https://academic.oup.com/qje/article-abstract/134/4/1675/5542244; Morten Bennedsen, Francisco Pérez-González, and Daniel Wolfenzon, "Do CEOs Matter? Evidence from Hospitalization Events," *Journal of Finance* 75, no. 4 (August 2020): 1877–911, https://onlinelibrary.wiley.com/doi/abs/10.1111/jofi.12897; and Simon Jäger and Jörg Heining, "How Substitutable Are Workers? Evidence from Worker Deaths" (working paper, Massachusetts Institute of Technology, Cambridge, MA, January 2019), https://economics.mit.edu/files/16635.

2. I am grateful to Michael R. Strain for framing this as a distinction between "productive" and "unproductive" surplus.

3. A growing empirical literature on monopsony and labor market concentration has emphasized this latter channel as a significant phenomenon across many labor markets in the United States. See, for example, José Azar et al., "Minimum Wage Employment Effects and Labor Market Concentration" (working paper, National Bureau of Economic Research, Cambridge, MA, July 2019), https://www.nber.org/papers/w26101.

4. This will be the case when there are no costs or benefits to parties outside the match. If there are, determining efficiency of preserving matches would also depend on those externalities.

5. This logic is developed by Robert E. Hall and Edward P. Lazear and usefully summarized by Henry S. Farber. See Robert E. Hall and Edward P. Lazear, "The Excess Sensitivity of Layoffs and Quits to Demand," *Journal of Labor Economics* 2, no. 2 (April 1984): 233–57, https://www.journals.uchicago.edu/doi/abs/10.1086/298032; and Henry S. Farber, "Mobility and Stability: The Dynamics of Job Change in Labor Markets," in *Handbook of Economics*, ed. Orley C. Ashenfelter and David Card, vol. 3B (Amsterdam, Netherlands: Elsevier, 1999), 2439–83, https://www.sciencedirect.com/science/article/abs/pii/S1573446399300237.

6. Pierre Cahuc, Fabien Postel-Vinay, and Jean-Marc Robin, "Wage Bargaining with On-the-Job Search: Theory and Evidence," *Econometrica* 74, no. 2 (March 2006): 323–64, https://www.jstor.org/stable/3598804.

7. Simon Jäger, Benjamin Schoefer, and Josef Zweimüller, "Marginal Jobs and Job Surplus: A Test of the Efficiency of Separations" (working paper, National Bureau of Economic Research, Cambridge, MA, January 2019), https://www.nber.org/papers/w25492.

8. José María Barrero, Nicholas Bloom, and Steven J. Davis, "COVID-19 Is Also a Reallocation Shock," Brookings Institution, Summer 2020, https://www.brookings.edu/bpea-articles/covid-19-is-also-a-reallocation-shock.

9. Farber, "Mobility and Stability."

10. Paul Oyer and Scott Schaefer, "Personnel Economics: Hiring and Incentives" (working paper, National Bureau of Economic Research, Cambridge, MA, May 2010), https://www.nber.org/papers/w15977.

11. Farber, "Mobility and Stability."

12. US Census Bureau, "Data—Longitudinal Employer-Household Dynamics," https://lehd.ces.census.gov/data/#qwi.

13. Farber, "Mobility and Stability."

14. Yusuf Mercan and Benjamin Schoefer, "Jobs and Matches: Quits, Replacement Hiring, and Vacancy Chains," *American Economic Review: Insights* 2, no. 1 (March 2020): 101–24, https://www.aeaweb.org/articles?id=10.1257/aeri.20190023; and Edward P. Lazear and James R. Spletzer, "Hiring, Churn, and the Business Cycle," *American Economic Review* 102, no. 3 (May 2012): 575–79, https://www.aeaweb.org/articles?id=10.1257/aer.102.3.575.

15. Henry R. Hyatt and James R. Spletzer, "The Recent Decline in Employment Dynamics," *IZA Journal of Labor Economics* 2, no. 5 (September 2013), https://izajole.springeropen.com/articles/10.1186/2193-8997-2-5.

16. The raw data are not seasonally adjusted. The plotted points are the output of a linear locally estimated scatterplot smoothing model applied to the raw data with

smoothing parameter 0.2. The long-run trends are not sensitive to these parameters.

17. Hyatt and Spletzer, "The Recent Decline in Employment Dynamics."

18. US Census Bureau, "Data—Longitudinal Employer-Household Dynamics."

19. Ian M. Schmutte and Meghan M. Skira, "The Response of Firms to Maternity Leave and Sickness Absence" (working paper, University of Georgia, Athens, GA, June 11, 2021), http://ianschmutte.org/files/SchmutteSkira_v2021-06-11.pdf.

20. Jäger and Heining, "How Substitutable Are Workers?"

21. Bennedsen, Pérez-González, and Wolfenzon, "Do CEOs Matter?"

22. Louis S. Jacobson, Robert J. LaLonde, and Daniel G. Sullivan, "Earnings Losses of Displaced Workers," *American Economic Review* 83, no. 4 (September 1993): 685–709, https://www.jstor.org/stable/2117574.

23. Marta Lachowska, Alexandre Mas, and Stephen A. Woodbury, "Sources of Displaced Workers' Long-Term Earnings Losses," *American Economic Review* 110, no. 10 (October 2020): 3231–66, https://www.aeaweb.org/articles?id=10.1257/aer.20180652.

24. John M. Abowd, Francis Kramarz, and David N. Margolis, "High Wage Workers and High Wage Firms" (working paper, National Bureau of Economic Research, Cambridge, MA, November 1994), https://www.nber.org/papers/w4917.

25. John A. Abowd and Thomas Lemieux, "The Effects of Product Market Competition on Collective Bargaining Agreements: The Case of Foreign Competition in Canada," *Quarterly Journal of Economics* 108, no. 4 (November 1993): 983–1014, https://www.jstor.org/stable/2118457; and John Van Reenen, "The Creation and Capture of Rents: Wages and Innovation in a Panel of U.K. Companies," *Quarterly Journal of Economics* 111, no. 1 (February 1996): 195–226, https://www.jstor.org/stable/2946662.

26. David Card et al., "Firms and Labor Market Inequality: Evidence and Some Theory," *Journal of Labor Economics* 36, no. S1 (January 2018): S13–S70, https://www.journals.uchicago.edu/doi/10.1086/694153. This study builds off previous work done by John Abowd, Francis Kramarz, and David Margolis. See Abowd, Kramarz, and Margolis, "High Wage Workers and High Wage Firms."

27. The chapter by Xavier Jaravel in this volume discusses the use of short-time work policies in France in response to the pandemic. Other chapters discuss policies in Australia (Jeff Borland and Jennifer Hunt) and Canada (Miles Corak) that subsidized wages for businesses that kept employees working and on payroll.

28. Several chapters in this volume focus on how such policies were implemented in different countries: Spain (Juan F. Jimeno), the Netherlands (Roel Beetsma and Raymond Gradus), the UK (Jonathan Cribb and Paul Johnson), and Germany (Tom Krebs).

29. Giulia Giupponi and Camille Landais, "Subsidizing Labor Hoarding in Recessions: The Employment & Welfare Effects of Short Time Work" (working paper, Centre for Economic Performance, London, UK, December 2018), https://cep.lse.ac.uk/pubs/download/dp1585.pdf.

30. Pierre Cahuc, Francis Kramarz, and Sandra Nevoux, "The Heterogeneous Impact of Short-Time Work: From Saved Jobs to Windfall Effects," Institute of Labor Economics, May 2021, https://www.iza.org/publications/dp/14381/the-heterogeneous-impact-of-short-time-work-from-saved-jobs-to-windfall-effects.

31. Morten Bennedsen et al., "Preserving Job Matches During the COVID-19 Pandemic: Firm-Level Evidence on the Role of Government Aid" (working paper, Global Labor Organization, June 20, 2020), https://www.econstor.eu/bitstream/10419/221802/1/GLO-DP-0588.pdf.

32. Jäger, Schoefer, and Zweimüller, "Marginal Jobs and Job Surplus"; and Ilse Lindenlaub and Fabien Postel-Vinay, "The Worker-Job Surplus" (working paper, National Bureau of Economic Research, Cambridge, MA, January 2021), https://www.nber.org/papers/w28402.

33. Fabien Postel-Vinay and Jean-Marc Robin, "Equilibrium Wage Dispersion with Worker and Employer Heterogeneity," *Econometrica* 70, no. 6 (November 2002): 2295–350, https://onlinelibrary.wiley.com/doi/10.1111/j.1468-0262.2002.00441.x; and Cahuc, Postel-Vinay, and Robin, "Wage Bargaining with On-the-Job Search."

34. See, for example, Christopher Taber and Rune Vejlin, "Estimation of a Roy/Search/Compensating Differential Model of the Labor Market," *Econometrica* 88, no. 3 (May 2020): 1031–69, https://onlinelibrary.wiley.com/doi/abs/10.3982/ECTA14441.

35. Jäger, Schoefer, and Zweimüller, "Marginal Jobs and Job Surplus"; and Cahuc, Kramarz, and Nevoux, "The Heterogeneous Impact of Short-Time Work."

36. Johannes F. Schmieder, Till von Wachter, and Stefan Bender, "The Effect of Unemployment Benefits and Nonemployment Durations on Wages," *American Economic Review* 106, no. 3 (March 2016), 739–77, https://www.aeaweb.org/articles?id=10.1257/aer.20141566.

37. Alexandre Mas and Amanda Pallais, "Valuing Alternative Work Arrangements," *American Economic Review* 107, no. 12 (December 2017): 3722–59, https://www.aeaweb.org/articles?id=10.1257%2Faer.20161500; Matthew Wiswall and Basit Zafar, "Preference for the Workplace, Investment in Human Capital, and Gender," *Quarterly Journal of Economics* 133, no. 1 (February 2018): 457–507, https://academic.oup.com/qje/article-abstract/133/1/457/4095201; Nicole Maestas et al., "The Value of Working Conditions in the United States and Implications for the Structure of Wages" (working paper, National Bureau of Economic Research, Cambridge, MA, October 2018), https://www.nber.org/papers/w25204; and Haoran He, David Neumark, and Qian Weng, "Do Workers Value Flexible Jobs? A Field Experiment," *Journal of Labor Economics* 39, no. 3 (July 2021): 709–38, https://www.journals.uchicago.edu/doi/pdf/10.1086/711226.

2

Did the Australian JobKeeper Program Save Jobs by Subsidizing Temporary Layoffs?

JEFF BORLAND AND JENNIFER HUNT

Geographic isolation, a willingness to seal national and state borders, and periodic lockdowns kept Australia's cumulative COVID-19 cases and deaths low by international standards for the first 18 months of the pandemic. Figure 1's smoothed plot of daily COVID-19 cases in selected countries (note log scale) shows Australia contained the initial COVID-19 outbreak by early May 2020, before a more severe but geographically limited outbreak in July–October 2020 brought national COVID-19 cases back to the previous peak. By October 2020, the caseload had returned to a low level, where it remained through mid-2021.

Figure 1. Daily COVID-19 New Cases per Million People

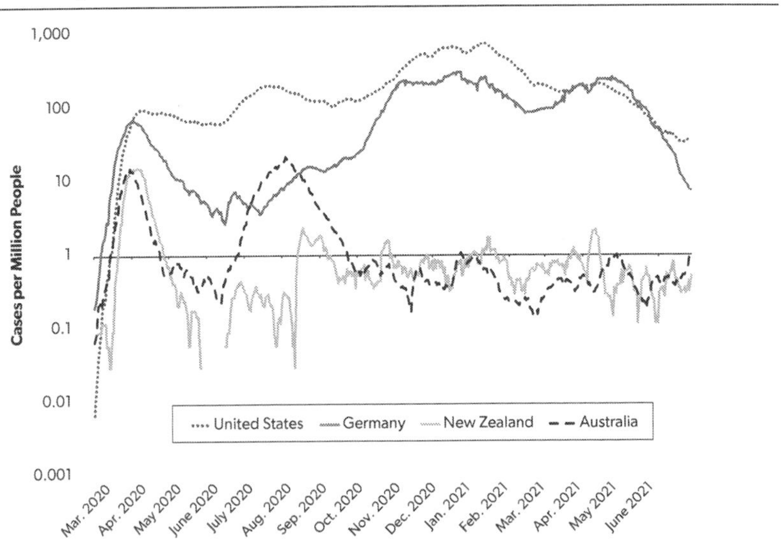

Note: Data are a seven-day moving average from March 1, 2020, to June 20, 2021.
Source: Our World in Data, COVID-19 Data, https://github.com/owid/covid-19-data/tree/master/public/data.

Figure 2. Real GDP in Australia and the United States

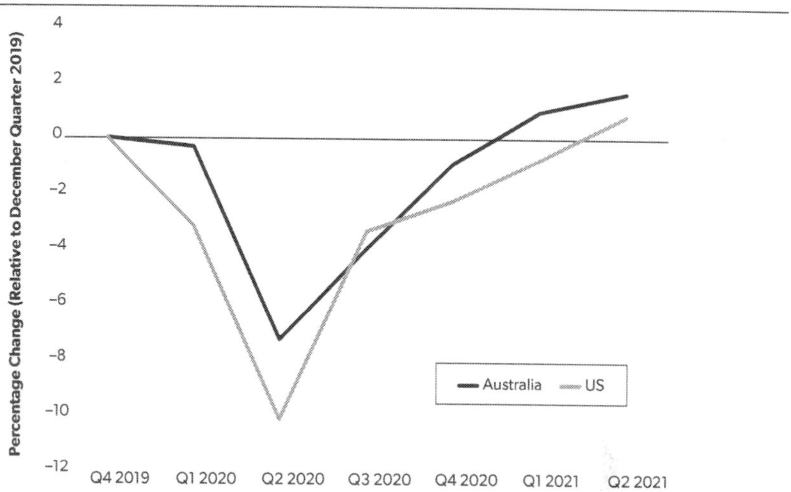

Note: Series are seasonally adjusted.
Source: Australian Bureau of Statistics, "Australian National Accounts: National Income, Expenditure and Product," June 1, 2021, Table 1, https://www.abs.gov.au/statistics/economy/national-accounts/australian-national-accounts-national-income-expenditure-and-product/jun-2021#data-download; and US Department of Commerce, Bureau of Economic Analysis, "National Data: National Income and Product Accounts," https://apps.bea.gov/iTable/iTable.cfm?reqid=19&step=2#reqid=19&step=2&isuri=1&1921=survey.

In March 2020, anticipating economic distress, federal and state governments implemented support and stimulus policies worth 8.6 percent of gross domestic product (GDP) by June 2020. This share is well above the median of advanced economies, though it is below the US share of 10.8 percent.[1] By June 2021, Australia's share had cumulated to 17.4 percent, compared to 22.2 percent for the United States.[2]

Because of public health and economic interventions, Australia's COVID-19-induced downturn in 2020 was short compared to past recessions (only one-quarter long), shallower than the US downturn (a 7.3 percent decline in GDP compared to 10.1 percent), and limited to the first wave of infections. (See Figure 2.)

In this chapter, we focus on the JobKeeper policy, a wage subsidy program. Its aims included mitigating employment decline and business insolvency, providing income support (in a way that relieved pressure on the existing public benefits system), providing macroeconomic stimulus, and setting propitious conditions for eventual recovery by maintaining employer-employee connections.

Our particular interest is the degree to which employer-employee connections maintained through JobKeeper dampened the employment cycle. That is, we focus on whether JobKeeper facilitated the use of temporary layoffs while recognizing that the program's effect in saving jobs will also have included maintaining some workers in jobs with positive hours. Our analysis relies partly on synthesizing results from existing academic papers and government reports. A key paper is "How Many Jobs Did JobKeeper Keep?" by James Bishop and Iris Day, who find that JobKeeper reduced employment losses by at least 700,000, or 5.4 percent of initial employment, in its first four months.

Description of JobKeeper and Other Measures

The JobKeeper wage subsidy program was announced on March 30, 2020. Initially, it was set to last six months. Program enrollment commenced on April 20. On July 21, it was announced that JobKeeper would be extended for six months, until the end of March 2021, with reduced payments and modified eligibility criteria.[3]

Accordingly, we distinguish between two phases of the program: phase one from March 30 to September 27, 2020, and phase two from September 28, 2020, to March 28, 2021. Despite considerable pressure in early 2021 for the JobKeeper program to be further extended, that did not happen.

The JobKeeper payment was made to eligible employers for employees covered by the program and eligible self-employed individuals (sole traders). Employees were covered by the program if they were working in full- or part-time permanent jobs or in a casual job and had been with their employer regularly for more than 12 months.[4]

In Australia, permanent employees have an advance commitment to ongoing employment, are entitled to paid leave, and must give or receive notice to end the employment, whereas casual employees (employed "at will" in US parlance) accept a job offer knowing there is no firm advance commitment to ongoing work with an agreed pattern of work.[5] A "one-in-all-in" rule meant that, once a business or nonprofit was nominated to receive JobKeeper, the payment was made to all its eligible employees. Employees retained eligibility so long as they remained with the same employer.[6]

Phase One. In phase one, the wage subsidy paid was AUD 750 per week per employee or self-employed individual. To qualify, employees needed to have been included in a firm's payroll records on or before March 1, 2020.[7] Employees who had been laid off after March 1 but then reattached after the program's announcement were eligible. The same flat subsidy of AUD 750 per week was paid for all recipients, regardless of their hours worked or earnings before or while JobKeeper was in effect.

Those working zero hours also received the full payment. Employees whose work hours were such that their total earnings were above AUD 750 per week had the difference between the subsidy and their total earnings paid by their employers. Australian labor law prevents employees' hourly wages from being reduced, and no exception was made for the pandemic.

The distribution of weekly earnings for all employed persons, including the self-employed, shows the expected bunching around AUD 750. These data are available annually in August, in categories. Figure 3 shows that the share of employed persons with weekly earnings in the range from AUD 600 to AUD 800 increased from 10.0 percent in August 2019 (before COVID-19 and JobKeeper) to 13.2 percent in August 2020 (during phase one). The same data indicate that 29.6 percent of workers earned AUD 800 or less in August 2019.

For employers to be able to claim JobKeeper for their employees during phase one, they needed to meet a turnover test. Eligibility required an organization to have experienced or to anticipate reduced turnover relative to a comparable period a year ago: a 15 percent reduction for a registered charity and a 30 or 50 percent reduction for businesses with turnover, respectively, less or more than AUD 1 billion. The reduced turnover was required to last for a minimum of one month between March and September 2020. Once eligibility was established, an organization then received JobKeeper until September 27, regardless of its turnover in subsequent months.[8]

Phase Two. Phase two changed the size of the wage subsidy and the eligibility criteria—in two stages: from September 28, 2020, to January 3, 2021,

Figure 3. Weekly Earnings Distribution, All Employed Persons, August 2019 and August 2020

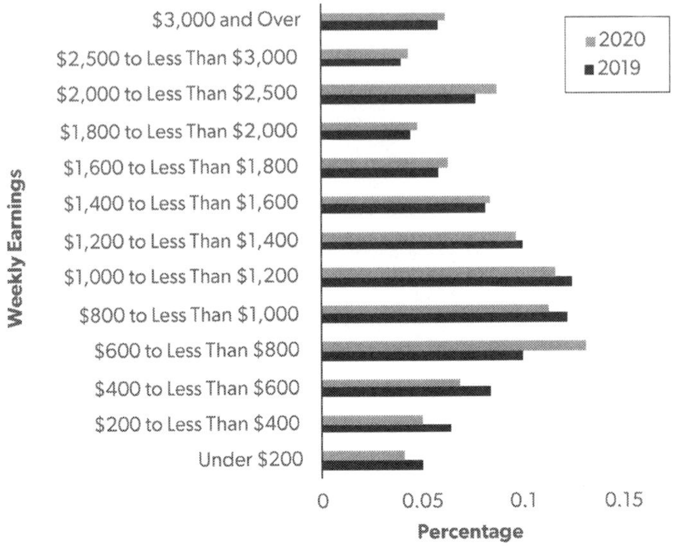

Source: Australian Bureau of Statistics, Characteristics of Employment, Australia, 2019 and 2020, https://www.abs.gov.au/statistics/labour/earnings-and-working-conditions/characteristics-employment-australia. This information was accessed via Australian Bureau of Statistics, TableBuilder, https://www.abs.gov.au/statistics/microdata-tablebuilder/tablebuilder.

and from January 4, 2021, to March 28, 2021.[9] The size of the wage subsidy was progressively reduced, and separate payments based on hours of work were introduced.

For September 28, 2020, to January 3, 2021, the payment was set at AUD 600 per week for all eligible employees and self-employed individuals who, in the four weekly pay periods before the reference period, were working for 20 hours or more a week on average, with the payment falling to AUD 500 per week from January 4 to March 28, 2021. Employees and self-employed individuals working fewer than 20 hours a week on average in the reference period had a payment rate of AUD 375 per week for September 28, 2020, to January 3, 2021, and AUD 325 per week from January 4 to March 28, 2021.

Furthermore, eligibility conditions for JobKeeper were tightened. Organizations seeking to claim the subsidy for fourth quarter (Q4) 2020

Table 1. Number of Individual Recipients of JobKeeper (Employees and Sole Traders)

	Number of JobKeeper Recipients	Persons Employed	JobKeeper Recipients as Percentage of Persons Employed
April 2020	3,368,680	12,413,000	27.2
May 2020	3,580,365	12,192,600	29.4
June 2020	3,639,526	12,392,500	29.4
July 2020	3,659,934	12,471,900	29.3
August 2020	3,642,790	12,562,700	29.0
September 2020	3,610,916	12,567,100	28.7
October 2020	1,633,406	12,735,400	12.8
November 2020	1,606,673	12,881,700	12.5
December 2020	1,569,009	12,995,500	12.1
January 2021	1,087,037	12,734,800	8.5
February 2021	1,072,520	13,036,200	8.2
March 2021	1,031,848	13,002,800	7.9

Source: Australian Government, Treasury, *Insights from the First Six Months of JobKeeper*, October 11, 2021, Table 4, https://treasury.gov.au/publication/p2021-211978; and Australian Bureau of Statistics, Labour Force, Australia, September 2021, Table 1, https://www.abs.gov.au/statistics/labour/employment-and-unemployment/labour-force-australia/sep-2021.

were required to reassess their eligibility with reference to their actual turnover in third quarter (Q3) 2020 compared to the same period in 2019. They were then required to again reassess their eligibility for JobKeeper payments in first quarter (Q1) 2021 by demonstrating that they met the relevant decline in the turnover test in Q4 2020. The reference date for an employee to be eligible for JobKeeper payments for phase two was updated to July 1, 2020.

Statistics on Receipt of JobKeeper. Table 1 provides information on the number of JobKeeper recipients. In phase one, the JobKeeper payment was made to about 3.5 million recipients, just over one-quarter of employed persons in Australia. A survey conducted in the week after enrollments in JobKeeper opened (April 22 to 28) found that about 95 percent of eligible businesses had or were planning to apply for JobKeeper.[10] With stricter eligibility requirements in phase two and the progress of economic recovery, the number of recipients fell to about 1.7 million in Q4 2020 and then to 1.1 million in Q1 2021.

Receipt of JobKeeper varied substantially by industry. In the hardest-hit industries, such as accommodation and food services and arts and recreation services, the JobKeeper subsidy accounted for almost 50 percent of employee compensation in second quarter (Q2) 2020. By contrast, in industries less affected by COVID-19, such as health care and social assistance, or where few businesses were eligible for JobKeeper, such as education and training, the share of employee compensation from the program was 10 percent or less.[11]

Because the recession was short, because phase-one eligibility could be based on expected rather than actual revenue declines and required a decline only in a single month, and because businesses' JobKeeper payments could continue unconditionally for months after eligibility was established, a significant share of JobKeeper payments went to businesses whose quarterly revenue when receiving JobKeeper was higher than it was one year previously. For example, in Q2 (April–June) and Q3 (July–September) 2020, 29 percent of JobKeeper payments went to businesses that had higher revenue than in the same quarter in 2019.[12]

Other Measures Introduced at the Onset of COVID-19. The announcement of the JobKeeper program followed an extensive set of policies already introduced by the Australian federal and state governments in mid-March 2020 in response to the onset of COVID-19.[13] The main federal government policies were supporting business via cash grants, underwriting loans and extra tax write-offs for investment, and increasing household incomes and spending capacity through higher welfare payments and permission to make withdrawals from pension funds.[14]

Theory

The theoretical impact of JobKeeper is complex. JobKeeper affected labor demand and labor supply in ways that differed for workers according to eligibility and initial earnings, and it likely inserted a wedge between demand and supply given the legal prohibition on reducing the hourly wage. We assume in our analysis that, because the economic disruptions and JobKeeper program were expected to be temporary, firms did not adjust the capital stock.

Static Analysis. The simplest analysis is a static model that assumes all workers are the same and initially earn more than the JobKeeper subsidy ("high earners"). For labor demand, the JobKeeper subsidy in isolation would increase a firm's optimal output (scale effect), which would tend to increase demand for labor. This scale effect would offset the output reduction's effect due to the decline in consumer demand from COVID-19. JobKeeper's influence on how a firm combines inputs to produce a given output, the substitution effect, depends on the net response of firm output to the decline in consumer demand, JobKeeper, and other government subsidies.

For the few firms experiencing no change or an increase in output, there would be no substitution effect, since the subsidy was not available for newly hired workers. On the other hand, for the more typical case of a firm reducing output, a worker's fixed cost is reduced by the per-worker subsidy, while the cost of an extra hour per worker remains unchanged, incentivizing the firm to substitute from hours per worker to heads (number of workers). JobKeeper would therefore mitigate the reduction in heads and total hours worked while reducing hours per worker. For this reason, some have referred to the program as a "short-time wage subsidy."[15]

This model ignores that some eligible workers initially earned less than the JobKeeper amount ("low earners"). In a more sophisticated model with heterogeneous workers, JobKeeper's effect on heads and total hours of high earners is ambiguous, since firms substitute from high earners to the fully subsidized low earners. While JobKeeper bolsters demand for total hours of the smaller group of low earners, its effect on the choice between hours per worker and heads is unclear.

Workers ineligible for JobKeeper must also be considered. For these workers, JobKeeper's effect on demand is ambiguous, as it is boosted by the scale effect but reduced by substitution to eligible workers (for firms reducing output). However, for ineligible workers, JobKeeper has no effect on the choice between hours per worker and heads. Overall, therefore, it is unclear whether JobKeeper incentivized firms to substitute from hours per worker to heads.

On the labor-supply side, some workers initially earning more than Job-Keeper will be unaffected by its introduction, while others would choose to reduce hours to zero and collect JobKeeper. Hours per worker stay the same, and heads (with positive hours) decline. All workers initially earning less than JobKeeper will choose to reduce hours to zero, while ineligible workers will not change their labor supply.

Putting supply and demand together in the static model, for workers initially earning more than JobKeeper, employment and total hours will fall as supply shifts and demand shifts or stays the same, and hours per worker will fall. Because the hourly wage cannot legally fall, workers will be underemployed (will want to work longer hours), but the relative size of the two shifts determines whether there is unemployment or a shortage of heads.

The market outcome for workers initially earning less than JobKeeper is more complex, since none will want to work positive hours unless they prefer work to leisure, but the demand for some will be positive. The program's temporary nature meant employers demanding positive hours of these workers might be able to persuade them to work due to worker fears of jeopardizing future promotions or being legally fired. The outcome would depend on the two parties' relative bargaining power.

Dynamic Analysis. Firms do not simply consider the present in responding to shocks. Dynamic considerations such as hoarding high-performing workers and weeding out low-performing workers—whose firing costs are lower when they can be justified by a loss of business—are likely important. JobKeeper was designed to encourage using temporary rather than permanent layoffs. If it is easy to permanently lay off workers and if it is easy to rehire "permanently" laid-off workers, there is no real distinction. In Australia, there are firing costs associated with "permanently" laying off a typical worker, and workers are more likely to search for another job if the layoff does not have a likely recall date.[16]

Temporary layoffs may thus preserve good matches and firm-specific human capital and reduce firing and search costs, albeit possibly at the cost of laid-off workers being idle when they might have been working in a new job. JobKeeper made temporary layoffs more appealing to workers because it paid about AUD 200 per week above the JobSeeker (unemployment) benefit. By lowering the likelihood of workers on temporary layoff searching for another job, and hence making it more likely that they would be available for recall, JobKeeper also increased employers' incentives to use temporary layoffs.

Data

Our analysis uses aggregate-level data from the Australian Bureau of Statistics (ABS) Labour Force Survey supplemented with other statistics provided by the federal government.[17] Understanding the data requires understanding certain features of the Australian labor market and associated concepts and terms.

Datasets. The ABS Labour Force Survey is undertaken monthly, for the two weeks before the Sunday that falls between the 12th and 18th of that month. Given the survey's timing, we interpret 2020 data for March as being pre-COVID-19 and April onward as during COVID-19, with data for April being pre-JobKeeper and for May as following the introduction of JobKeeper.

Other data we draw on are from ABS's Payroll Jobs and Wages Survey, Characteristics of Employment survey, special household and business surveys relating to COVID-19, and National Accounts. These are supplemented with material drawn from government reports and research studies that have used official and proprietary data sources not available to us. For example, government reports on JobKeeper have been able to use Australian Taxation Office data that link organization- and employee-level measures, allowing organizations participating in the JobKeeper program and individual payment recipients to be identified.[18]

Concepts. The concept of employment in Australia differs from the concept in the United States and Canada in an important way for this study. An Australian worker may be "stood down" if their firm experiences a work stoppage for reasons beyond its control. The practice is similar to the practice of temporary layoffs in the US: Stood-down workers work no hours, are not paid, and may not have a specific recall date.

The crucial difference is that, unlike temporarily laid-off US workers, stood-down Australian workers are still considered employed (legally and statistically), and the employer therefore cannot simply fail to recall them.[19] If the employer does not want to recall a stood-down worker, they must go through the normal dismissal process usually involving a notice period or pay in lieu of notice, severance pay, and justification of why the worker cannot be redeployed in another job at the company. Exceptions to this include casual workers and permanent workers with short tenure.[20]

We refer to stand-downs as temporary layoffs and approximate workers on temporary layoff in the Labour Force Survey as those responding that they were employed and working zero hours for the reason of "no work, not enough work available, or stood down."[21] We use this estimate to create alternative employment and unemployment series, including and excluding temporarily laid-off workers.

Decomposition of the Decline and Recovery of GDP

The initial onset of the virus brought a severe economic contraction in Australia, due to government-imposed lockdowns and "fear" effects on households' willingness to engage in activities in which there was risk of contracting the virus. After that period of lockdown, however, economic activity has largely been able to resume, as shown in Figure 1.

To understand JobKeeper's role, it is helpful to start by establishing the dimensions along which the economy adjusted in the downturn and recovery. Accordingly, we use quarterly data to decompose additively the changes in GDP into changes in labor productivity (*GDP/Hrs*), labor input, and population size (*Pop*). Labor input is further subdivided into hours worked per employed person (*Hrs/Emp*), share of the labor force employed (*Emp/LF*), and the labor force participation rate (*LF/Pop*):

$$\Delta ln(GDP) = \Delta ln(GDP/Hrs) + \Delta ln(Hrs/Emp) + \Delta ln(Emp/LF) + \Delta ln(LF/Pop) + \Delta ln(Pop).$$

Table 2 shows that the 7.2 percent decrease in GDP from Q1 to Q2 2020 and the 8.3 percent recovery from Q2 2020 to Q1 2021 (when JobKeeper ended and GDP had returned to its original level) were primarily

Table 2. Decomposition of Change in Real GDP (Percentage), Q1 2020 to Q1 2021

	ΔGDP (1)	ΔGDP/ Hrs (2)	ΔHrs/ Emp (3)	ΔEmp/LF (4)	ΔLF/Pop (5)	ΔPop (6)
Downturn Q1 2020–Q2 2020	−7.2	+1.4	−3.2 [0]	−1.8 [−5.0]	−3.9	+0.3
Recovery Q2 2020–Q1 2021	+8.3	+1.1	+2.0 [−1.2]	+1.0 [+4.2]	+4.1	+0.1

Note: We treat workers who are temporarily laid off as employed, except for in numbers in square brackets, where we treat those workers as unemployed. Data are seasonally adjusted.
Source: Australian Bureau of Statistics, "Australian National Accounts: National Income, Expenditure and Product," June 1, 2021, Table 1, https://www.abs.gov.au/statistics/economy/national-accounts/australian-national-accounts-national-income-expenditure-and-product/jun-2021#data-download; Australian Bureau of Statistics, Labour Force, Australia, June 2021, Tables 1 and 19, https://www.abs.gov.au/statistics/labour/employment-and-unemployment/labour-force-australia/jun-2021#data-download; and Australian Bureau of Statistics, Labour Force, Australia, Detailed, June 2021, EM2a, https://www.abs.gov.au/statistics/labour/employment-and-unemployment/labour-force-australia-detailed/jun-2021.

associated with changes in labor input. Withdrawal from the labor force accounts for about half (3.9 percent, Column 5) the GDP decline, while entry into the labor force accounts for about half (4.1 percent, Column 5) the GDP recovery.

The adjustment roles of hours per employed person and (un)employment (Columns 3 and 4) depend on how workers on temporary layoff are classified. When they are counted as employed, changes in average hours (Column 3) make a larger contribution than changes in unemployment (*Emp/LF*, Column 4) do, but when they are counted as unemployed, changes in unemployment dominate: Increases in unemployment account for 5.0 percent of the decline in GDP, while decreases account for 4.2 percent of the recovery in GDP (Column 4, in square brackets). Labor productivity grew in both periods (Column 2), probably reflecting a composition effect as shares of output from industries intensive in low-skill labor (such as accommodation and food services) decreased due to COVID-19. Population growth was negligible (Column 6) due to a halt in migration.

The decomposition hints that temporary layoffs could have played an important role in the cycle, albeit more so in the downturn than the recovery, while "work sharing" (reducing work hours to positive hours) may not have.

Monthly Evolution of the Labor Market

Before examining the connection between temporary layoffs and JobKeeper, we provide further useful descriptive information on the labor market, including on temporary layoffs and hours per worker, using monthly data for more accurate timing.

Worker Hours, Employment, and Unemployment. The monthly employment series during COVID-19 are presented in Figure 4. Worker hours fell by 9.5 percent from early March to early April 2020. The month from early April to early May was transitional, coinciding with the introduction of JobKeeper, with worker hours improving slightly to 8.9 percent below the early March level. That was followed by a steady and rapid recovery to late 2020, after which the growth in worker hours continued at a slower rate.[22]

By June 2021, worker hours were 1 percent above the level immediately before COVID-19. The path of persons employed is almost identical (except for the January 2021 dip) if workers on temporary layoff are classified as not employed; if they are classified as employed, the initial decrease and subsequent recovery in employment are dampened. According to the ABS payroll jobs series, the jobs trough was the week of April 12–18, 2020.[23]

Data from the ABS Characteristics of Employment survey show that the employment declines were concentrated among low-tenure and casual workers. Between August 2019 and August 2020, employment of workers with less than one year of tenure fell 17.7 percent for permanent workers and 21.9 percent for casual workers. This indicates hiring freezes. Employment of casual workers with more than one year of tenure fell 5.8 percent, suggesting employer-initiated separations, while employment of permanent workers with more than one year of tenure actually rose 3.8 percent.

The impact of COVID-19 by industry was highly uneven—reflecting that the extent of social contact and scope for virus transmission between workers and customers, and hence impact of government lockdowns and "fear" effects, varied by industry. In Australia, almost 50 percent of initial job losses (excluding temporary layoffs, based on the Payroll Jobs and

Figure 4. Employment and Worker Hours, March 2020–June 2021

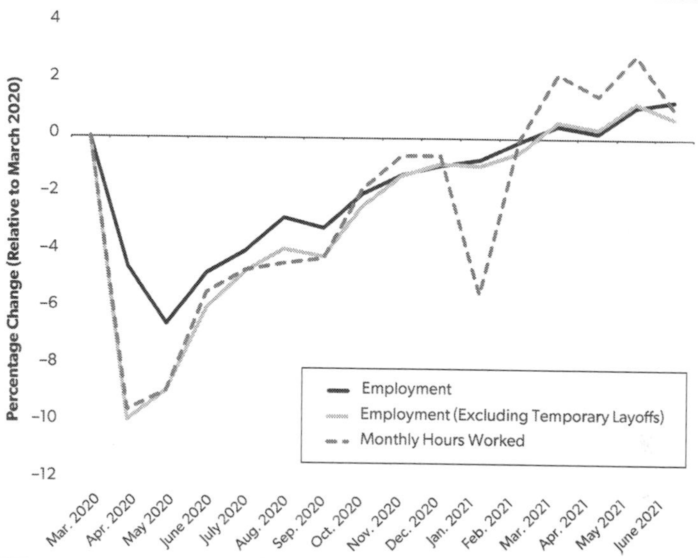

Note: Including or excluding temporarily laid off workers means including or excluding workers on zero hours for reason of "no work, not enough work available, or stood down." Data are seasonally adjusted. Source: Australian Bureau of Statistics, Labour Force, Australia, June 2021, Table 1, https://www.abs.gov.au/statistics/labour/employment-and-unemployment/labour-force-australia/jun-2021#data-download; and Australian Bureau of Statistics, Labour Force, Australia, Detailed, June 2021, EM2a, https://www.abs.gov.au/statistics/labour/employment-and-unemployment/labour-force-australia-detailed/jun-2021.

Wages Survey) came from just three industries (which before the pandemic accounted for only 18.7 percent of jobs): accommodation and food services, arts and recreation services, and retail trade.

Movement in Australia's official rate of unemployment was muted given the large fall in official employment. It peaked at 7.4 percent in mid-2020, compared to 5.3 percent before COVID-19 (Figure 5). The relatively small increase in the official rate of unemployment is explained by the large flow out of the labor force and the classification of persons on temporary layoff as employed. If workers who are on temporary layoff are instead classified as unemployed, the peak rate of unemployment becomes 12.2 percent. (See Figure 5.)

Figure 5. Rate of Unemployment, March 2020 to June 2021

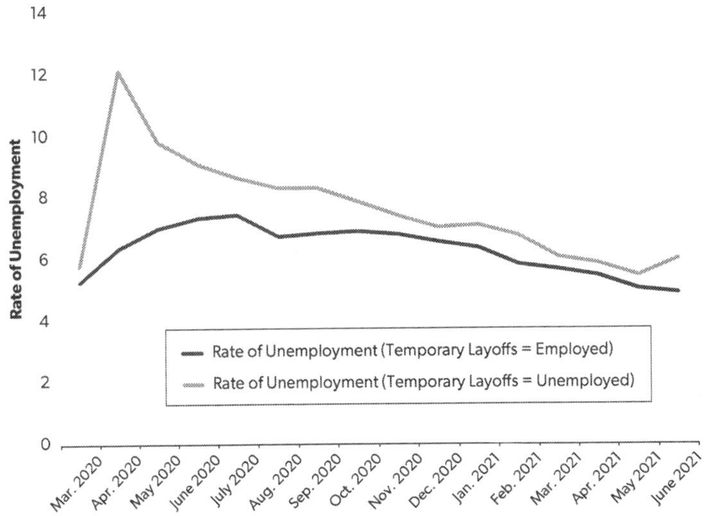

Note: Including or excluding temporarily laid off workers means including or excluding workers on zero hours for reason of "no work, not enough work available, or stood down."
Source: Australian Bureau of Statistics, Labour Force, Australia, June 2021, Tables 1 and 19, https://www.abs.gov.au/statistics/labour/employment-and-unemployment/labour-force-australia/jun-2021#data-download; and Australian Bureau of Statistics, Labour Force, Australia, Detailed, June 2021, EM2a, https://www.abs.gov.au/statistics/labour/employment-and-unemployment/labour-force-australia-detailed/jun-2021.

Hours per Worker and the Extent of Work Sharing. The quarterly decomposition of GDP hinted that work sharing was not a significant margin of adjustment stimulated by JobKeeper. Monthly data in Figure 6 show that, using the official definition of employment, hours per worker fell considerably from early March to early April 2020, before returning to their original level over the next two months.

However, this definition includes workers on temporary layoff with zero hours. When we exclude these workers, we find that hours per worker oscillated, rising somewhat from early March (31.5 hours per week) to early April (32.0 hours per week), before falling back to their original level between early April and early May as JobKeeper was introduced (31.3 hours per week).

Figure 6. Average Actual Weekly Hours Worked, March 2020 to June 2021

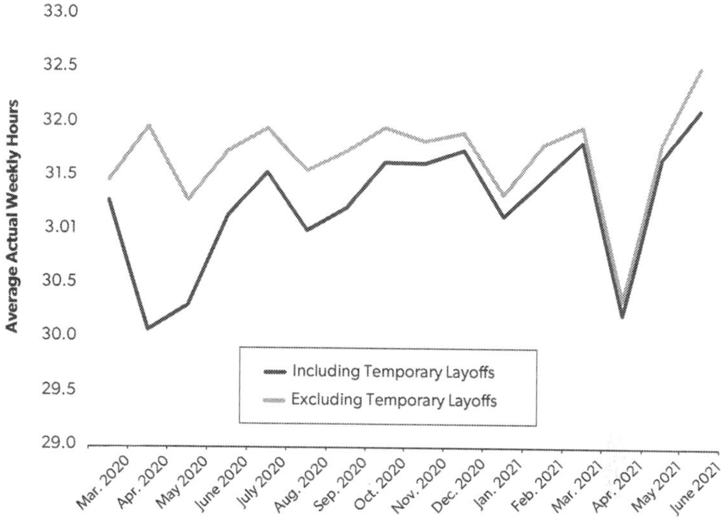

Note: Data have been manually seasonally adjusted using average monthly deviations from the annual mean for 2015–19. Including or excluding temporarily laid off workers means including or excluding zero-hours workers for the reason of "no work, not enough work available, or stood down" relative to March 2020.
Source: Australian Bureau of Statistics, Labour Force, Australia, Detailed, June 2021, Table 09 and EM2a, https://www.abs.gov.au/statistics/labour/employment-and-unemployment/labour-force-australia-detailed/jun-2021.

Since employment exclusive of those on temporary layoff changed little between early April and early May (Figure 4), the change in the composition of employment may be small, and the decline of 0.7 hours per week may genuinely indicate a small reduction in hours per worker (to positive values) stimulated by JobKeeper. Consistent with this, the share of workers saying they want to work more hours (the underemployment rate), exclusive of those temporarily laid off, rose somewhat from 7.9 percent to 10.1 percent over the same period (Figure 7). These hours adjustments may have played a modest role in arresting the employment decline in April.[24]

Figure 7. Rate of Underemployment, March 2020 to June 2021

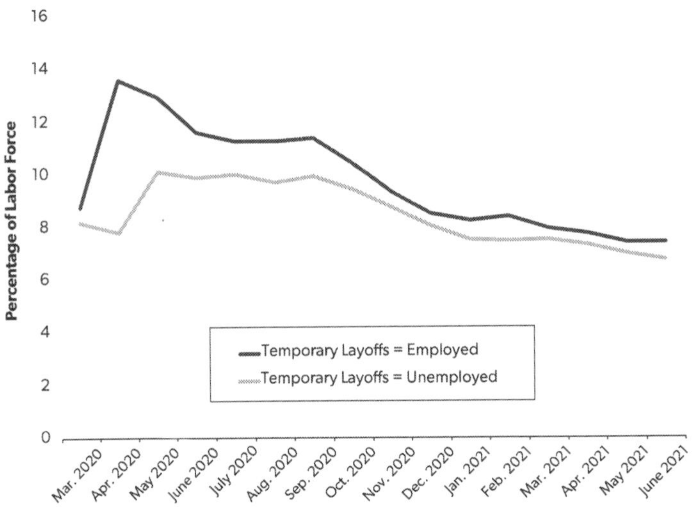

Note: Including or excluding temporarily laid off workers means including or excluding zero-hours workers for the reason of "no work, not enough work available, or stood down."
Source: Australian Bureau of Statistics, Labour Force, Australia, June 2021, Table 22, https://www.abs.gov.au/statistics/labour/employment-and-unemployment/labour-force-australia/jun-2021#data-download; and Australian Bureau of Statistics, Labour Force, Australia, Detailed, June 2021, EM2a, https://www.abs.gov.au/statistics/labour/employment-and-unemployment/labour-force-australia-detailed/jun-2021.

JobKeeper's Overall Effect on Employment

Before turning to the role of temporary layoffs in saving jobs, we consider JobKeeper's overall effect. Because the policy was national and introduced simultaneously for all workers, it is difficult to develop a counterfactual scenario in which JobKeeper was not introduced.

Bishop and Day use the best possible approach, estimating JobKeeper's impact as the difference in the change in employment outcomes for casual workers with fewer than 12 months' tenure at their employer, who were not eligible for JobKeeper, and casual workers with at least 12 months' tenure, who were eligible. Using this approach involves an assumption that the estimated impact for casual workers extends to permanent workers. Bishop and Day estimate that JobKeeper saved at least 700,000 jobs, based on data through May 2020 (mostly downturn) and counting workers placed on temporary layoff as employed.[25]

The Role of Temporary Layoffs over Downturn and Recovery

We next scrutinize temporary layoffs more carefully, using our data and external estimates to answer the questions at the heart of the chapter: whether JobKeeper encouraged temporary layoffs; if so, whether these temporary layoffs substituted for permanent layoffs; and if so, whether the employer-employee connection provided by JobKeeper spurred a faster recovery.[26]

Downturn. The combination of COVID-19 and government policies clearly encouraged temporary layoffs in the downturn. While workers on temporary layoff as a share of all workers had not risen above 0.7 percent in the previous six years for which data on the number of employed persons working zero hours for reason of "no work, not enough work available, or stood down" are available, this share peaked at 6.2 percent in April 2020. Unfortunately, we cannot identify which workers on temporary layoff were receiving JobKeeper payments, and even if we could, there is no obvious identification strategy for estimating how many workers on temporary layoff and receiving JobKeeper payments would have been permanently laid off without JobKeeper. Furthermore, these workers on temporary layoff would be only an estimate of jobs saved if they were all recalled in the upturn.

The most informative statistic comes from the Australian Treasury, which found that in May 2020, 375,000 individuals were on firm payrolls with JobKeeper as their only monetary compensation.[27] This was slightly after the trough in mid-April in the ABS index of payroll jobs.[28] If all 375,000 would have been permanently laid off and never rehired at the same employer without JobKeeper and if they all returned to positive hours with the same employer, this would constitute an accurate measure of jobs saved by JobKeeper via temporary layoffs. Therefore, 375,000 workers (2.9 percent of March 2020 employment) is the upper bound on employment saved. Relative to pre-COVID-19 (early March

2020), the decline in employment, counting temporary layoffs as employed, was 6.6 percent. Hence, this implies a reduction in employment lost in the downturn of 31 percent (2.9/(2.9 + 6.6)).

With the available data, we can contextualize this number. Figure 8 plots the number of workers on temporary layoff from March 2020 to June 2021 (not all of whom were necessarily receiving JobKeeper payments when the program was operating). In the March 2020 Labour Force Survey, pre-COVID-19, the number was 76,200. It surged to 766,600 in the April survey, when JobKeeper was announced, before subsiding to 368,400 a month later and generally declining thereafter, returning to its March level in November.[29]

An estimate of the number of temporary layoffs due to JobKeeper in the downturn is the difference between the number a month after JobKeeper was announced (at the employment trough) and the pre-COVID-19 number (368,400 – 76,200 = 292,200, or 2.2 percent of pre-COVID-19 employment and an 18 percent reduction in jobs lost). Similarly, Bishop and Day calculate from the Labour Force Survey micro-data that, in early May, 310,000 people were classified as away from work for more than four weeks but still paid by their employer (most likely receiving JobKeeper payments).[30]

Our estimate could be smaller than the Treasury estimate because the stock of workers on temporary layoff increased between early and mid-May, but this seems unlikely given the evidence that the job market improved in May. A different possibility is that the 70,000–80,000 workers on temporary layoff in normal times were able to obtain JobKeeper in May despite not being on layoff due to COVID-19, thus biasing upward jobs saved based on the Treasury statistic. On the other hand, these normal temporary layoffs may not have occurred during COVID-19, and all May temporary layoffs may have been associated with COVID-19 and JobKeeper, in which case Figure 8 would suggest 368,400 jobs were saved, essentially the same as the Treasury's estimate.[31]

Recovery. The study of the downturn in isolation suggests 292,000–375,000 jobs were saved by JobKeeper-induced temporary layoffs, but we also want to know how many resumed positive hours with the same employer in the recovery. Although we cannot measure this directly, we can investigate whether workers returning from temporary layoff appear

Figure 8. Number of Workers on Temporary Layoff

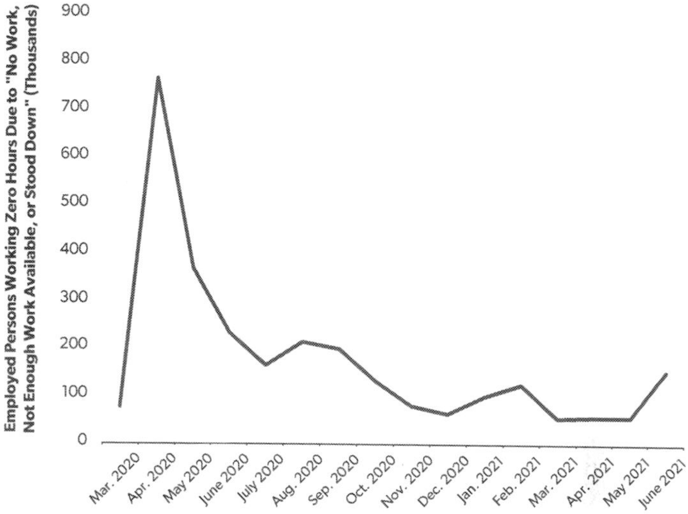

Source: Australian Bureau of Statistics, Labour Force, Australia, Detailed, June 2021, EM2a, https://www.abs.gov.au/statistics/labour/employment-and-unemployment/labour-force-australia-detailed/jun-2021.

to have been the earliest and largest source of increased worker hours in the recovery. Speeding the recovery in this way was an objective of JobKeeper; if for some reason temporarily laid-off workers remained at zero hours until late in the recovery, the objective would not have been attained.

The monthly changes in numbers of workers in various labor market states, shown in Figure 9, cast doubt on the importance of temporary layoffs for the recovery. Considering the downturn first, the figure shows that, during the pre-JobKeeper month of March, employment (excluding workers on temporary layoff) fell approximately equally due to temporary layoffs and exits from the labor force.[32] During the transitional month of April, the number of workers on temporary layoff fell considerably, as already seen in Figure 8, but exits from the labor force continued, and unemployment increased slightly as it had in March.[33]

The third set of bars in Figure 9 represent May, the first month of unambiguous recovery. Workers on temporary layoff decreased by only 136,200, less than half the stock shown in Figure 8, and we estimate below that about one-quarter of these transitioned to nonemployment. A

Figure 9. Changes in the Number of Workers in Different Labor Market States over Time

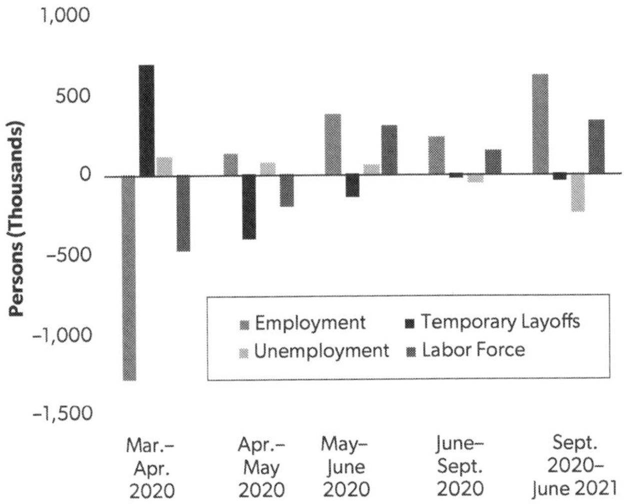

Note: The categories are mutually exclusive. Temporary layoffs refers to working zero hours for reasons of "no work, not enough work available, or stood down."
Source: Australian Bureau of Statistics, Labour Force, Australia, June 2021, Table 1, https://www.abs.gov.au/statistics/labour/employment-and-unemployment/labour-force-australia/jun-2021#data-download; and Australian Bureau of Statistics, Labour Force, Australia, Detailed, June 2021, EM2a, https://www.abs.gov.au/statistics/labour/employment-and-unemployment/labour-force-australia-detailed/jun-2021.

conservative definition of jobs saved in the way hoped for could thus be merely 0.75 x 136,200 = 102,150.

Focusing on only the first recovery month may seem restrictive, but in each of the next three months (which we group together in the figure), the stock of temporarily laid-off workers changed little, and employment rose due to an expanding labor force. Only from September did the source of employment increase become more balanced among labor force expansion, unemployment decline, and recalls from temporary layoffs.

We have access to tables based on longitudinal data that can make us more confident in the interpretation of the cross-section data in Figure 9: monthly matrices for individuals' transitions among not employed, employed at zero hours, and employed at positive hours. The category of employed at zero hours includes workers on temporary layoff, and during

Figure 10. Monthly Transition Rates out of Positive-Hour Employment and from Zero-Hour Employment to Nonemployment

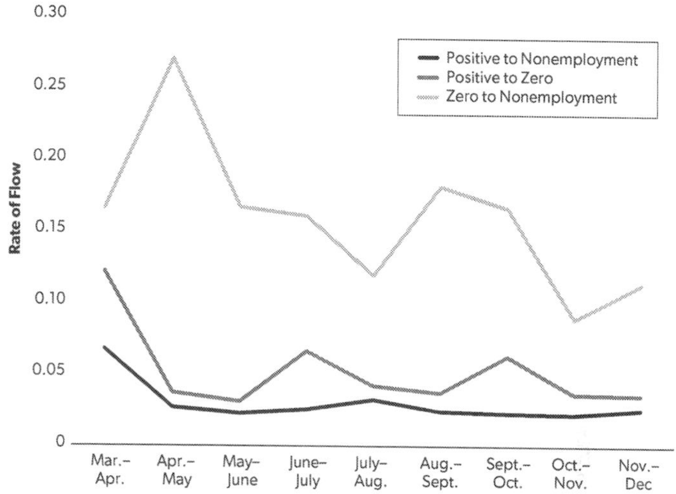

Source: Australian Bureau of Statistics, "Insights into Hours Worked," April to December 2020, https://search.abs.gov.au/s/search.html?form=simple&collection=abs-search&query=insights+into+hours+worked.

the initial months after the onset of COVID-19, transitions to and from this category were mainly from temporary layoffs.[34]

Unfortunately, the matrices are not available before March to April 2020, so the most recent matrices must be used as a proxy for normal times, and seasonal adjustment is not possible. The transition rates are displayed in graphical form in Figures 10–12. (The y-axis scales differ across figures.)

Figure 10 confirms the high rate of transitions from positive-hour employment to both zero-hour employment and nonemployment between the pre-COVID-19 period in early March 2020 and after the onset of COVID-19 in early April 2020. The spike in transitions from zero-hour employment to nonemployment between early April and early May confirms what we had inferred from cross-section data above: that a large fraction of those who, in early April, were working zero hours due to "no work, not enough work available, or stood down" were in fact recent permanent layoffs. Hence, the high early April stock of these workers is not an accurate indicator of jobs saved by temporary layoffs.

Figure 11. Monthly Transition Rates out of Nonemployment and from Zero-Hour to Positive-Hour Employment

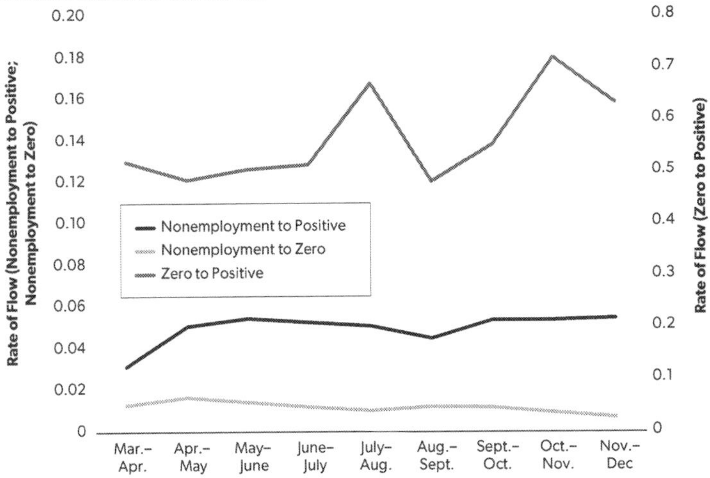

Source: Australian Bureau of Statistics, "Insights into Hours Worked," April to December 2020, https://search.abs.gov.au/s/search.html?form=simple&collection=abs-search&query=insights+into+hours+worked.

Positive-hour employment increased between April and May and between May and June (see Figure 4) as the stay rate in positive-hour employment returned to a normal level (Figure 12), a constant inflow rate from zero hours (Figure 11) operated on an elevated stock of zero-hours workers, and the transition rate from nonemployment to positive-hour employment rose (Figure 11).[35] The May–June transition matrix indicates that 75 percent of those leaving zero-hour employment in that period moved to positive-hour employment, a number we applied above to the stock of temporarily laid-off workers identified by the Treasury.

In summary, analysis of the downturn alone almost certainly overestimates jobs saved by JobKeeper-induced temporary layoffs: Our analysis of the recovery suggests that as few as 100,000 workers may have been recalled from temporary layoffs in the first month of the recovery, compared to an employment increase of 375,000 workers, and only small numbers were recalled in the subsequent three months. Instead, recovery was driven by hiring workers directly from out of the labor force, some of whom may have been rehired by their previous employer.

Figure 12. Monthly Stay Rates in Positive-Hour Employment and Nonemployment

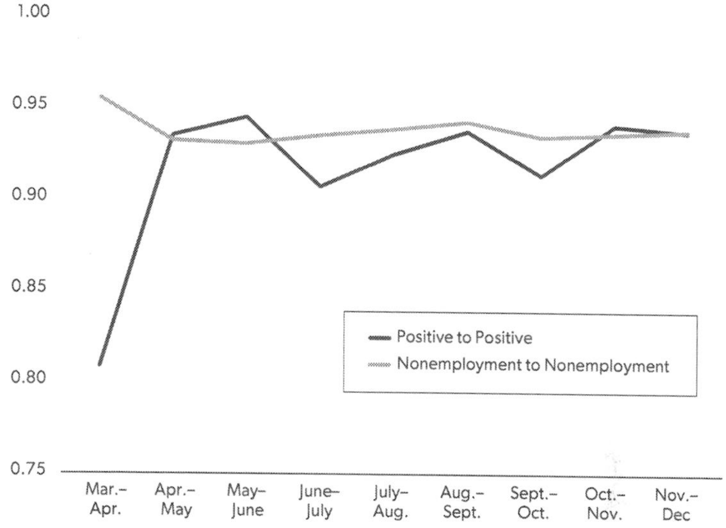

Source: Australian Bureau of Statistics, "Insights into Hours Worked," April to December 2020, https://search.abs.gov.au/s/search.html?form=simple&collection=abs-search&query=insights+into+hours+worked.

Our conclusion is consistent with the Treasury's analysis, which found that in May 2020, 375,000 workers were receiving JobKeeper payments for zero hours of work and that in September 2020 that number had declined to only 235,000.[36] This implies, at most, 140,000 recalls from JobKeeper-induced temporary layoffs in the first several months of the recovery.

How Disruptive Was Phasing Out JobKeeper?

Phasing out a subsidy could be associated with increased separations of workers from firms (involuntary and voluntary). The size of that increase might indicate the extent to which the subsidy was stimulating labor demand by keeping output artificially high (offsetting the drag of continuing COVID-19-related restrictions on economic activity) or disincentivizing reallocations of workers to more productive firms or industries.

The transition from phase one to the less generous phase two of JobKeeper occurred when most of Australia had recovered from the

Figure 13. Outflow Rate from Employment

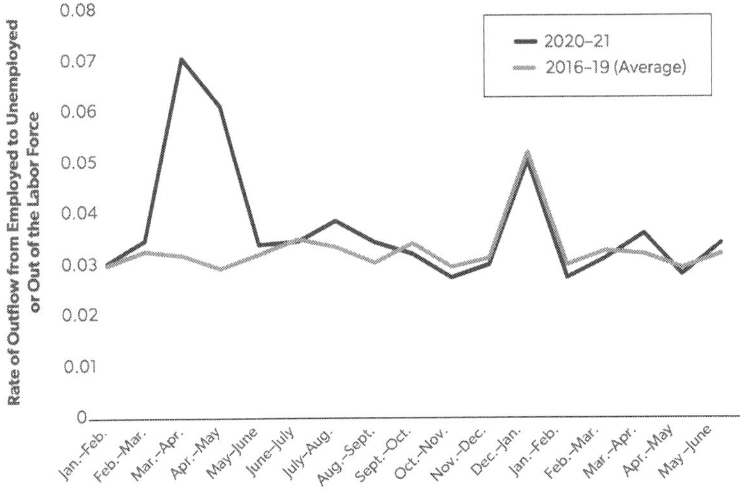

Note: Data are not seasonally adjusted.
Source: Australian Bureau of Statistics, Labour Force, Australia, June 2021, GM1, https://www.abs.gov.au/statistics/labour/employment-and-unemployment/labour-force-australia/jun-2021#data-download.

downturn, except for the locked-down state of Victoria. By the time JobKeeper ended, the economy was performing well throughout the country, and COVID-19 rates were low.

Plots of outflows from employment in Figure 13 show that any effect of the transition from phase one to phase two at the end of September 2020 was imperceptible and that the outflows rose only 13 percent (by 45,000 people), compared to previous years, when the program ended at the end of March 2021.[37] This suggests that, once the economy recovered, JobKeeper was primarily increasing firm profits (though stimulus effects on consumer demand are unlikely to be detectable from this figure).

Benefit-Cost Assessment

JobKeeper created social benefits in several main ways. First, by providing macroeconomic stimulus, the program promoted increased economic activity and allowed smoothing of income over time. Second, increasing incomes of workers who would otherwise have experienced lower or zero hours of work had a positive distributional impact. Third, by increasing the survival rate of viable businesses that would have ceased to exist without JobKeeper and decreasing the costs of job search and hiring in recovery due to job connections preserved, the program reduced adjustment costs associated with COVID-19.

JobKeeper's monetary cost was AUD 88.8 billion. Accounting for the fact that workers whose jobs were saved by JobKeeper would otherwise have been receiving the JobSeeker (unemployment) benefit gives a direct cost of AUD 75.5 billion.[38] A further indirect cost may have been to "freeze" firm and worker dynamics and hence lower labor productivity. For example, firms may have been discouraged from churning their workforces because the payment was available only for employees already working with the employer.

At this stage, it is not possible to make an overall benefit-cost assessment of JobKeeper. We can, however, address several aspects that are relevant to that overall assessment. First, the cost of preserving job connections via JobKeeper appears relatively high. Dividing AUD 75.5 billion by the estimate of 700,000 jobs saved gives an average cost per job saved of AUD 107,900 (about USD 80,500).[39] This is relatively high by comparison with previous international programs; for example, the American Recovery and Reinvestment Act of 2009 is estimated to have had an average cost per job saved of about USD 50,000.[40] It is, however, much less than the estimated cost of USD 224,000 per job supported by the Paycheck Protection Program, implemented by the US government to deal with COVID-19.[41]

Second, it seems indubitable that JobKeeper provided substantial macroeconomic stimulus in Australia during 2020–21. The relatively short duration of economic downturn and fast pace of recovery were likely partly due to JobKeeper raising household and business incomes and improving confidence. For example, consumer and business confidence increased rapidly following the announcement of JobKeeper.[42] At this stage, however, it is not possible to separate JobKeeper's precise effect on macroeconomic activity from other government stimulus measures and successful management of COVID-19.

Third, who received the JobKeeper payments matters. When employment losses peaked in May 2020, an estimated one-quarter of payments went to labor as increased income, and three-quarters went as a transfer to businesses and nonprofits.[43] As employment recovered in subsequent months, the share of payments going to labor is likely to have fallen, and the share to business is likely to have increased. That business received the greater share of payments was partly due to the program's one-in-all-in feature and partly due to the economic downturn caused by COVID-19 being less severe than the initial scenario for which JobKeeper was designed.

The distribution of JobKeeper payments between labor and business has implications for the extent and timing of macroeconomic stimulus. Whereas the payments going to labor likely brought a relatively immediate increase in consumption spending, the impact of the payments that constituted a transfer to businesses and nonprofits is less certain. The distributional consequences of such a large transfer to business cannot be assessed until more data are available. However, analysis by the Australian Treasury shows that the income component of JobKeeper went predominantly to individual workers at the bottom of the income distribution.[44]

Fourth, JobKeeper's costs deriving from freezing firm and worker dynamics were likely minimal. Annual labor productivity growth from 2012 to 2019 in Australia was 1.1 percent yearly.[45] The share of productivity growth that can be attributed to employment reallocation—based on reviews of microeconomic studies of firm-level productivity—is about one-quarter to one-half.[46]

Hence, taking into account that JobKeeper covered only one-fourth of the Australian workforce at its peak, even if the program had prevented all employment reallocation among recipients, the cost of missing productivity growth would be equal to, at most, 0.1 to 0.15 percent of GDP.[47] In fact, the minimal job destruction that occurred in the transition from phase one to phase two and when the program ended in March 2021 suggest that the negative effect on productivity would have been even less.

Lessons from JobKeeper

JobKeeper was introduced at short notice in the face of a crisis whose duration and severity were unclear, and hindsight can inform improvements in preparation for a future sudden economic downturn. One key question is whether the cost per job saved could be reduced from AUD 100,000 by adjusting the program. The Australian government did adjust JobKeeper when the program was renewed in September 2020, notably reducing costs by reducing payments to part-time workers. Lower payments to part-time workers may not have changed the microeconomic incentives meaningfully but would have reduced the stimulus to consumption.

If inframarginal payments to firms do not produce much stimulus, the second phase of JobKeeper would have been a better program to use initially. Had JobKeeper been introduced earlier, its impact on jobs may also have been larger and hence the cost per job lower.

Another cost concern is the relatively large proportion of JobKeeper subsidies that flowed to businesses that had revenue decreases smaller than the intended threshold for eligibility. Whether a program such as JobKeeper should incorporate built-in features allowing spending to adapt to the severity of the downturn it is seeking to address therefore will likely be an important topic of policy debate.

Given the importance of a quick policy response and the limited degree to which JobKeeper appears to have shared the available work hours among workers, a short-time work program such as those used in Germany, Switzerland, and elsewhere in Europe could also be worth considering for Australia. The long-standing German program, for example, has the twin objectives of reducing employment loss and retaining employer-worker matches. It can be used at any time by individual firms suffering revenue declines affecting a sufficiently large share of workers, and though it is used principally in recessions, it does not need to be activated in response to a recession.[48] A short-time program seems likely to save jobs at lower cost than JobKeeper did due to lower deadweight loss and seems likely to reduce hours per worker more equitably.[49]

Conclusion

Australia's JobKeeper program provided a lump-sum wage subsidy to workers via employers, to be paid even if the workers' hours were reduced to zero. Theoretically, JobKeeper should subsidize labor hoarding and speed recovery through its promotion of temporary layoffs and should mitigate output decline (except when the output decline is due directly to COVID-19 restrictions). Theory may also seem to predict that JobKeeper is a work-sharing program, in which jobs are saved by cuts in hours per worker to positive hours, but once one considers worker groups with differing eligibility, the prediction no longer holds.

The best empirical evidence in the literature suggests that the subsidy may have reduced total employment losses by at least 700,000 in the downturn, equivalent to 5.2 percent of March 2020 employment, implying a reduction in employment losses of 44 percent (5.2/(5.2 + 6.6)).[50] Our examination of the downturn indicates that the subset saved due to putting workers on temporary layoff was 292,000–375,000.

However, our analysis of the recovery suggests that as few as 100,000 workers were recalled from temporary layoffs in the first month of the recovery and small numbers were recalled in the subsequent three months, with recovery driven by workers hired directly from out of the labor force. Temporary layoffs facilitated by JobKeeper seem not to have sped recovery, raising the question of how many workers were in fact recalled to positive hours of work.

JobKeeper does not appear to have operated as a short-time work (work-sharing) program: There was little reduction of worker hours to positive hours. Adjustment came through hiring freezes and temporary and permanent layoffs, particularly of casual and low-tenure permanent workers with lower firing costs. Given this and the high costs per job saved by JobKeeper, we believe that, in preparation for the next recession, Australia should consider setting up a short-time work system similar to those used in Germany and Switzerland.

Acknowledgments

Jennifer Hunt is grateful for the University of Sydney's hospitality while she and Jeff Borland were writing this chapter, and she is also affiliated with the Centre for Economic Policy Research and the Institute of Labor Economics. We thank James Bishop for stimulating discussions and supplemental figures, Samuel Fang for research assistance, and Deborah

Cobb-Clark, James Graham, Dean Hyslop, Andrew Leigh, Dave Maré, Dean Paatsch, and participants in the University of Sydney Microeconomic and Public Policy seminar for helpful input.

Notes

1. International Monetary Fund, Fiscal Monitor: Database of Country Fiscal Measures in Response to the COVID-19 Pandemic, June 2020, https://www.imf.org/en/Topics/imf-and-covid19/~/media/Files/Topics/COVID/FM-Database/june-2020-fiscal-monitor-database-of-fiscal-measures-in-response-to-covid19.ashx. The shares comprise additional spending and forgone revenue, exclusive of additional health expenditures.

2. International Monetary Fund, Fiscal Monitor: Database of Country Fiscal Measures in Response to the COVID-19 Pandemic, July 2021, https://www.imf.org/en/Topics/imf-and-covid19/~/media/Files/Topics/COVID/FM-Database/july-2021-country-fiscal-measures-database-publication-v2.ashx.

3. Josh Frydenberg, Scott Morrison, and Anne Ruston, "JobKeeper Payment and Income Support Extended," press release, July 21, 2020, https://ministers.treasury.gov.au/ministers/josh-frydenberg-2018/media-releases/jobkeeper-payment-and-income-support-extended; and Australian Government, Treasury, "JobKeeper Payment Extension," October 15, 2020, https://treasury.gov.au/sites/default/files/2020-10/Fact_sheet-JobKeeper_Payment_extension_0.pdf.

4. Australian Government, Fair Work Ombudsman, "Casual Employees," https://www.fairwork.gov.au/employee-entitlements/types-of-employees/casual-part-time-and-full-time/casual-employees.

5. Eligibility also required an employee to be an Australian citizen, the holder of a permanent visa, a protected Special Category visa holder, a non-protected Special Category visa holder who has been residing continually in Australia for 10 years or more, or a Subclass 444 Special Category visa holder. Eligibility for JobKeeper was also restricted via ruling some types of organizations to be outside the program's scope—for example, government agencies, universities, and major banks.

6. When an employee had multiple jobs at which they were eligible to receive JobKeeper payments, they were required to nominate a "primary employer" to whom the subsidy would be paid.

7. Self-employed individuals needed to have been operating their businesses on March 1, been able to meet requirements relating to having a registered business, and submitted recent tax statements.

8. For further details on businesses' eligibility for phase one of JobKeeper, see Australian Government, Taxation Office, *JobKeeper Payment—Decline in Turnover Test*, April 9, 2020, https://www.ato.gov.au/law/view/pdf/pbr/lcr2020-001.pdf.

9. Australian Government, Treasury, "JobKeeper Payment Extension."

10. Australian Bureau of Statistics, "Business Indicators, Business Impacts of COVID-19," May 4, 2020, https://www.abs.gov.au/statistics/economy/business-indicators/business-conditions-and-sentiments/apr-2020.

11. Australian Bureau of Statistics, "Government Support for Business," September 2, 2020, Figure 2, https://www.abs.gov.au/articles/government-support-business#jobkeeper-payments-by-industry.

12. Australian Government, Treasury, *The JobKeeper Payment: Three-Month Review*, July 21, 2020, https://treasury.gov.au/publication/jobkeeper-review; and Australian Government, Treasury, *Insights from the First Six Months of JobKeeper*, October 11, 2021, Table 3, https://treasury.gov.au/publication/p2021-211978.

13. For details of these policies, see Prime Minister of Australia, "Economic Stimulus Package," press release, March 12, 2020, https://www.pm.gov.au/media/economic-stimulus-package; Prime Minister of Australia, "Supporting Australian Workers and Business," press release, March 22, 2020, https://www.pm.gov.au/media/supporting-australian-workers-and-business; and Prime Minister of Australia, "$130 Billion JobKeeper Payment to Keep Australians in a Job," press release, March 30, 2020, https://www.pm.gov.au/media/130-billion-jobkeeper-payment-keep-australians-job.

14. Recipients of government welfare payments had their incomes raised through one-off cash payments and temporary increases in benefit levels. For example, the flat amount for JobSeeker (unemployment) payments was initially increased by AUD 275 per week (raising the overall payment for a single person to AUD 562.85 per week).

15. Rebecca Cassells and Alan Duncan, "JobKeeper: The Efficacy of Australia's First Short-Time Wage Subsidy," *Australian Journal of Labour Economics* 23, no. 2 (September 2020): 99–128, https://bcec.edu.au/publications/jobkeeper-the-efficacy-of-australias-first-short-time-wage-subsidy.

16. We calculate that 84 percent of employees eligible for JobKeeper had permanent status and hence would have been costly for employers to lay off.

17. See Australian Bureau of Statistics, Labour Force, Australia, https://www.abs.gov.au/statistics/labour/employment-and-unemployment/labour-force-australia.

18. For example, see Australian Government, Treasury, *The JobKeeper Payment: Three-Month Review*, July 21, 2020, https://treasury.gov.au/publication/jobkeeper-review; and Australian Government, Treasury, *Insights from the First Six Months of JobKeeper*.

19. Australian Fair Work Commission, "Standing Down Employees," April 7, 2021, https://www.fwc.gov.au/industrial-action-benchbook/payments-relating-industrial-action/standing-down-employees. The standing-down rules were clarified in the COVID-19 context. See Australian Government, Fair Work Ombudsman, "JobKeeper Enabling Stand Down Directions," May 24, 2021, https://coronavirus.fairwork.gov.au/coronavirus-and-australian-workplace-laws/changes-to-workplace-laws-during-coronavirus/jobkeeper-scheme-overview/jobkeeper-enabling-stand-down-directions.

20. Australian Government, Fair Work Ombudsman, "Ending Employment and the JobKeeper Scheme," May 24, 2021, https://coronavirus.fairwork.gov.au/coronavirus-and-australian-workplace-laws/changes-to-workplace-laws-during-coronavirus/jobkeeper-scheme-overview/ending-employment-and-the-jobkeeper-scheme.

21. Australian Bureau of Statistics, "People Working Fewer Hours," May 21, 2020, https://www.abs.gov.au/articles/people-working-fewer-hours.

22. The large decrease in monthly hours worked in January 2021 was due to an exceptionally large number of people taking vacation during that summer month (above the usual number incorporated into the seasonal adjustment).

23. Jeff Borland and Andrew Charlton, "The Australian Labour Market and the Early Impact of COVID-19: An Assessment," *Australian Economic Review* 53, no. 3 (September 2020): 297–324, https://papers.ssrn.com/sol3/papers.cfm?abstract_id=3703715#.

24. Our unreported analysis of data over the longer period from February to May 2020 indicates that changes in industry composition slightly moderated the decrease in average weekly hours worked that would otherwise have occurred. (We are obliged to consider this longer period because industry-level data are available only quarterly.)

25. James Bishop and Iris Day, *How Many Jobs Did JobKeeper Keep?*, Reserve Bank of Australia, November 2020, https://rba.gov.au/publications/rdp/2020/pdf/rdp2020-07.pdf. It is not possible to track employment of workers earning above and below the JobKeeper payment as earnings are available in publicly available data only for August of each year.

26. Bishop and Day do test sensitivity to the definition of employment and to extending the data through July to include some of the recovery. Comparing these results in principle allows a calculation of the role of temporary layoffs, but the differences among the estimates do not have a clear pattern and are small compared with the standard errors. See Bishop and Day, *How Many Jobs Did JobKeeper Keep?*

27. Australian Government, Treasury, *Insights from the First Six Months of JobKeeper*.

28. Australian Bureau of Statistics, "Weekly Payroll Jobs and Wages in Australia," July 22, 2021, https://www.abs.gov.au/statistics/labour/earnings-and-work-hours/weekly-payroll-jobs-and-wages-australia/week-ending-3-july-2021.

29. In the April survey, the category of "no work, not enough work available, or stood down" also includes permanent layoffs. This is because a worker who is permanently laid off and did not work in the Labour Force Survey reference week, but who received payment for work in the past four weeks, is counted as employed. For more details, see the definition of "employment" in Australian Bureau of Statistics, "Questionnaires Used in the Labour Force Survey," https://www.abs.gov.au/statistics/research/questionnaires-used-labour-force-survey.

30. Bishop and Day, *How Many Jobs Did JobKeeper Keep?*

31. Bishop and Day speculate that their number differs from the Australian Treasury's number due to JobKeeper recipients temporarily laid off from one job but being paid (non-JobKeeper earnings) at another firm. For the purposes of counting jobs saved, it is unclear how such workers should be classified. See Bishop and Day, *How Many Jobs Did JobKeeper Keep?*

32. What we refer to as the month of March is the period from the March to April Labour Force Surveys. Similarly, references to the months of April and May refer to the periods from the April to May and May to June Labour Force Surveys, respectively.

33. As noted in endnote 22, this decrease included recent permanent layoffs that had been included in April in the category of employed on zero hours for the reason of "no work, not enough work available, or stood down."

34. In the cross-section data, for March to April, April to May, and May to June, 65 percent, 46 percent, and 72 percent, respectively, of the changes in the total number of workers employed on zero hours were due to changes in the category of "no work, not enough work available, or stood down."

35. The timing of the employment recovery in May versus June, in Figure 4, does not correspond exactly to the changes implied by Figure 9, due to the discrepancy between temporarily laid-off workers and all workers with zero hours.

36. Australian Government, Treasury, *Insights from the First Six Months of JobKeeper*, 29.

37. Steven Kennedy, "Opening Statement—Economics Legislation Committee" (speech, Parliament House, Canberra, Australia, March 24, 2021), https://treasury.gov.au/speech/opening-statement-economics-legislation-committee-2021.

38. This estimate is based on assumptions that one-fifth of JobKeeper recipients would otherwise have received JobSeeker and that the JobSeeker payment was about three-quarters of the JobKeeper payment throughout both programs.

39. This is a best-case scenario, based on a peak estimate of jobs saved. Robert Breunig and Timothy Watson estimate that the cost per job retained by JobKeeper in the first six months was between AUD 70,000 and AUD 102,000. See Robert Breunig and Timothy Watson, "Strengthening JobKeeper," Asia and the Pacific Policy Society, June 16, 2020, https://www.policyforum.net/strengthening-jobkeeper.

40. Gabriel Chodorow-Reich, "Geographic Cross-Sectional Fiscal Spending Multipliers: What Have We Learned?," *American Economic Journal: Economic Policy* 11, no. 2 (May 2019): 1–34, https://www.aeaweb.org/articles?id=10.1257/pol.20160465.

41. David Autor et al., "An Evaluation of the Paycheck Protection Program Using Administrative Payroll Microdata" (working paper, Massachusetts Institute of Technology, Blueprint Labs, Cambridge, MA, July 2020), 24, https://blueprintlabs.mit.edu/research/an-evaluation-of-the-paycheck-protection-program-using-administrative-payroll-microdata.

42. Australian Government, Treasury, *Insights from the First Six Months of JobKeeper*, 26.

43. Australian Government, Treasury, *Insights from the First Six Months of JobKeeper*, 28.

44. Australian Government, Treasury, *Insights from the First Six Months of JobKeeper*, 31.

45. Australian Bureau of Statistics, "Australian National Accounts: National Income, Expenditure and Product," December 1, 2021, Table 1, https://www.abs.gov.au/statistics/economy/national-accounts/australian-national-accounts-national-income-expenditure-and-product/latest-release.

46. Lucia Foster, John Haltiwanger, and C. J. Krizan, "Aggregate Productivity Growth: Lessons from Microeconomic Evidence" (working paper, National Bureau of Economic Research, Cambridge, MA, November 1998), Table 4, https://www.nber.org/papers/w6803.

47. The minimal job destruction that occurred between phase one and phase two and then when the program ended in March 2021 suggest that JobKeeper's negative effect on productivity would have been even less. Dan Andrews, Andrew

Charlton, and Angus Moore suggest, from a review of employment reallocation during COVID-19 in Australia, "that the reallocation-productivity link remained intact amongst the JobKeeper eligible workforce suggests that the JRS did not completely distort natural market selection." Dan Andrews, Andrew Charlton, and Angus Moore, "COVID-19, Productivity and Reallocation: Timely Evidence from Three OECD Countries" (working paper, Organisation for Economic Co-operation and Development, Paris, France, 2021), 28, https://www.oecd-ilibrary.org/economics/covid-19-productivity-and-reallocation-timely-evidence-from-three-oecd-countries_d2c4b89c-en.

48. For a description of short-time work in Germany during COVID-19, see International Monetary Fund, "Kurzarbeit: Germany's Short-Time Work Benefit," June 15, 2020, https://www.imf.org/en/News/Articles/2020/06/11/na061120-kurzarbeit-germanys-short-time-work-benefit.

49. Michael C. Burda and Jennifer Hunt, "What Explains the German Labor Market Miracle in the Great Recession?," *Brookings Papers on Economic Activity* (Spring 2011): 273–319, https://www.brookings.edu/wp-content/uploads/2011/03/2011a_bpea_burda.pdf; and Giulia Giupponi and Camille Landais, "Subsidizing Labor Hoarding in Recessions: The Employment & Welfare Effects of Short Time Work," London School of Economics and Political Science, Centre for Economic Performance, May 26, 2020, https://econ.lse.ac.uk/staff/clandais/cgi-bin/Articles/STW.pdf.

50. See Bishop and Day, *How Many Jobs Did JobKeeper Keep?*

3

The Canada Emergency Wage Subsidy as an Employer-Based Response to the Pandemic: First Steps, Missteps, and Next Steps

MILES CORAK

Many members of the Royal Ottawa Golf Club may have been relieved, perhaps even pleasantly surprised, after hearing the club treasurer summarize the financial statements for 2020, the pandemic year. The Royal Ottawa is the club of the elite in Canada's national capital region, with former prime ministers and cabinet ministers, high commissioners and ambassadors, business leaders, and even players in the National Hockey League among its well-heeled membership: a well-financed operation that nonetheless applied for and received a $1.019 million wage subsidy from the federal government.

Based on the audited financial statements and a recording of the annual general meeting, the Canadian Broadcasting Corporation reported that the membership had many suggestions for the use of the moneys—lowering fees, transferring to the capital account, accelerating expenditures, and paving the parking lot—but the club treasurer reported that the executive decided to "park" the funds. The entire amount "ended up on the bottom line" and contributed to a "very strong financial position," the club weathering the first year of the pandemic nicely with an $825,000 surplus, somewhat higher than the $43,000 recorded for the 2019 fiscal year.[1]

This golf club, like many other businesses, was clearly aware of the many fast-paced developments in the policy response to COVID-19. Most notably, on April 1, 2020, the Department of Finance Canada issued a press release titled "Government Announces Details of the Canada Emergency Wage Subsidy to Help Businesses Keep Canadians in Their Jobs." The release stated:

> To help Canadians and businesses get through these tough economic times, the Prime Minister, Justin Trudeau, announced that the Government is proposing to introduce a wage subsidy of 75 per cent for qualifying businesses, for up to 3 months, retroactive to March 15, 2020.[2]

With this announcement and the passing of legislation on April 11, the Canada Emergency Wage Subsidy (CEWS) started taking applications on April 27. The Royal Ottawa Golf Club was among the roughly 300,000 applications received during each of the remaining months of the year. The CEWS's stated objective was to support businesses "hardest hit by the COVID-19 pandemic" and thereby "protect the jobs Canadians depend on during these difficult times."[3]

I tell the story of the Royal Ottawa because it so clearly illustrates the failure to appreciate three basic lessons from standard economic principles that should govern the design and evaluation of programs intended to maintain a tie between workers and firms—principles that eventually will, or should, guide more-detailed cost-benefit assessments of this program. In the first section of this chapter, I describe the CEWS, how it evolved throughout the pandemic, and how it has been wound down.

In the second section, I reflect on why we might in retrospect be cautious in considering its design as a model for the future. I look at its failure to (1) address the factors that influence a firm's decision to shut down, (2) recognize that the legal incidence of a subsidy is not necessarily its economic incidence, and (3) target policy at the margin.

But in assessing the Canadian pandemic response, we must also recognize three matters of policy practice. In the third section, I use these to evaluate the challenges policymakers faced in crafting the Canadian response and highlight how existing programs were in one sense more suited but also hampered in their capacity to respond. These include a federally operated non-experience-rated unemployment insurance program that has long offered ongoing wage subsidies to employers and special provisions within this program for work sharing during significant economic shocks. In evaluating the CEWS's effectiveness and charting options for the future, policymakers will need to recognize not only core economic principles but the challenges posed by program delivery, program substitution, and policy drift arising from the political economy of discretionary decisions.

I conclude that, when the final evaluations are in, the CEWS might not pass a cost-benefit test because other programs proved more effective in offering real-time income support to affected workers. I also conclude that the political economy of the small-business lobby may have shaped a less-than-optimal response. Policymakers found the CEWS necessary because of the bottlenecks in the delivery of existing and better-suited programs. Challenges in the service-delivery side of government created the need and drove hasty policy choices.

In the Canadian case, one positive consequence of the pandemic is long-needed investments in the modernization of program delivery that will reduce the need for discretionary policy in the future. If this lesson is not to be lost, governments should offer ongoing investment for the continual modernization of service delivery in good times and bad. With this modernization in place, future Canadian public policy would be well-advised to rely on the unemployment insurance program, particularly on the work-sharing provisions it offers, to more effectively target support directly to workers. The CEWS may reasonably be thought of as an experiment not to be repeated.

The Evolution of the CEWS

The CEWS represents a significant part of the federal government's pandemic response. The 2021 federal budget estimates total spending of $111 billion on this program over fiscal years 2019–20 and 2021–22, amounting to 38.6 percent of the total direct pandemic support measures of $286 billion and significantly exceeding the next highest item, the $73 billion Canada Emergency Response Benefit (CERB).[4]

As originally announced, potentially all employers of all sizes in all sectors of the economy (excluding the public sector) were eligible to apply for a 75 percent subsidy of the first $58,700 normally earned by an employee, a maximum benefit of $847 per week. It was also announced that this benefit would be in place for 12 weeks, from March 15 to June 6, 2020. The Department of Finance made clear that "entitlement to this wage subsidy will be based entirely on the salary or wages actually paid to employees." It even went so far as to suggest, as an act of moral suasion rather than legislative requirement, that "all employers would be expected to at least make best efforts to top up salaries to 100% of the maximum wages covered."[5]

The legislation that enacted these provisions received royal assent on April 11, 2020, as Bill C-14. The bill stipulated that employers were eligible if their revenues declined by at least 15 percent between March 15 and April 11 relative to March 2019 but by 30 percent between April 12 and May 9 or between May 10 and June 6 relative to April or May 2019.[6] A business could also qualify if gross revenues fell by the same percentages relative to average revenues between January and February 2020 if it was not active on March 1, 2019.[7]

In line with the prevailing sentiment among policymakers in many countries, a sentiment strongly promoted by the Paris-based Organisation for Economic Co-operation and Development, the government clearly intended this program to channel income support to workers through their employers. This would prevent the layoffs that would otherwise inevitably result from the pandemic-induced collapse of demand for products and services in many sectors. The guiding metaphor was of "freezing" the economy and businesses to prevent job and income losses during the lockdowns necessitated by the pandemic and then to begin again where the economy had left off once the health shock had passed or been contained. Indeed, at the time, many economists speculated about the shape of the recession and recovery, the best-case scenario being a "V-shaped" recession that would be sharp and quick on the downswing but equally sharp and quick on the upswing—a "plucking" model of the business cycle, to borrow a term used decades ago by Milton Friedman and his coauthors.[8]

That said, the prime minister was also clear in repeated press conferences that the government was crafting its policies step-by-step in the face of uncertainty about the nature and extent of the health shock and its economic impacts. It aimed for two quick steps forward while being aware of inevitable missteps necessitating a rethink, followed by another move forward as better evidence accumulated. The socioeconomic challenges of COVID-19 called for real-time policymaking and delivery, and the government was the first to admit that programs of a scale never before designed, put into place at a speed never before attempted, would require reconsideration and refinement as the situation evolved, experience was gained, and delivery capacity was developed. The government may well have been in a hard-pressed position of facing suboptimal policy choices between supporting too few or too many Canadians.[9]

So, it is in some sense understandable that a wage-subsidy program intended to prevent, or at least soften, a sharp decline in employment and incomes would be refined and even extended as the first wave of the pandemic turned into a second wave before wide-scale vaccination was possible. The enabling legislation stipulated that the CEWS payments could be collected no later than September 30, 2020. But the CEWS was repeatedly extended with changes, most notably in the federal budget released on April 19, 2021, that extended the program with the intention to wind it down on September 25 while seeking legislative authority to extend it through regulations to as long as November 20 if the government saw fit. Indeed, on July 30, 2021, the government announced proposed changes and an extension to October 23, 2021, before confirming on October 21 that the program would end.[10]

The program's actual structure, however, can be summarized as moving through three distinct phases. The subsidy rate as a function of the revenue drop required to qualify is depicted in Figure 1, a different shade corresponding to each phase. The first phase is the program as originally launched, having the most stringent eligibility rule but a high subsidy rate. Applications to the program were required for each of a series of monthly claim periods. This version of the program combined a sharp discontinuity in the eligibility rule, requiring a revenue fall of at least 15 percent during the first claim period and 30 percent during the next two, with a generous and flat subsidy rate of 75 percent regardless of the revenue loss beyond the minimum required to qualify.

This design was replaced with the claim period beginning on July 5, 2020, one that repeated through subsequent claim periods for a year. During this phase, the rules permitted employers with any revenue fall to qualify for the subsidy, significantly eroding the targeting of program eligibility. Further, employers were not obligated to demonstrate that their revenue loss was related to COVID-19. The subsidy rate increased linearly with the amount of the revenue loss up to a loss of 50 percent, beyond

Figure 1. Three Phases in the Evolution of the CEWS: Wage Subsidy Rate and Revenue Fall Required to Qualify

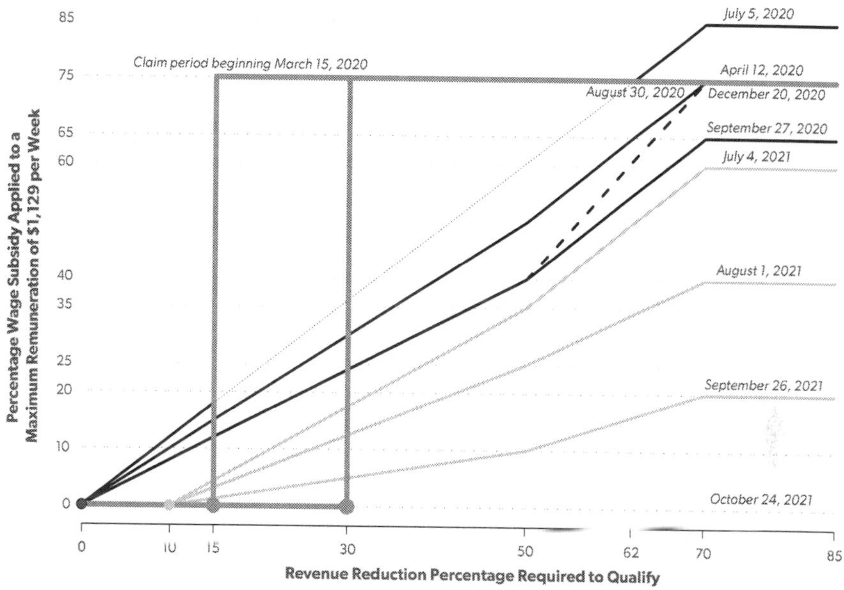

Source: Created by the author using information available at the time of writing from the Canada Revenue Agency and Department of Finance Canada.

which it was "topped up," increasing at a higher rate to a maximum, which introduced an attempt to target program generosity on the most-impacted businesses.

This maximum varied slightly with changes over some of the claim periods. The first claim period of this structure, that beginning on July 5 and extending to August 30, was the most generous version of the CEWS. All employers with any revenue drop were eligible, and the subsidy reached a maximum rate of 85 percent for the most affected businesses. Also, if the subsidy rate calculated by the piecewise linear rule was lower than what would have been received during the previous claim period, then the employer could take advantage of, to use the government's words, a "safe harbour" and claim the higher subsidy rate. The region over which the safe harbour applied is indicated by the dashed line in Figure 1 for the July 5 claim period.[11]

The maximum subsidy rate was reduced to 65 percent for the claim period beginning on September 27 but then returned to 75 percent with the December 20 claim period, where it remained until July 4, 2021. This claim period represents the start of the program's third structure, which is characterized by a minimum 10 percent reduction of revenues to qualify and a gradually declining maximum subsidy rate, though still embodying a top-up of that rate if the revenue decline is 50 percent or greater. With the government's July 30 announcement, the maximum subsidy rate stood at 20 percent, with the claim period beginning on September 26, 2021. The program was eliminated beginning on October 24.

The wage subsidy could be claimed for not just existing employees but also those hired after March 15, 2020. The subsidy rate applied to weekly per-employee remuneration to a maximum of $1,129, implying a maximum subsidy of $959.65 when the 85 percent rate was in place and $846.75 for the 75 percent rate. In addition, beginning in the claim period starting on June 6, 2021, well after a year since the initial launch, the government introduced "the executive compensation wage subsidy repayment rule," requiring repayment of any or all the wage subsidy to publicly listed or traded employers whose aggregate executive compensation during 2021 exceeded that in 2019.

On October 21, 2021, the government confirmed that the CEWS would end and be replaced by two more-targeted programs: the Tourism and Hospitality Recovery Program and the Hardest-Hit Business Recovery Program. Program eligibility would be determined by not just significant revenue losses in the current month but also average monthly losses over the first 12 months of the pandemic: a 40 percent decline in revenues over each time span for businesses in tourism and hospitality and 50 percent for other businesses. The maximum subsidy rate for the Tourism and Hospitality Recovery Program was set at 75 percent, increasing one-for-one for each percentage point loss in revenues above the qualifying threshold. For the Hardest-Hit Business Recovery Program, it was set at 50 percent but started at 10 percent and only reached the maximum for businesses experiencing a 75 percent reduction in revenues.[12]

Figure 2. Business Closures in Canada, Seasonally Adjusted from January 2019 to June 2021

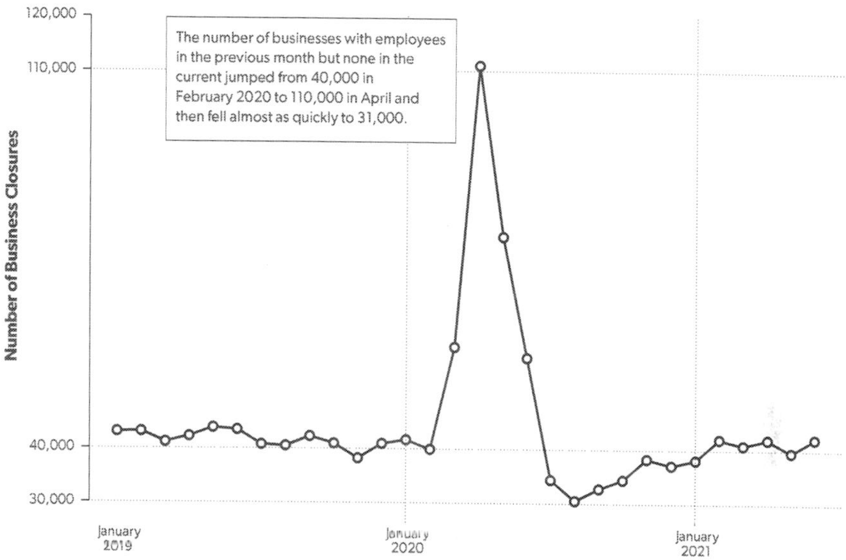

Note: Business closures refer to business establishments transitioning from having at least one employee in the previous month to no employees in the current month, an establishment being the unit of production within an enterprise. The figure shows these seasonally adjusted data from January 2019 to June 2021.

Source: Created by the author using information from Statistics Canada, "Experimental Estimates for Business Openings and Closures for Canada, Provinces and Territories, Census Metropolitan Areas, Seasonally Adjusted," November 29, 2021, https://www150.statcan.gc.ca/t1/tbl1/en/tv.action?pid=3310027001.

Evaluating the CEWS

Figure 2 depicts the pattern of monthly business closures in the country from the beginning of 2019 through June 2021, the most recently available data at the time of writing. A "business closure" refers to an establishment having at least one paid employee in the previous month that reports no employees in the current month. Just short of 41,700 establishments closed during the average month of 2019, about 4.6 percent of the 905,000 employers typically active. The numbers for January and February 2020 were no different, with 41,440 and 39,725 closures, respectively. But in April 2020, closures jumped to 110,000, following 58,500 in March, itself

Figure 3. Number of Employed Canadians, Seasonally Adjusted from January 2019 to September 2021

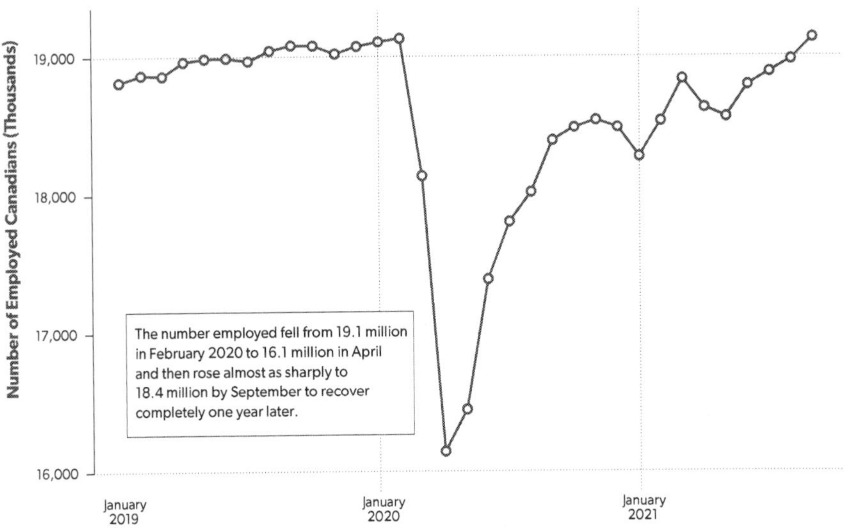

Note: The figure shows the seasonally adjusted number in thousands of Canadians age 15 and older—the working-age population, classified as employed by the Labour Force Survey conducted by Statistics Canada. The data refer to the reference week of each month, usually the week containing the 15, from January 2019 to September 2021.

Source: Created by the author using information from Statistics Canada, "Labour Force Characteristics, Monthly, Seasonally Adjusted and Trend-Cycle, Last 5 Months," December 3, 2021, https://www150.statcan.gc.ca/t1/tbl1/en/tv.action?pid=1410028701.

being an unprecedented jump. Consequently, the number of active firms fell to a low of 795,000 in May. These closures translated directly into the deepest employment losses experienced during the pandemic.[13]

The Labour Force Survey, the monthly Statistics Canada household survey used to track employment and unemployment rates, reports that the number of employed Canadians in 2020 fell by three million. Those employed dropped from 19.1 million in January and February to a low of 16.1 million in April, with the employment-population ratio dropping about 10 percentage points from 61.8 percent to 52.1 percent. Figure 3 shows the speed and depth of the drop in the number of employed. By mid-April, the pandemic had burst through the economy; the damage to employment was done in a matter of six weeks. But this sharp fall in employment was followed by sharp increases during each of the following months, with fully two-thirds of the employment drop being recovered by September.

The 2021 budget states that

> federal support measures have protected jobs and helped limit the number of permanent business closings. . . . The Canada Emergency Wage Subsidy has, at times, supported a quarter of private sector employment, and an even higher share in some hard-hit industries like accommodation and food services.[14]

But this falls short of a program evaluation, which requires more than an "audit study," a documentation of how much was spent and how it was spent. A full evaluation requires an assessment of the degree to which the stated goals were achieved and the impact of this spending: Did CEWS reduce firm closures and attenuate the loss of jobs? How big was this impact? At what cost?

Statistics Canada reports that while CEWS support was indeed concentrated in the hardest-hit industries, these industries, particularly the businesses in them receiving CEWS, also suffered the largest declines in employment. The CEWS take-up rate in accommodation and food services was 66 percent, and in arts and entertainment, it was 56 percent, well above the economy-wide take-up rate of 36 percent.[15] But as Figure 4 illustrates, these sectors also experienced the sharpest falls in employment—31 and 36 percent, respectively. These declines were well beyond the experience in the next most-affected industries: education services at 14 percent, administrative and support industries at 12 percent, and retail trade and real estate both at 11 percent.

Statistics Canada also reports that employment fell more among CEWS recipients than among non-recipients in these industries. Indeed, this was the case in all industries except construction. But this perspective, a description of outcomes and one that invites a comparison between firms receiving and not receiving CEWS support, also falls short of a proper program evaluation. It does not tell us what employment would have been among CEWS-receiving firms if they had not participated. The factors determining participation in the program are also certain to influence

Figure 4. Take-Up of the CEWS by Percentage Change in Industry Employment

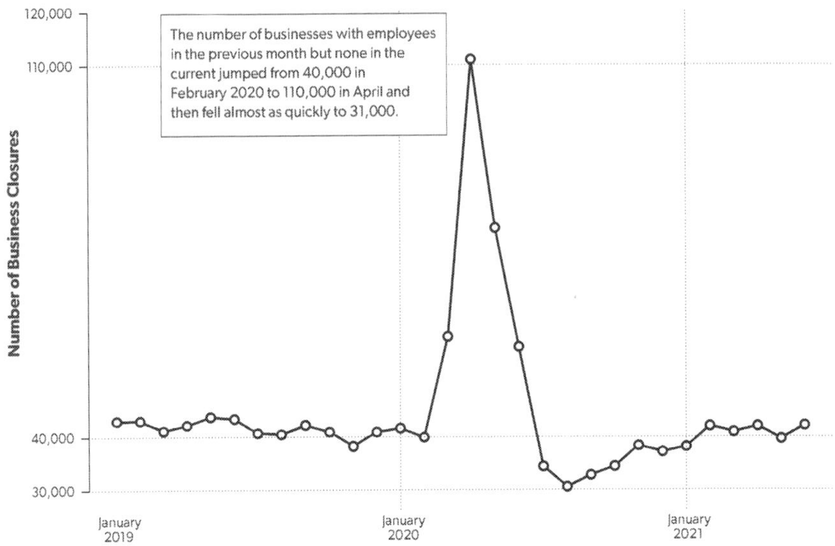

Note: The figure shows the relationship between the take-up rate of the CEWS and the percentage change in industry employment for broad industry categories. Take-up rates are defined as the number of CEWS recipient businesses as a percentage of the total number of active businesses in the industry. The change in employment refers to the percentage change in industry employment from between April 2019 and March 2020 and that between April 2020 and October 2020.
Source: Created by the author using information from Huju Liu, Yuqian Lu, and Michael Willox, *Use of the Canada Emergency Wage Subsidy Program by Employer Businesses in 2020*, Statistics Canada, June 23, 2021, 4, Chart 1, https://www150.statcan.gc.ca/n1/pub/36-28-0001/2021006/article/00006-eng.htm.

employment outcomes and therefore generate a self-selected sample that biases any simple comparison.

Proper program evaluation requires a clear counterfactual of what would have happened to closures and employment without CEWS, all other things constant. Careful evaluations with a quasi-experimental design will certainly be the subject of future research. But this may be challenging given that the pandemic had wide-ranging impacts across the entire economy and that there were many policy responses with new programs interacting and having overlapping eligibility rules.[16] Any speculation about whether this program passes a basic cost-benefit analysis must necessarily be contingent.

Perhaps the best evaluation that can be done in its immediate aftermath is to rely on judging it in terms of its stated objectives, its adherence to some basic lessons from economic theory, and some back-of-the-envelope calculations based on these principles.

Shutdown Decision. The CEWS's stated objective was clear: to prevent business closures and keep employees "in place"—that is, in some way attached to their employer to channel income support to them. Preventing business closures was part of the "freezing the economy" metaphor, so program design should, in the first instance, be informed by what economic theory teaches about the shutdown decision.

It is hard to imagine that the program significantly prevented closures during the early weeks and months of the pandemic, when the decline in total employment was greatest, for the simple reason that it did not receive legal status until mid-April and the government did not start accepting applications until April 27. Once open, applications were slow to start coming in from eligible businesses, even if they could be made retroactively.[17] Unprecedented business closures and major job loss had, in large measure, taken place even before the CEWS was effectively up and running. Meanwhile, the CERB had already been available for three weeks, with strong uptake among the surge of workers laid off during the previous six weeks. The availability of timely and direct support through this program likely cut off the demand and urgency for support through a wage subsidy.

Furthermore, the CEWS did not offer support for the costs that influence businesses' closure decisions. A wage subsidy may be seen as a policy to maintain employer-employee attachment only if the firm has decided not to permanently close down. As such, the first course of action in maintaining employer-employee attachment must be preventing permanent business closures. This shutdown decision depends on being able to cover fixed costs, which don't vary with production. This is distinct from decisions over the rate of production.

Businesses will keep operating in the short term if they cover their variable costs, even if fixed costs can't be covered by operating revenues. But eventually, over weeks or months depending on the structure of the capital involved, fixed costs need to be covered. If public policy is concerned about permanent closures, it needs to address fixed costs such as rents, financing, and some parts of the wage structure, particularly those associated with overhead employees and firm-specific skills.

These are costs to which, at least on paper, the CEWS did not address. Indeed, the government's first instinct was to bolster support to the financial sector and several facilities for business credit. These measures were announced as early as March 13, 2020.[18] But support for rent and other expenses directly associated with lockdowns evolved more slowly and was less generous and slow to be taken up.

Even if CEWS is unlikely to have significantly prevented firms from closing in the early weeks and months of the pandemic, it may have had an impact afterward. Business closures did fall rapidly in the months after their April 2020 peak and were below 2019 levels from June 2020 onward, through subsequent waves of the pandemic. Indeed, as Figure 2 shows, for most of 2020, they were significantly below the previous year, reaching a low of 31,000 in August, fully one-quarter below the 2019 average.

Legal Incidence of a Subsidy. The CEWS may well have contributed to this extraordinarily low rate because its design did not recognize a second principle of basic theory: that the legal incidence of a subsidy may not be the same as its economic incidence. In some measure, firms may have used the funds for purposes other than just supporting the payroll of workers directly engaged in the production process, including management and other supervisory or overhead workers. Clearly, this possibility is hinted at by the fact that the government introduced the repayment rule for executive compensation. This was a response to media coverage of profitable large businesses simultaneously increasing executive compensation and collecting CEWS support. Even if the data are not available to accurately assess the impact on executive compensation, these reports raise the possibility of more wide-ranging support of business expenses beyond just production workers to include management at all levels, not just senior executives.

In some measure, this may have been a blessing in disguise, but it leaves open the question of whether reducing closures to a level significantly lower than the 2019 level, a business-cycle peak, also leads to economic inefficiencies. Joseph Schumpeter's view of recessions—as cold showers inherently involving structural changes that move the economy forward as recovery promotes more productive firms—is also useful as a metaphor for understanding the long-term consequences of the pandemic. A metaphor of emptying and then refilling the bathtub, one encouraged by Friedman's plucking model, does not offer a complete guide to public policy in pandemic or other times. Schumpeter encourages us to view public policy that overshoots in supporting firms that would otherwise close as thwarting, or at least postponing, the structural changes that the pandemic moved forward in time.

For example, it is reasonable to suggest that the pandemic called for a greater online presence in all sectors, including retail and food services, or a reduction in a broad array of public-facing business models, even a smaller or different restaurant sector or a more sophisticated and responsive human resources strategy among small businesses. A generous, broad-based wage subsidy might serve to support firms that had already been slow to adapt to an evolving climate and that instead buckled down during the pandemic and its aftermath to rely on even lower wages.

Targeting Policy at the Margin. This raises the third principle that the CEWS violated: the need to target behavior at the margin—that is, to support firms that would otherwise have shut down operations without supporting those that would not have shut down despite the pandemic nor those that would have shut down regardless. The targeting of program eligibility and benefit generosity was at best coarse. The CEWS was not in any way targeted at the margin, particularly with the reduction of the eligibility rule allowing enterprises with any revenue reduction, or as little as a 10 percent fall, to qualify, there being no obligation to document that the fall was pandemic related. It was also easily manipulated by accounting or other adjustments to revenue. It may well be difficult to target policy on the margin with this sort of program, as it is virtually impossible for government administrators to attribute revenue declines specifically to the pandemic.

Putting aside the dynamic inefficiencies that Schumpeter's view raises, this would lead to a significant deadweight loss and waste of public moneys. Michael Smart of the University of Toronto finds, based on the first six months of the CEWS, that the average subsidy for each approved application was $300,000. He argues that the "problem is that CEWS payments are paid for *all* workers at affected businesses, not just those facing the prospect of earnings losses. That makes the program an expensive way of helping workers hit by the lockdown."[19] (Emphasis in original.) His back-of-the-envelope calculations, based on an elasticity of labor demand of 0.15, suggest that each person-month of employment support by CEWS came at a cost of $25,000, with only one in 12 employees owing their jobs to the program.

The story of the Royal Ottawa Golf Club succinctly illustrates how the CEWS's operation had little relation to these three basic principles that should have informed optimal program design. This was an enterprise at no risk of shutting down, which diverted the funds received to other purposes and ultimately did not materially change employment. If, as Smart suggests, the program offered about $2,000 support per employee covered but cost $25,000 per job saved, then many enterprises like the Royal Ottawa were supported in this program's net.

Public Policy Practices and Next Steps

The irony of Canada's employer-based policy response to the pandemic is that the existing labor market and social policy architecture was, in principle, well-suited to offer wage subsidies to many employers and promote labor retention during sharp economic downturns. The problem was one of practice, of the capacity to deliver: The scale of the shock to employment swamped the infrastructure of existing programs and necessitated discretionary and fast-paced development of work-arounds like the CEWS.

Social policy—from childcare and education to income assistance and workplace regulation—is delivered by the provinces and is a provincial responsibility even if it often involves a significant financial contribution from the federal government. The federal government can influence the design of these programs and the setting of national standards through cost-sharing agreements negotiated separately with the 10 provinces, often a challenging and time-consuming process. But this is not the case for the unemployment insurance program, called Employment Insurance, which lies entirely in the federal government's domain and can be changed with federal legislation for the country as a whole.

Employment Insurance is financed through a uniform payroll tax on firms based on the payroll of their insured workers to maximum insurable earnings. The program results in significant cross-subsidization among regions, industries, and firms. Because it is not experience rated, all firms face the same contribution rate regardless of their layoff history and the extent to which their employees rely on benefits. Many firms never receive a net transfer from the program, and others always do, with the resulting cross-subsidization caused, in large measure, by greater-than-average separation rates, particularly temporary layoffs, among lower-wage, always-subsidized firms. This implies a long-standing wage subsidy in which many of these employers regularly lay off workers in the face of demand shocks but are confident that the workers will remain available to be recalled. The program encourages an attachment between employers and employees through an implicit contract: giving employees enough work to qualify for unemployment insurance and recalling them before they exhaust their benefits. This is a de facto wage subsidy.[20]

Whatever the inefficiencies associated with this design and whatever its implications for interregional, inter-industry, and inter-firm income transfers, it is well-suited, in a macro sense, to maintain an attachment between employers and their employees in the face of a temporary shock to product demand. Furthermore, features of Employment Insurance make it even more suited to the particular objectives the government was pursuing through CEWS. The Employment Insurance program includes a provision called "Work-Sharing." As a government of Canada monitoring report states:

> Work-Sharing is an adjustment program designed to help employers and employees avoid layoffs when there is a temporary reduction in the normal level of business activity that is beyond the control of the employer. Layoffs are avoided by offering temporary EI [Employment Insurance] income support to employees eligible for EI regular benefits willing to work a temporarily reduced work week while their employer recovers. The goal of the program is for all participating employees to return to normal working hours by the end of the Work-Sharing agreement.[21]

In other words, this is exactly what the government's pandemic response was calling for: a way of supporting employee incomes through their employers and maintaining an attachment between them by using reductions in hours of work to avoid layoffs. Work-Sharing was effectively used during the 2007–08 Great Recession, and it is no surprise that the government's first announcements of pandemic emergency measures on March 15, 2020, before CEWS was conceived and launched, promoted and expanded this part of Employment Insurance.[22]

However, it became immediately clear that the simultaneous pursuit of these two goals, income support and employer-employee attachment, could not be achieved entirely through Employment Insurance for two reasons. The first illustrates the influence that the program-delivery side of public policy had on the policy-development side: The administrative capacity of the Employment Insurance was incapable of handling the pandemic caseloads. The program was constrained by its infrastructure and not able to meet the unprecedented demands placed on it by the millions of pandemic-induced claims. The minister responsible for the program reported at the time that proceeding at the usual rate, the backlog would take up to 18 months to process.[23] An automatic stabilizer, whose original objective was to respond in real time to big shocks, choked, struggled, and stalled. Decades of patchwork fixes and layers of complexity added to its application process and delivery windows simply not being up to the task.[24]

The CEWS, in some measure, can be thought of as a stopgap discretionary measure to work around capacity constraints in programs otherwise manifestly better designed to meet the stated goals. The lesson going forward for public policy concerns the need to invest in delivery infrastructure in a way that continually modernizes the workings of automatic stabilizers that can respond close to real time. One positive outcome of this experience is that the government has done just that, allocating funds in the last budget to accelerate "Benefit Delivery Modernization," an investment related to the IT infrastructure of Employment Insurance and other programs.

The second reason Employment Insurance fell short in responding to the pandemic is limitations in coverage. Many workers, particularly low-wage workers, were not employed in "insurable jobs" and, along with recent labor market entrants, did not necessarily have the required hours of past work to qualify for benefits. This also required the government to enhance its capacity to make income-support payments directly to individuals and in real time, leading to the creation and implementation of the CERB.

Eligibility for the program did not depend on contributions based on insurable employment. It simply required that the applicant had $5,000 of work income during 2019 or in the 12 months before the application and had not quit to collect the benefit.[25] This direct payment was an immediate success. It offered benefits to low-income Canadians suffering an income loss through a simple and quick application procedure leading to biweekly payments in a matter of days. The "trust then verify" principle used in its administration encouraged applications and sped up benefit delivery. As suggested, the CERB's flexibility and speed may in fact be one reason CEWS applications were slow to get started, as this "program substitution" was an aspect of the practical side of public policy that likely limited the CEWS's impact. A significant wage subsidy to employers as a way of channeling income support to workers is less necessary when direct payments to affected workers are already being delivered quickly and transparently.

The third policy practice influencing the CEWS's effectiveness is "policy drift" associated with the political economy of discretionary program development. Best practice in the making of discretionary fiscal policy requires, among other things, one-off interventions that avoid the development of vested interests that may reshape the policy and extend expenditure beyond its original need for purposes beyond its original intent. In some measure, this has happened to the CEWS, as the government extended the program repeatedly and most recently within weeks before calling a federal election. It is hard not to imagine that in some degree this reflects an ascending small-business community, which through extensive media attention and lobbying of members of Parliament contributed to shifting the framing of public discourse from concerns for essential workers to those of small business.[26] Throughout its many versions, the CEWS subsidy has also been applied to not just payroll associated with existing employees but also workers who have been rehired.

Constraints in program delivery, the scope for program substitution, and the possibility of policy drift are all practical forces that have not only influenced the CEW's design and effectiveness but also offered lessons. When big, unexpected shocks happen in the future, the policy response should not be to resurrect a program like the CEWS, which likely has not passed a reasonable cost-benefit analysis. Rather, policymakers should look to reinforce what should now be fine-tuned and robust automatic stabilizers. Principal among them should be an unemployment insurance program that has sufficient capacity to process worst-case scenario caseloads in real time and offer quick adoption of Work-Sharing provisions, a design that avoids discretionary intervention and is eminently better suited for enhancing employer-employee attachment and targeting support on the margin.[27] Going forward, the Employment Insurance program needs to be reformed to expand coverage to currently uninsured employment and otherwise ineligible workers, redesigned in its eligibility rules to be more sensitive to macroeconomic downturns, and, if necessary, complemented with other programs inspired by the CERB's success.[28]

Conclusion

In evaluating public policy addressed to mitigating business closures and layoffs throughout the pandemic, particularly during the early months, we must recognize two important matters. The first is the uncertainties that Canadian policymakers—indeed, policymakers in many countries—were facing about the scale and duration of the economic fallout. The second is that speed trumped perfection, as governments struggled to offer real-time support of a magnitude never before attempted. This said, it is exactly during uncertain times—when the challenges are new, the data aren't in, and experiments, trials, and pilots can't be conducted—that clarity of objectives and guidance from basic principles are most needed.

As an employer-based response to the pandemic intended to prevent business closures and layoffs, the CEWS was certainly a program constructed in haste but perceived to be necessary in the face of limits in the capacity of better-designed existing programs, particularly the national unemployment insurance program. Even so, the program was not informed by fundamental lessons from economic theory. It was not addressed to the fixed costs that actually determine business closures, it did not recognize that a subsidy nominally directed to worker payroll can be shifted to other purposes, and it was not, or in principle could not be, targeted on the margin or on businesses that would indeed have closed without support.

This implies that the job losses actually prevented are much lower than the actual payroll covered, with each person-month of employment saved costing $25,000 according to one estimate. Income support of this magnitude paid directly to affected workers would likely not be considered politically acceptable among informed citizens. Therefore, it is hard to imagine that the program would pass any reasonable cost-benefit analysis.

Going forward, it will also be important to recognize the practical considerations that shaped, and perhaps even motivated, this program. Their downsides should be recognized. They call for policymakers to be as concerned with program delivery as they are with program design, offering ongoing investments in modernizing physical and human capacity to deliver benefits. One positive consequence of the Canadian experience is that these investments have been promised to overcome limitations in the capacity of the country's unemployment insurance program. The expectation should be that in the future, this program will play an even bigger role should it be necessary, particularly provisions within it designed to promote work sharing, which reduces the reliance on layoffs by offering benefits for adjustments to work hours.

The practical experiences during the pandemic also call for policymakers to recognize that programs may interact and should be designed to complement each other. Other programs making real-time direct payments to individuals suffering income losses, notably the CERB, were in some measure a substitute for the CEWS, which was slower out of the starting gate and undersubscribed when it mattered most to the most-vulnerable businesses during the first weeks and month of the pandemic. Success in making direct transfers to individuals to some degree made the wage subsidy less relevant; delays in getting it off the ground made it less necessary.

Finally, the practical considerations of public policy also call for policymakers to avoid policy drift—that is, the development of vested interests that can prolong the duration of a program after its need has passed or pervert its intent by skewing its design. This calls for increased reliance on programs structured as automatic stabilizers rather than on discretionary interventions.

Acknowledgments

The final draft of this chapter was written in late October 2021 and reflects the design of the Canada Emergency Wage Subsidy and the data available at that time. I am grateful for the helpful comments on an earlier draft from an anonymous referee and from Keith Banting, Kevin Milligan, Benoit Robidoux, Jennifer Robson, and Mikal Skuterud while acknowledging that I am entirely responsible for the content and any errors it may contain.

Notes

1. Jonathon Gatehouse, "Exclusive Golf Course Books $1 Million Surplus, Aided by Federal COVID-19 Relief," CBC News, December 18, 2020, https://www.cbc.ca/news/canada/royal-ottawa-golf-club-million-dollar-cews-windfall-1.5846001.

2. Government of Canada, Department of Finance Canada, "Government Announces Details of the Canada Emergency Wage Subsidy to Help Businesses Keep Canadians in Their Jobs," press release, April 1, 2020, https://www.canada.ca/en/department-finance/news/2020/04/government-announces-details-of-the-canada-emergency-wage-subsidy-to-help-businesses-keep-canadians-in-their-jobs.html.

3. Government of Canada, Department of Finance Canada, "Government Announces Details of the Canada Emergency Wage Subsidy to Help Businesses Keep Canadians in Their Jobs."

4. The Canada Emergency Response Benefit (CERB) offered direct support to individuals who had an annual income of at least $5,000 in the previous year, who experienced a significant pandemic-related fall in their income, and who were not able to receive support through the unemployment insurance program. It amounted to a maximum of $2,000 over any four-week period, $500 per week, between March 15 and September 26, 2020. This program evolved throughout the pandemic, most notably to be superseded by the Canada Recovery Benefit, accounting for an additional $26.7 billion in spending. Government of Canada, "Budget 2021," April 19, 2021, 604–8, https://www.budget.gc.ca/2021/home-accueil-en.html.

5. Government of Canada, Department of Finance Canada, "Government Announces Details of the Canada Emergency Wage Subsidy to Help Businesses Keep Canadians in Their Jobs."

6. March 15, 2020, marked the date of the first countrywide emergency orders, suggesting to policymakers that falls in business revenue might not be visible until the full following month.

7. For more details and a legislative summary of the bill, see COVID-19 Emergency Response Act, No. 2, S.C. 2020, c. 6, https://www.parl.ca/DocumentViewer/en/43-1/bill/C-14/royal-assent.

8. The original quote reads:

> Output is viewed as bumping along the ceiling of maximum feasible output except that every now and then it is plucked down by a cyclical contraction. . . . Since there is no physical limit to the decline short of zero output, the size of the decline in output can vary widely. When subsequent recovery sets in, it tends to return output to the ceiling; it cannot go beyond, so there is an upper limit to output and the amplitude of the expansion tends to be correlated with the amplitude of the contraction.

Milton Friedman et al., "The Monetary Studies of the National Bureau," in *The National Bureau Enters Its Forty-Fifth Year* (Cambridge, MA: National Bureau of Economic Research, January 1964), https://www.nber.org/books-and-chapters/national-bureau-enters-its-forty-fifth-year.

9. In fact, when announced, the Canada Emergency Wage System (CEWS) replaced a more modest program that had been launched less than two weeks earlier. On March 18, 2020, the federal government announced that effective immediately, small businesses would be offered a 10 percent wage subsidy for 90 days (to June 19) to a maximum of $1,375 per employee and $25,000 per employer. See Government of Canada, Department of Finance Canada, "Canada's COVID-19 Economic Response Plan: Support for Canadians and Businesses," March 18, 2020, https://www.canada.ca/en/department-finance/news/2020/03/canadas-covid-19-economic-response-plan-support-for-canadians-and-businesses.html.

10. For a timeline of the program evolution, see Government of Canada, "Canada Emergency Wage Subsidy (CEWS): What the Changes Are," October 22, 2021, https://www.canada.ca/en/revenue-agency/services/subsidy/emergency-wage-subsidy/cews-what-changes.html. For a detailed list of frequently asked questions that describes the program and its evolution, see Government of Canada, "Frequently Asked Questions—Canada Emergency Wage Subsidy (CEWS)," September 24, 2021, https://www.canada.ca/en/revenue-agency/services/subsidy/emergency-wage-subsidy/cews-frequently-asked-questions.html. For a description of the July 30 post-budget announcement, see Government of Canada, Department of Finance Canada, "Extending Business Support Measures Through the Pandemic," July 30, 2021, https://www.canada.ca/en/department-finance/news/2021/07/extending-business-support-measures-through-the-pandemic.html. For a description of the final announcement confirming that the program would not be extended any further, see Government of Canada, Department of Finance Canada, "Government Announces Targeted COVID-19 Support Measures to Create Jobs and Growth," press release, October 21, 2021, https://www.canada.ca/en/department-finance/news/2021/10/government-announces-targeted-covid-19-support-measures-to-create-jobs-and-growth.html.

11. Applications made in the claim period beginning on September 27, 2020, through to the period beginning November 22, 2020, were also subject to a "safe harbour" rule not depicted in Figure 2.

12. For more details on these programs and other changes introduced with the October 21 announcement, including their phasing out and the expansion of the Canada Recovery Hiring Program and Canada Emergency Rent Subsidy, see Government

of Canada, Department of Finance Canada, "Targeting COVID-19 Support Measures," October 21, 2021, https://www.canada.ca/en/department-finance/news/2021/10/targeting-covid-19-support-measures.html.

13. The pattern depicted in Figure 2 is a little different if the data are expressed as rates. The percentage of businesses closing in the average month of 2019 was 4.6, spiked to 13.5 percent in April 2020, and fell to a low of 3.7 percent in August 2020, staying below the 2019 average until February 2021, where it remained.

14. The document goes on to note that "business insolvencies have, so far, remained low and below historic levels." In fact, insolvencies were not just lower but significantly lower, about one-third lower during the 2020 pandemic months compared to the same months in the previous year, particularly so during March and April 2020. This said, insolvencies are a more stringent measure than the indicator used in Figure 2 and are measured in the hundreds, bouncing around 300 per month over 2019 and 200 during the pandemic months of 2020, though they reached a low of about 150 in April. See Government of Canada, Department of Finance Canada, "Budget 2021: A Recovery Plan for Jobs, Growth, and Resilience," April 19, 2021, 82, Chart 2.4, https://www.budget.gc.ca/2021/home-accueil-en.html. The budget document does not translate this into an impact on employment.

15. The "take-up rate" refers to the number of CEWS recipients divided by the number of active recipients in the industry, and the fall in employment refers to the percentage difference between industry employment during April 2019 to March 2020 and April to October 2020. See Huju Liu, Yuqian Lu, and Michael Willox, *Use of the Canada Emergency Wage Subsidy Program by Employer Businesses in 2020*, Statistics Canada, June 23, 2021, 4, 6, Chart 1, Table 1, https://www150.statcan.gc.ca/n1/pub/36-28-0001/2021006/article/00006-eng.htm.

16. These studies may well benefit from adopting cross-national or interregional comparisons. The authors of the working paper "Did the Paycheck Protection Program Hit the Target?" offer one example of a US-based evaluation of the Paycheck Protection Program, a program similar to the CEWS, partly basing their identification strategy on regional variation. Some of their findings suggest that the program's impact on employment was small. Joao Granja et al., "Did the Paycheck Protection Program Hit the Target?" (working paper, Becker Friedman Institute for Economics at the University of Chicago, Chicago, September 21, 2021), https://bfi.uchicago.edu/working-paper/did-the-paycheck-protection-program-hit-the-target. For a preliminary analysis of this program with a distinct identification strategy, see David Autor et al., "An Evaluation of the Paycheck Protection Program Using Administrative Payroll Microdata" (working paper, Blueprint Labs at Massachusetts Institute for Technology, Cambridge, MA, July 2020), https://blueprintlabs.mit.edu/research/an-evaluation-of-the-paycheck-protection-program-using-administrative-payroll-microdata.

17. Jennifer Robson, "Radical Incrementalism and Trust in the Citizen: Income Security in Canada in the Time of COVID-19," *Canadian Public Policy* 46, no. S1 (July 2020): S10, https://utpjournals.press/doi/10.3138/cpp.2020-080.

18. Government of Canada, Department of Finance Canada, "Canada Outlines Measures to Support the Economy and the Financial Sector," press release, March 13, 2020, https://www.canada.ca/en/department-finance/news/2020/03/canada-outlines-

measures-to-support-the-economy-and-the-financial-sector.html.

19. Michael Smart, "Boos for CEWS," Finances of the Nation, September 20, 2020, https://financesofthenation.ca/2020/09/20/boos-for-cews.

20. Miles Corak and Wen-Hao Chen, "Firms, Industries, and Unemployment Insurance: An Analysis Using Employer-Employee Data" (working paper, Institute for the Study of Labor, Bonn, Germany, June 2003), https://docs.iza.org/dp811.pdf.

21. Government of Canada, Employment and Social Development Canada, *Employment Insurance Monitoring and Assessment Report for the Fiscal Year Beginning April 1, 2019 and Ending March 31, 2020*, May 19, 2021, https://www.canada.ca/en/employment-social-development/programs/ei/ei-list/reports.

22. This involved expanding employer eligibility, doubling the permitted length of work-sharing agreements to 78 weeks, and easing the application process. See Government of Canada, Employment and Social Development Canada, *Employment Insurance Monitoring and Assessment Report for the Fiscal Year Beginning April 1, 2019 and Ending March 31, 2020*, 126. As of the time of writing, these provisions, originally slated to end in September 2021, are to remain in effect until September 25, 2022.

23. Robson, "Radical Incrementalism and Trust in the Citizen," S3.

24. Miles Corak, "Ottawa Is Struggling to Be a Just-in-Time Government," *Globe and Mail*, March 30, 2020, https://www.theglobeandmail.com/opinion/article-ottawa-is-struggling-to-be-a-just-in-time-government.

25. Jennifer Robson notes that the "goal of the policy was not to encourage work but to allow workers to reduce their [labour] supply to protect public health." See endnote 4 and Robson, "Radical Incrementalism and Trust in the Citizen," S6–S9.

26. Bill Curry and Chris Hannay, "Ottawa in Discussions to Extend Pandemic Aid Beyond Oct. 23 Deadline," *Globe and Mail*, October 6, 2021, https://www.theglobeandmail.com/politics/article-freeland-signals-openness-to-extending-some-pandemic-support-programs.

27. The program requires employers to show that layoffs are unforeseen and temporary in nature, rather than seasonal or part of planned production cycles, and that they have a reasonable plan to return to normal employment. Targeting support on the margin is also enhanced by requiring employers to have been in operation for at least two years and a "cooling off" period between repeated reliance on the program.

28. In my online post "Employment Insurance for the Future of Work, Right Now," I discuss inadequacies in employment insurance and offer suggestions for reform. See Miles Corak, "Employment Insurance for the Future of Work, Right Now," March 9, 2021, https://milescorak.com/2021/03/09/employment-insurance-for-the-future-of-work-right-now.

4

Whatever It Takes: Subsidizing Short-Time Work During the COVID-19 Pandemic in France

XAVIER JARAVEL

In response to the COVID-19 pandemic, the French government established several policies to support the economy throughout the crisis. Subsidies for short-time work were a key policy, accounting for over half the cost of emergency and stimulus measures to date. The purpose of this program was partly to preserve employer-employee links and, more broadly, to address the uncertainty at the beginning of the crisis and implement targeted transfers.

According to the French national accounts, in August 2021, private-sector employment in France had just reached its precrisis level, suggesting that the policy package was effective. But the recovery features a tight labor market, with an increase in the number of vacancies per job-seeking individual. This recent evolution raises concerns that short-time work subsidies may have contributed to reducing job search and increasing labor market tightness, which may impede the economic recovery.

In this chapter, I first provide a comprehensive description of the short-time work program introduced in France, how it evolved with the pandemic's changing circumstances, and its macroeconomic significance among the broader set of emergency measures the government introduced during the crisis. The short-time work program was a program of unprecedented scale, establishing the French government's commitment to do "whatever it takes" to protect workers and jobs during the COVID-19 crisis.[1]

Second, I provide a simple framework to assess the cost-benefit analysis of the short-time work subsidy program, drawing on evidence at the micro- and macroeconomic levels. At the micro level, I analyze the economic effects of the short-time work program, compared with those of other emergency measures, by leveraging recent evidence on each policy's take-up and ability to target firms and individuals that were most in need, firms' stated levels of satisfaction with the policy, and the policy's propensity to inefficiently support "zombie firms," defined as firms that are likely to go bankrupt in the long run without public support. Although some firms appeared to have windfall gains, the short-time work program seems to have performed better than some of the other support programs—in particular, deferred tax and social contribution payments.

At the macro level, I argue that the program's main benefit was likely to drastically reduce uncertainty and preserve consumer confidence and business investment going forward, which allowed for a quick rebound of the French economy.[2] As of the fall of 2021, the recovery in France appears strong, but the country faces two new macroeconomic challenges. First, the job market has become tight. Second, public support programs were so strong that firms' bankruptcy rates have fallen by half, creating the potential for a wave of "catch-up bankruptcies" if public support programs are withdrawn too soon or for a fall in allocative efficiency if the programs are not withdrawn quickly enough. To strike this balance, the French government is transitioning from a "whatever it takes" approach to a tailor-made approach to public support programs.[3]

The remainder of the chapter is organized as follows: The next section describes the parameters of short-time work programs and their evolution during the crisis, and the third section presents my analysis of their economic effects. The fourth section concludes.[4]

Short-Time Work Programs in France During the COVID-19 Pandemic

In this section, I describe short-time work programs in France during the COVID-19 pandemic, first highlighting their macroeconomic importance and then describing the characteristics of the subsidies.

Short-Time Work Subsidies Played a Major Role in the Macroeconomic Stabilization Strategy. The economic and health crises brought about by the COVID-19 pandemic were unprecedented. In 2020, French gross domestic product (GDP) fell by 7.9 percent, compared with 6.9 percent in the rest of the eurozone. Excess mortality between March 2020 and February 2021 was 13.1 percent. In the United States, the recession was smaller (–3.5 percent in 2020), but excess mortality was larger (22.1 percent between March 2020 and February 2021).[5]

To mitigate the economic consequences of lockdowns, in March 2020 the French government launched four main programs to mitigate the economic crisis: a short-time work policy, a solidarity fund, state-backed loans for firms, and deferred or reduced tax payments for firms. Between March 2020 and June 2021, these four programs amounted to €212 billion, or about 10 percent of France's GDP, including €35.2 billion for short-time work, €31.2 billion for the solidarity fund, €140 billion for state-backed loans,[6] and €5.6 billion for deferred or reduced taxes.[7] The solidarity fund became more important later into the crisis, with a total amount of €0.7 billion for the first wave compared with €7 billion for the second wave. These programs were all introduced quickly.

Economically, these policies can be divided into two types: Liquidity policies are meant to be reimbursed, while the solidarity fund, short-time work policies, and tax reductions are subsidies, which are not meant to be refunded.

Characteristics of Short-Time Work Subsidies. I now describe the main parameters of the short-time work policy in France and then highlight several changes to the policy and implementation choices throughout the pandemic.

Main Parameters of the Short-Time Work Policy. Short-time work policies with public subsidies existed in France even before the COVID-19 crisis. The policies work based on three interrelated principles. First, employers are no longer obligated to give work to their employees; the workload can be reduced to zero hours.

Second, employees receive a benefit amounting to 70 percent of their pretax wage, paid by the employer, up to 4.5 times the minimum wage.[8] This benefit is subject to lower taxes, with an overall rate of 6.7 percent;[9] in particular, the benefit is exempt from income tax and social insurance contributions. As a result, for the average worker, the benefit of 70 percent of the pretax wage accounts for 84 percent of the posttax wage. Furthermore, the benefit has a floor equal to the minimum wage, such that workers paid at the minimum wage receive 100 percent of their posttax wage.[10]

Third, the employer receives a benefit equal to 70 percent of the employee's pretax wage, with a floor equal to the minimum wage. In this way, the employer is fully refunded for the benefit the employee receives.

The Evolution of the Policy During the Crisis. The policy evolved during the crisis, especially regarding the third principle. During the first lockdown from March to May 2020, all employers were fully refunded for short-time work. In the second phase of the crisis, employers were refunded only 85 percent of the employee benefit, except for firms that kept a full refund, subject to eligibility criteria—namely, if (1) they were shut down due to regulations, their industry (e.g., with a state-ordered closure of restaurants, gyms, night clubs, etc.), or their location (e.g., with a regional lockdown) or (2) they were part of a set of sectors particularly affected by the crisis (including travel and leisure, hotels, restaurants, etc.). The differential treatment by industries or location during this phase of the crisis was deemed necessary to ensure that shutdowns remained politically and socially acceptable.[11] The policy did not impose any constraints on quits or layoffs.

In October 2020, a new, less generous regime was defined for the short-time work policy, but its deployment was delayed several times. With the new parameters, the employee benefit was set to 60 percent of the pretax wage (rather than 70 percent), and the employer had to cover 40 percent of the benefit (rather than 0 percent in the first version of the policy and 10 percent in the second version). Moreover, the floor was reduced to 90 percent of the minimum wage (rather than 100 percent).

This regime started being enforced on July 1, 2021, except for a set of firms that retained a full refund, subject to the same two eligibility criteria described above—that is, being subject to a state-ordered closure or being part of a struggling sector. In those cases, the employee benefit remains at 70 percent of the pretax wage. As the economic recovery firms up, the subsidy rate will be gradually reduced for all sectors and all firms. It is planned that, as of December 2021, employers should have to cover 40 percent of the short-time work benefit in all sectors and regardless of the evolution of their sales.

Finally, on July 28, 2020, a new "long-term part-time work program" ("*activité partielle de longue durée*") was introduced. This program, which requires a signed agreement between the employer and its employees, allows for a reduction of work time up to 40 percent over the total duration of the agreement, which can cover up to 24 months over a period of three years. Contrary to the policies described above, which can be used only up to a year, the long-term part-time work program is meant to support sectors that may be underperforming for several years—for example, the travel or aircraft manufacturing industries. Use of the program is subject to the obligation to avoid layoffs.

In the initial version of this policy, which was active until June 1, 2021, the employee received 70 percent of the pretax wage, and the employer obtained a full refund. The floor for the pretax wage was set to the minimum wage—that is, €8.11—and a ceiling was set at €27.68. Since July 2021, the employer has to cover 10 percent of the employee benefit, and the floor is set to 90 percent of the minimum wage.

Implementation Choices and the Importance of Fraud Detection. A key feature of short-time work programs was that they could be deployed quickly. In this case, employers had up to 30 days *after* putting their employees on short-time work to apply for the subsidy, and they could be refunded retroactively.

The large take-up of the part-time work program during the crisis dramatically increased the workload of civil servants at the Labor Ministry to process these requests, which was an organizational challenge but was necessary so that firms could be refunded quickly. During the lockdown in March 2020, 1.1 million firms applied for short-time work, but only 100,000 firms were previously registered in the history of the program. Before the crisis, 84 full-time civil servants were involved in processing requests for short-time work. During the crisis, the Labor Ministry allocated about 1,200 civil servants to this task, both in the central administration in Paris and in the local branches of the ministry throughout the country, including 300 new short-time workers who were recruited specifically for this task.[12]

Despite this effort, it proved difficult to address all applications in time. Starting in April 2020, the Labor Ministry decided to automatically approve applications under 48 hours; much of the oversight was done automatically using existing databases, and fraud detection was organized ex post. Starting in October 2020, the delay to validate applications increased from two days to two weeks, with increased oversight.

The fraud detection program was launched in May 2020 and strengthened in September 2020. The strategy combines ex ante and ex post audits based on firms' balance sheets and random audits. As of June 2021, the Labor Ministry had carried out 47,700 audits. In 62 percent of cases, the audits revealed no fraud and no inaccuracies. In 31 percent of cases, the audit revealed that the firm had provided an incomplete or inaccurate application; in 87 percent of those cases, the firm had to partly reimburse public funds. Finally, 7 percent of cases appeared to constitute outright fraud—for example, involving identity theft or the creation of fictitious firms.

To carry out these audits, the ministry focused on applications (1) with high wages per hour; (2) in sectors that had a high take-up rate for short-time work, such as construction; (3) from firms with a majority of white-collar workers, for whom remote work was likely possible; and (4) from new firms. About 400 civil servants were involved in these audits, which led to wide-ranging cooperation among several ministries including the Ministry of Labor, the Ministry of Budget, and the Justice Ministry. The relatively high rates of inaccuracies or fraud indicate that preparing better fraud-detection policies, with the ability to be quickly scaled up, would be an important task to prepare for the next crisis.

Short-Time Work Subsidies During the First Lockdown. To measure the take-up of the short-time work policy, the main available data source is a survey run by the statistical division of the Labor Ministry, the ACEMO-Covid survey.[13] This survey has a sample of 38,000 companies, representative of all firms with at least 10 employees. Using this survey, as of May 2021, the cumulative number of hours involving a short-time work subsidy reached 3.363 billion hours, corresponding to €35.2 billion, about 1.6 percent of GDP.

As shown in Figure 1, take-up reached its peak in April 2020, when 29 percent of private-sector workers received short-time work benefits, while the French economy was in full lockdown. It then fell gradually to reach 2 percent in September 2020. In the second lockdown, the take-up rate increased again to 8 percent of private-sector workers. It then hovered around that level and declined to 5 percent in May 2021.

Take-up was heterogeneous across sectors. Hotels and restaurants accounted for about one-fourth of (full-time-equivalent) employees who benefited from the program, while they account for only 6 percent of total private-sector employment. Take-up was also heterogeneous by firm size. Small and medium-sized firms were the main beneficiaries of the program. Firms with more than 250 employees account for 41.2 percent of private-sector employment but only 28.7 percent of the hours subsidized by the program.

Other data sources paint a similar picture about the broad use of the short-time work subsidies. A survey conducted at the end of June 2021, whose results are reported in Table 1, shows that eight in 10 firms have used at least one of the public support programs during the crisis. Short-time work programs were by far the most prevalent; close to two-thirds of firms used them.

According to a recent study of the statistical division of the Labor Ministry,[14] workers benefiting from short-time work subsidies tend to be younger and have lower incomes. These differences are largely due to the composition of sectors that used short-time work subsidies most—in particular, hotels and restaurants. White-collar workers accounted for about 10 percent of workers on short-time work arrangement during the first lockdown; their share increased to 20 percent (i.e., close to their share in total private-sector employment) during the summer of 2020 and started falling back to 10 percent after October 2020. Overall, the policy was redistributive in favor of lower-income workers, and there was no bias by gender.

Economic Effects of the Short-Time Work Subsidy Program

In this section, I provide an analysis of the economic effects of short-time work policies, first discussing a conceptual framework and then providing firm-level and macro-level empirical evidence.

Conceptual Framework for the Cost-Benefit Analysis of Short-Time Work Subsidies. Using tools from economics, the standard approach for

Figure 1. Share of Employees on Short-Time Work Across Sectors, March 2020–May 2021

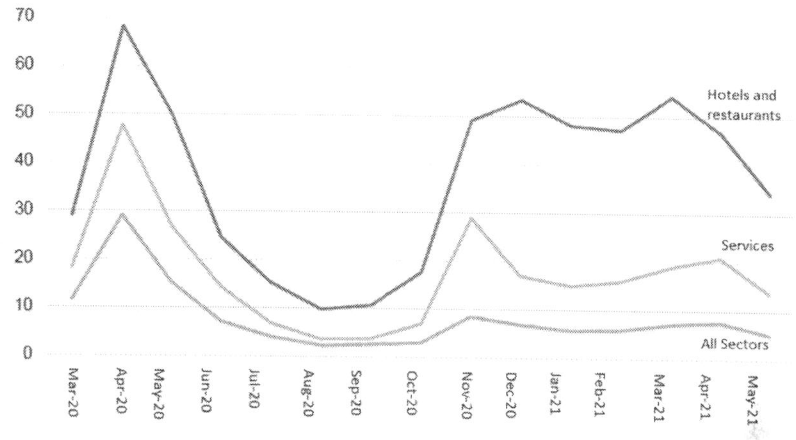

Source: Benoît Coeuré, "Premier rapport du Comité d'évaluation du plan France Relance," France Stratégie and the Inspection Génerale des Finances, October 26, 2021.

cost-benefit analysis of short-time work subsidies proceeds in two steps: (1) isolating the motives for public intervention by explaining why the social optimum diverges from the private optimum and (2) setting the optimal subsidy level by equating the social marginal cost of subsidies to their social marginal benefit. A growing literature in economics follows this approach[15] and has highlighted two main market failures that may justify subsidies for short-time work: inefficient layoffs due to liquidity constraints and inefficient search due to slack labor markets.

The idea that there may be inefficient layoffs stems from training costs and firm-specific human capital making it costly for firms to replace workers and for workers to change jobs. In principle, the private equilibrium may be able to achieve the optimum amount of labor hoarding during a crisis. But in the presence of liquidity constraints, firms may have to resort to inefficient layoffs, which short-time work subsidies can help alleviate. Thus, short-time work subsidies may be set optimally to address the liquidity constraints that would otherwise cause excess sensitivity of employment to productivity shocks. However, in France, firms' liquidity levels actually increased during the COVID-19 crisis, thanks to state-backed

Table 1. Share of Firms Using Public Support Programs During the COVID-19 Crisis

	Used	Did Not Use	N/A
Short-Time Work	65%	35%	0%
State-Backed Loans	37%	63%	0%
Deferred Taxes and Social Contributions	35%	64%	1%
Solidarity Fund	27%	72%	1%

Source: Benoît Coeuré, "Premier rapport du Comité d'évaluation du plan France Relance," France Stratégie and the Inspection Génerale des Finances, October 26, 2021.

loans.[16] Therefore, it appears difficult to take this theoretical justification as grounding for short-time work subsidy programs.

A second potential theoretical justification is based on the idea of inefficient job search. Recessions are usually characterized by slackness in the labor market—that is, many workers are searching for jobs, and firms post few vacancies, such that the equilibrium level of job search may be too high relative to the social optimum. In such a case, short-time work subsidies may be optimal because they discourage job search by subsidizing low levels of labor supply. However, the French labor market has remained tight during the COVID-19 pandemic, with an increase in labor market tightness in 2021 (as discussed later), which casts doubt on the relevance of this potential theoretical grounding for public intervention.

In practice, it appears that the widespread use of short-time work subsidy programs during the crisis stemmed from two sources: fairness concerns and uncertainty management. Indeed, short-time work was primarily used as a response to state-ordered shutdowns of several sectors of the French economy. To prevent the spread of the epidemic, President Emmanuel Macron announced mandatory home lockdowns for 15 days starting at noon on March 17, 2020, which was extended twice and ended on May 11, 2020. It appeared "fair" to alleviate the costs to business owners and workers, which short-time work subsidies helped achieve.

Furthermore, lockdowns created high levels of uncertainty. Given the widespread use of the program, support to firms and workers through short-time work subsidies might have dramatically reduced uncertainty and helped maintain aggregate demand. This is in contrast with the standard view of social insurance during a recession, which, according to economic research, usually cannot prop up aggregate demand simply because too few people benefit from it.[17]

Thus, the unprecedented nature and magnitude of the COVID-19 crisis makes it difficult to carry out a cost-benefit analysis of short-time subsidy programs based on maximization and optimization at the margin. Short of such a framework for optimal short-time work subsidies, in the remainder of the chapter, I ask two questions to shed light on the program's performance.

First, were there obvious design flaws of the short-time subsidy program? Using firm-level data in the next section, I assess several potential flaws regarding (1) whether the level of support was deemed sufficient by firms that used the subsidies, (2) whether non-take-up resulted from design flaws, (3) the extent of windfall gains for firms that did not need the program but received transfers, and (4) the extent of allocative efficiency costs through support for zombie firms. In conducting this analysis, I compare the performance of short-time work subsidy programs to that of the other major support policies used during the crisis.

Second, do short-time work subsidies contribute to addressing the overall macroeconomic challenges faced by the French economy? In the "Macro-Level Analysis" section, I address this question by documenting the state of the recovery to date, with a particular focus on the large fall in bankruptcy rates and the increase in labor market tightness.

Firm-Level Analysis. I now discuss firm-level evidence shedding light on the performance of the short-time work subsidy policy.

Firms' Stated Levels of Satisfaction with Short-Time Work Subsidies. Large-scale surveys of firms can help inform the cost-benefit analysis of public support programs in real time. A survey conducted at the end of 2021[18] helps analyze whether the level of support for firms that used the programs was calibrated appropriately and the reasons for non-take-up among other firms.

Table 2, Panel A documents that most firms that used short-time work subsidies found the program useful. Fifty-two percent of firms state that it was "key to weather the crisis." Thirty-eight percent of firms mention that the program was "useful but largely insufficient." Finally, 10 percent mention that the program was "not useful at all." These results suggest that the program was calibrated appropriately for a majority of firms.

However, the fact that 10 percent of firms state that the program was not at all useful is potentially an important concern, given the program's financial implications. The available survey evidence does not indicate the share of short-time work subsidies that these firms account for. To obtain an upper bound, one can assume these firms account for at most a proportional share of the funds that were disbursed through short-time work subsidy programs—that is, €3.5 billion (or 0.16 percent of GDP). An important direction for policy going forward would be to assess why these firms did not consider the funds useful, as the implications for public finances are potentially large.

Table 2, Panel B documents the reasons firms did not use the program. Of the firms that did not take up the program, 77 percent state that the main reason was because this program was not necessary for them, as their sales had not decreased much or had increased. These results are encouraging since they suggest that non-take-up was not caused by major issues with the program's implementation.

How Large Were Windfall Gains for Firms? The short-time work support programs were accessible without strict eligibility criteria (in contrast with other policies such as the solidarity fund, which could be used only by firms with a fall in sales compared with the prior year). Loose eligibility criteria made it possible to support all firms quickly, at the cost of subsidizing firms that may not have needed it. Because the cost of public funds is above one due to distortionary taxation, it is useful to assess to what extent certain firms may have received public support that was not necessary (for example, firms with an *increase* in sales) or whether certain firms' financial difficulties were more than offset by public support (for example, firms with subsidies that *more than offset* the fall in operating surplus). Put another way, were short-time work subsidies adequately targeted?

To assess whether public support programs were targeted adequately toward firms that needed it most, a simple approach is to see whether firms with the highest fall in gross operating surplus were the main beneficiaries of public support programs. Gross operating surplus is defined as value added minus wages and taxes on production, plus production

Table 2. Survey Evidence on Firms' Satisfaction with Short-Time Work Programs

Panel A. Firms' Assessment of Short-Time Work Subsidies Conditional on Take-Up

	What role did short-time work subsidies play for your company?
Short-time work subsidies were key to weather the crisis.	52%
Short-time work subsidies were useful but largely insufficient.	38%
Short-time work subsidies were not useful at all to face the crisis.	10%

Panel B. Firms' Motivations for Not Taking Up Short-Time Work Subsidies

	Why didn't your company use short-time work subsidies?
It was not useful because sales increased or did not decrease much.	77%
You were not eligible.	8%
You didn't want to become dependent upon public subsidies.	7%
Your application was rejected.	4%
The application procedure was too complex.	1%
N/A	3%

Source: Benoît Coeuré, "Premier rapport du Comité d'évaluation du plan France Relance," France Stratégie and the Inspection Génerale des Finances, October 26, 2021.

subsidies. According to the French national accounts, between the second quarter of 2020 and the first quarter of 2021, gross operating surplus fell by 4.0 percent (–€28.4 billion, or 1.29 percent of GDP).

According to the Coeuré commission, the aggregate emergency policies helped offset about 45 percent of the fall in gross operating surplus during the first wave (from March 2020 to September 2020) and fully offset it during the second wave (from October 2020 until March 2021). At the macro level, short-time work subsidies and the solidarity fund helped offset about 75 percent of the fall in gross operating surplus. This finding shows that short-time work programs could not have been used in isolation.

In a few sectors, on average, subsidies contributed to a *net increase* in gross operating surplus; that is, even absent these subsidies, these sectors would have done well, and the gross operating surplus would have increased at the sectoral level. This is the case for three sectors: IT, agriculture, and leisure-related activities (including sports, arts, and museums). In these sectors, short-time work support programs and the solidarity fund contributed equally to the "overshooting" of public subsidies.

Using firm-level data, one can measure the distribution of the changes in operating surplus across firms. The aggregate fall in gross operating surplus could result from either concentrated losses in a small number of firms or more equally spread losses. The data show that, in fact, a majority of firms (59 percent) incurred a fall in gross operating surplus. For 20 percent of firms, the fall in gross operating surplus was above 25 percent. Assuming that without short-time work programs workers would have been paid at their normal rates (an extreme assumption), micro-simulations show that 72 percent of firms would have incurred a fall in gross operating surplus. The short-time work subsidy program is used more strongly at the bottom of the distribution of changes in operating surplus, more so than state-backed loans but not as much as the solidarity funds and deferred tax payments.

The results are broadly similar when analyzing changes in sales, rather than changes in gross operating surplus. During the first wave, over 80 percent of subsidies went to companies with a fall in sales, compared with 75 percent during the second wave.

Overall, the Coeuré commission's analysis shows that the support programs appear to have been targeted primarily at struggling firms but that there were some windfall gains, both because the fall in firms' gross operating surplus was more than offset by public support programs in some sectors and because some firms used the programs while they had an *increase* in their sales. To assess whether it was efficient to support struggling firms, it is necessary to analyze to what extent these firms can be viewed as zombie firms.

How Large Was the Support to Zombie Firms? To assess the role of zombie firms in the take-up of the program, it is instructive to document take-up depending on the firm's financial characteristics. A first proxy for zombie firms uses measures of creditworthiness. The Bank of France assigns credit scores to all firms in the French economy. Using precrisis (2019) credit scores, the Coeuré commission's analysis shows that take-up rates for short-time work vary non-monotonically with creditworthiness. Take-up is lower for firms with an excellent credit score or a poor credit score, compared with firms at an intermediate level. In contrast, other government support programs, such as deferred tax payments, have the highest take-up among firms with the lowest credit scores. This suggests that short-time work subsidies may be less likely than other support programs to support firms that are not creditworthy and are artificially sustained by public support.

Second, one can leverage balance sheet data to build a proxy for zombie firms. Using data from the National Institute of Statistics and Economic Studies, zombie firms are defined as firms that are at least 10 years old and were unable to cover their interest charges with their gross operating surplus for at least three consecutive years. To assess the role of zombie firms for the short-time work program and compare it with the impact of other support policies, one can use the latest available comprehensive balance sheet information to define the set of zombie firms. In 2018, these firms accounted for 7.2 percent of all mature firms (i.e., older than 10 years), 4 percent of value added, 7.5 percent of employment, and 8.1 percent of capital. From March 2020 to June 2021, about half of zombie firms used one of the public support programs.

As shown in Table 3, during the first wave (March–September 2020), 4.5 percent of the funds disbursed as short-time work subsidies went to zombie firms, compared with 3.6 percent for the solidarity fund, 3.4 percent for state-backed loans, and 8.1 percent for deferred tax payments. These percentages remained stable during the second wave, from October 2020 to March 2021: The share of zombie firms is 4.3 percent for short-time work subsidies, 2.5 percent for the solidarity fund, 3.4 percent for state-backed loans, and 8.1 percent for deferred tax payments. Thus, short-time work subsidies do better than deferred tax payment in avoiding zombie firms, but they do not perform as well as state-backed loans or the solidarity fund.

Overall, these figures imply that about €1.56 billion of public subsidies for short-time work may have been directed toward zombie firms. Although there may be an efficiency loss from subsidizing these firms, to the first order these funds constitute a transfer toward these firms' workers. In other words, the €1.56 billion figure can certainly be taken as an upper bound for the potential efficiency cost.

Table 3. Share of Zombie Firms Across Support Programs

	First Wave, March–September 2020	Second Wave, October 2020–March 2021
Short-Time Work Subsidies	4.5% (out of €14 billion)	4.3% (out of €6 billion)
Solidarity Fund	3.6% (out of €0.7 billion)	2.5% (out of €7 billion)
State-Backed Loans	3.4% (out of €90 billion)	3.4% (out of €90 billion)
Deferred Taxes and Social Contributions	8.1% (out of €8 billion)	8.1% (out of €8 billion)

Source: Benoît Coeuré, "Premier rapport du Comité d'évaluation du plan France Relance," France Stratégie and the Inspection Génerale des Finances, October 26, 2021.

Third, to assess the importance of zombie firms, one can assess whether firms that actually went bankrupt during the crisis benefited from public support programs. As shown in Table 4, €279 million from short-time work subsidies were used by companies that went bankrupt between March 2020 and March 2021 (i.e., about 0.80 percent of short-time work subsidies and 0.013 percent of GDP). In total, firms going bankrupt during this period used about €1.1 billion of public subsidies.

As previously mentioned, deferred tax payments are the main source of windfall gains, and short-time work subsidies do relatively well compared with their macroeconomic importance. These numbers are a lower bound for the amount of public subsidies going to bankrupt firms, given that the bankruptcy rates fell dramatically during the crisis, as discussed further in a later section.

Macro-Level Analysis. For the macro-level analysis of the short-time work policy, I argue that three main features are relevant: The economic recovery was surprisingly swift, bankruptcy rates fell dramatically, and the labor market has been tight.

A Surprisingly Swift Recovery. Although the economic crisis was deep and generated much uncertainty in March and April 2020, the economic recovery has been surprisingly swift.

The evolution of macroeconomic aggregates during the crisis can be summarized as follows. First, consumption expenditure fell while

Table 4. Use of Support Programs by Firms That Went Bankrupt Between March 2020 and March 2021 (Millions of Euros)

	First Wave, March–September 2020	Second Wave, October 2020–March 2021	Both Waves
All Programs	241	868	1,109
Short-Time Work Subsidies	78	201	279
Solidarity Fund	51	59	110
State-Backed Loans	13	243	257
Deferred Taxes and Social Contributions	98	364	462

Source: Benoît Coeuré, "Premier rapport du Comité d'évaluation du plan France Relance," France Stratégie and the Inspection Génerale des Finances, October 26, 2021.

household income was preserved, leading to a large increase in household savings, which increased from 15.1 percent of disposable income in 2019 to 21.4 percent in 2020. This accumulated wealth has not decreased in 2021.

Second, corporate investment has performed better than expected, with a fall close to that of GDP, while in previous recessions, investment had been pro-cyclical, with a fall about twice as large as that of GDP.

Third, employment has outperformed expectations by far. At the end of the first quarter in 2021, employment was only 1.2 percent below its level at the end of 2019, or a loss of 243,000 jobs; the forecasts early in the crisis were much worse. By September 2021, employment had returned to its precrisis level.

Fourth, firms' profitability has increased. For example, margins have increased by 1.5 percentage points in 2020, compared to 2019.

Fifth, business activity was almost back to its precrisis level by September 2021. According to the survey of business leaders conducted by the Bank of France,[19] in September 2021 the level of activity was back to 99.5 percent of its normal level, as depicted in Figure 2.

Sixth, state-backed loans led to an increase in both the level of liquidity and net debt for firms. France started from a situation with a higher level of corporate debt, at 73 percent of GDP, compared with 63 percent in Italy, 57 percent in the UK, and 41 percent in Germany.

Figure 2. The Swift Rebound of Business Activity

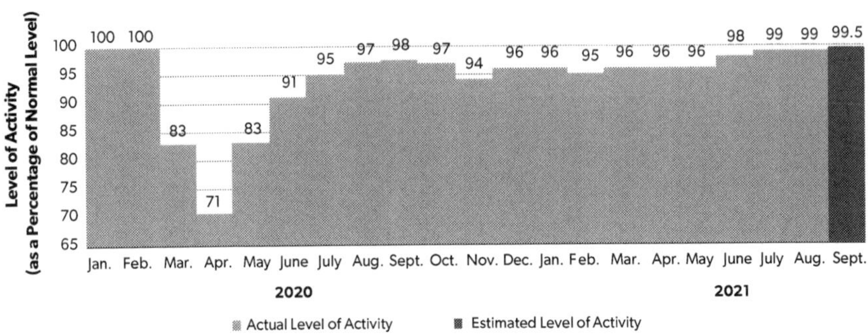

Source: Bank of France, "Update on Business Conditions in France at the Start of September 2021," September 13, 2021, https://www.banque-france.fr/sites/default/files/media/2021/09/24/update_on_business_conditions_in_france_start_of_september_2021_0.pdf.

Overall, the macroeconomic cost of the crisis was shared between public administrations, which shouldered 75 percent of the cost, and companies, which incurred 25 percent of the overall shock. Households were fully offset on average, notably thanks to short-time work programs, which prevented an increase in unemployment. Survey evidence suggests that firms were adequately supported during the crisis. In the representative sample of the Coeuré commission, 21 percent of firms state that the public support they received was "absolutely sufficient," and 56 percent state that it was "rather sufficient"; 16 percent of firms answer "rather insufficient," 2 percent say "totally insufficient," and 2 percent do not answer.[20]

This evidence and the swift recovery in France suggest that the emergency measures, including short-time work, achieved their goals. Economic activity has bounced back after each lockdown, as measured with real-time bank account data. Short-time work programs likely played a key role, especially early in the crisis, to preserve consumer confidence and business investment by reducing uncertainty and thus maintaining aggregate demand.

However, France now faces new macroeconomic challenges, which I discuss next. In this new macroeconomic context, it appears necessary to gradually wind down short-time work programs.

Figure 3. Changes in Bankruptcy Rates over Time

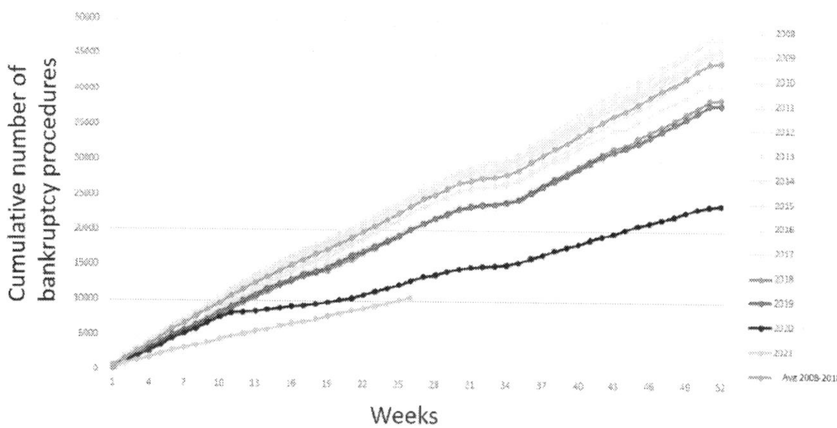

Source: Benoît Coeuré, "Premier rapport du Comité d'évaluation du plan France Relance," France Stratégie and the Inspection Génerale des Finances, October 26, 2021.

An Unprecedented Fall in Bankruptcy Rates. Due to the generosity of public support policies, including short-time work policies, the bankruptcy rate has fallen substantially in France since the beginning of the crisis, raising the possibility of a wave of "catch-up bankruptcies." The large fall in bankruptcy rates in 2020 and 2021, shown in Figure 3, suggests that many firms that would have gone bankrupt absent a crisis were saved thanks to public subsidies.

The number of bankruptcies fell in 2020 in most European countries, but the decline was larger in France, with a fall of about 40 percent. Using harmonized data sources, recent work by the Organisation for Economic Co-operation and Development (OECD)[21] compares the change in bankruptcy rates across countries. The estimates are shown in Table 5. Only Austria experienced a larger decline in bankruptcy than France did. In the United States, the divergence relative to pre-COVID-19 bankruptcies was much less substantial, with a fall of about 5 percent.

Table 5 also shows that, perhaps paradoxically, there is a positive correlation between the change in GDP and the change in bankruptcy rates in 2020, even though bankruptcies are normally pro-cyclical. Policy decisions regarding shutdowns may explain this pattern. Countries where

Table 5. Changes in Bankruptcy Rates and GDP During the Pandemic Across Countries

Country	Cumulative Percentage Change in Bankruptcies, March–December 2020 Relative to 2019	Year-on-Year Percentage Change in GDP, Q4 2020
Austria	–40.62%	–6.1%
France	–39.65%	–4.3%
United Kingdom	–38.78%	–7.1%
Denmark	–33.75%	–0.5%
Belgium	–32.00%	–4.4%
Italy	–31.62%	–6.6%
Korea	–29.23%	–1.1%
Canada	–23.23%	–3.1%
Finland	–18.60%	–1.7%
Germany	–18.35%	–2.9%
Netherlands	–17.04%	–3.1%
Spain	–14.45%	–8.8%
Japan	–5.39%	–0.8%
United States	–5.39%	–2.3%
Sweden	–1.00%	–1.8%

Source: Organisation for Economic Co-operation and Development, *OECD SME and Entrepreneurship Outlook 2021*, June 28, 2021, https://www.oecd-ilibrary.org/sites/97a5bbfe-en/index.html?itemId=/content/publication/97a5bbfe-en.

shutdowns were less stringent (and where excess mortality was often higher), such as the United States or Sweden, suffered from a smaller fall in GDP. These countries offered less generous public support programs, such that bankruptcy rates fell more in countries with a larger fall in GDP in 2020. These patterns suggest that generous public support programs, including short-time work subsidies, were a key ingredient to make it politically acceptable to shut down large sectors of the economy, leading to an unprecedented fall in bankruptcy rates in several countries despite a large fall in economic activity.

The large decrease in firm bankruptcies in France suggests that public support programs overshot relative to the level of support that was required; indeed, a rule of thumb is that optimal stabilization policy should attempt to smooth bankruptcy rates over time. A challenge of the COVID-19 crisis is the large uncertainty that existed at the beginning about the depth and duration of the crisis. The quick development of vaccines helped strengthen the recovery in a way that was difficult to predict. For this reason, the sustained fall in bankruptcy rates may be interpreted as a symptom that the recovery of fundamentals was unexpectedly fast, rather than as a symptom of overly generous public support programs. Put another way, public support programs, including short-time work subsidies, may appear too generous ex post primarily because fundamentals recovered faster than expected due to unexpectedly quick vaccine development, rather than because the public support programs were too generous relative to the expected shock.

Regardless of the interpretation, a new macroeconomic challenge for France and other high-income countries is to manage the rise in bankruptcy rates going forward. Allowing for an increase in bankruptcy rates going forward appears necessary for allocative efficiency and requires winding down subsidy programs like short-time work programs (while liquidity policies such as state-backed loans could be maintained for a longer period to accompany the recovery). Thus, it is important for the new long-term part-time work program, which was established at the end of July 2021 (as discussed earlier), to avoid being overgenerous going forward. At this stage, the rate set for the employer (which has to cover 10 percent of the employee benefit) remains generous, and it would seem appropriate to consider increasing employers' contributions gradually going forward.

A Large Increase in Labor Market Tightness. The French economy is currently characterized by a strong increase in the job vacancy rate and labor market tightness. The job vacancy rate, defined as the number of job vacancies or vacant positions on the last business day of the month expressed as a percentage of labor demand (occupied positions and vacant positions), has been on an upward trajectory for several years in France, as shown in Figure 4. The increase has continued during the crisis, after a small decline at the beginning of the crisis.

As illustrated in the figure, the increase in vacancy rates is a relatively long-term trend in the French economy. It is unlikely that subsidies for

Figure 4. Changes in Vacancy Rates over Time

Source: French Labor Ministry.

short-time work contributed to the increase in labor market tightness. Recent work by the OECD[22] shows that job search, measured in real time using Google Trends data, has remained elevated throughout the crisis. If anything, the level of job search has remained higher than in the United States. Google Trends data also suggest that job searches haven't been redirected toward sectors with increasing demand during the crisis (e.g., toward education and health and away from tourism and restaurants).

Based on the available evidence to date, the increase in labor market tightness appears to be best interpreted as a structural problem in the French economy, potentially reflecting a mismatch between labor demand and skills and relatively generous unemployment benefits. Short-time work benefits should not be viewed as the main cause of the increase in labor market tightness, but maintaining them for an extended period appears inefficient in this context.

Conclusion

Short-time work subsidies were widely used in France during the COVID-19 crisis. Based on the available data, the policy appears to have achieved its main goals: to compensate workers and firms for state-ordered shutdowns and to reduce uncertainty to maintain aggregate demand. It was instrumental in supporting a quick economic recovery. However, short-time work subsidies do not seem to be a useful tool to address the new macroeconomic challenges facing the French economy, in particular the increase in labor market tightness and the necessary increase in bankruptcy rates to preserve allocative efficiency.

To address these new challenges, it appears necessary to promote structural reforms in the French labor market and avoid maintaining short-time work subsidies for too long. In particular, policymakers must be careful to avoid an overly generous long-term short-time work program. Estimates of fraud rates to date suggest that strengthening fraud-detection programs is another important direction to prepare for the next crisis.

Short-time work subsidies were a key ingredient to make it politically acceptable to shut down large sectors of the economy and order home lockdowns in France. Other countries like the United States reacted less strongly and incurred higher excess mortality and a smaller recession. In this sense, the cost-benefit analysis of short-time work is fundamentally tied to the broader cost-benefit analysis of each country's health and economic strategies during the pandemic.[23]

There is perhaps one obvious aspect in which short-time work subsidies fail a simple and pragmatic cost-benefit test—namely, the next-best alternative use of funds. The COVID-19 pandemic has led to large stimulus packages, but international solidarity has been largely lacking, as illustrated by vaccine nationalism and export restrictions. While France spent over €35 billion in short-time work subsidies (about 1.6 percent of GDP) to date, advanced economies donated less than €10 billion[24] to deliver vaccines in low-income countries.

In a recent International Monetary Fund working paper, Ruchir Agarwal and Gita Gopinath estimate that $35 billion, in the form of grants to low-income countries, would suffice to end the COVID-19 pandemic by promoting vaccination, testing, tracing, and other public health measures.[25] By preventing the rise of novel COVID-19 variants and their health and economic consequences worldwide, it appears to be in the enlightened economic self-interest of France and other high-income nations to promote these policies. This could be achieved with a fraction of the budget that was devoted to short-time work subsidies around the world, or with the amount spent in France alone. Going forward, one can only hope that the "whatever it takes" mindset will start applying across borders, in particular to vaccinate the world.

Notes

1. The idea that public support programs would be established "whatever it takes" ("*quoi qu'il en coûte*") was promoted by President Emmanuel Macron in a public address at the onset of the crisis, on March 12, 2020.

2. Indeed, the scale of the program was such that there could be a large impact. This stands in contrast with typical crises, in which social insurance policies have been shown to barely affect spending at the aggregate level, simply because they affect too few people. See, for example, Alisdair McKay and Ricardo Reis, "The Role of Automatic Stabilizers in the U.S. Business Cycle," *Econometrica* 84, no. 1 (January 2016): 141–94, https://onlinelibrary.wiley.com/doi/abs/10.3982/ECTA11574.

3. The idea that public support programs should become more targeted and tailor-made ("*sur-mesure*") was promoted by Finance Minister Bruno Le Maire in a series of press, TV, and radio events at the end of August 2021.

4. Throughout this chapter, I draw extensively on a comprehensive report reviewing the emergency programs to support the French economy, which was presented in July 2021 to the French prime minister; the report was written by France Stratégie and the Inspection Génerale des Finances under the direction of Benoît Coeuré. See Benoît Coeuré, "Premier rapport du Comité d'évaluation du plan France Relance" [First Report of the Commission in Charge of Assessing the Efficiency of the French Economic Stimulus Package], France Stratégie and the Inspection Génerale des Finances, October 26, 2021.

5. Coeuré, "Premier rapport du Comité d'évaluation du plan France Relance."

6. In the first quarter of 2021, the Bank of France's estimate of default rates for state-backed loans was 5 percent, implying an expected fiscal cost of €7 billion.

7. Deferred tax payments account for €2.6 billion, and reduced tax payments account for €3.6 billion.

8. The minimum wage was €8.03 in 2020 and €8.11 in 2021.

9. The tax rates are the "contribution sociale géneralisée," equal to 6.2 percent, and the "contribution au rem-boursement de la dette sociale," equal to 0.5 percent.

10. Because of this floor, the benefit is above 84 percent of the posttax wage for all workers earning up to 1.2 times the minimum wage.

11. According to recent evidence from the French Council of Economic Analysis, sectors that were most affected by the crisis and benefited from continued government support, in particular through continued short-time work policies, may have been overcompensated for their losses. Indeed, analysis of firms' bank records reveals that net

debt and liquidity *improved* for small and medium-sized firms in these sectors (e.g., for restaurants, hotels, movie theaters, and museums). See Anne Epaulard et al., "The Financial Situation of SMEs in August 2021 Based on Their Bank Account," September 2021.

12. These statistics and the statistics in the remainder of this section are taken from Coeuré, "Premier rapport du Comité d'évaluation du plan France Relance."

13. France Ministry of Labor, "ACEMO-Covid: Labor Force Activity and Working Conditions During the COVID-19 Health Crisis," https://www.casd.eu/en/source/labor-force-activity-and-working-conditions-during-the-covid-19-health-crisis.

14. See Laetitia Otte, "En 2020, l'activité partielle a concerné tous les secteurs et tous les profils de salaries" [In 2020, Short-Time Work Was Used in All Sectors and All Occupations], France Ministry of Labor, April 20, 2021, https://dares.travail-emploi.gouv.fr/publication/en-2020-lactivite-partielle-concerne-tous-les-secteurs-et-tous-les-profils-de-salaries.

15. For a recent review, see Giulia Giupponi, Camille Landais, and Alice Lapeyre, "Should We Insure Workers or Jobs During Recessions?," *Journal of Economic Perspectives* 36, no. 2 (Spring 2022): 29–54, https://www.aeaweb.org/articles?id=10.1257/jep.36.2.29.

16. For example, the French Council of Economic Analysis has shown the increase in firms' liquidity using real-time data on a large sample of firms' bank accounts.

17. Absent a structural model, it is difficult to quantify the importance of this channel, but doing so is an important task for future research. See, for example, McKay and Reis, "The Role of Automatic Stabilizers in the U.S. Business Cycle."

18. This survey was also used for Figure 1 and is taken from Coeuré, "Premier rapport du Comité d'évaluation du plan France Relance."

19. The Bank of France publishes a range of monthly and quarterly economic surveys that provide a snapshot of the French economy in the form of business climate indicators and short-term forecasts. Here I use the results of the September 2021 survey: Bank of France, "Update on Business Conditions in France at the Start of September 2021," September 13, 2021, https://www.banque-france.fr/sites/default/files/media/2021/09/24/update_on_business_conditions_in_france_start_of_september_2021_0.pdf.

20. Results of Coeuré, "Premier rapport du Comité d'évaluation du plan France Relance."

21. Organisation for Economic Co-operation and Development, *OECD SME and Entrepreneurship Outlook 2021*, June 28, 2021, https://www.oecd-ilibrary.org/sites/97a5bbfe-en/index.html?itemId=/content/publication/97a5bbfe-en.

22. See Organisation for Economic Co-operation and Development, *OECD Employment Outlook 2021: Navigating the COVID-19 Crisis and Recovery*, July 7, 2021, https://www.oecd-ilibrary.org/employment/oecd-employment-outlook-2021_5a700c4b-en.

23. In this respect, economic analysis can merely provide some orders of magnitude. For example, a simple exercise consists in attributing differences in outcomes between France and the United States to differences in their health and economic strategies; that is, a French-style strategy would reduce excess deaths by a factor of two while amplifying the fall in gross domestic product (GDP) by a factor of two. According to these illustrative estimates, implementing a US-style strategy in France could have increased

excess deaths by 55,000 while reducing the fall in GDP by €100 billion. Setting an average age at death of 80 years for COVID-19 victims and a life expectancy of 89, these estimates imply a cost per year of life saved of €200,000, which is surprisingly similar to leading estimates of the statistical value of life.

24. This amount was provided through COVID-19 Vaccines Global Access, abbreviated as COVAX, a worldwide initiative aimed at equitable access to COVID-19 vaccines directed by Gavi, the Vaccine Alliance, the Coalition for Epidemic Preparedness Innovations, and the World Health Organization.

25. Ruchir Agarwal and Gita Gopinath, *A Proposal to End the COVID-19 Pandemic*, International Monetary Fund, May 2021, https://www.imf.org/en/Publications/Staff-Discussion-Notes/Issues/2021/05/19/A-Proposal-to-End-the-COVID-19-Pandemic-460263.

5

German Labor Market Policy During and After the COVID-19 Recession

TOM KREBS

The COVID-19 crisis reached Germany in March 2020, when infection rates rose quickly and economic activity dropped dramatically. The German government reacted to the economic crisis by implementing a mix of economic stabilization policies. One central instrument of the policy mix was the short-time work (STW) program that makes it attractive for companies to reduce working hours without laying off workers. In other words, STW provides income insurance for workers and preserves existing employer-employee links in the face of adverse economic shocks.

The German government had already relied on STW insurance during the global financial crisis of 2007–09, and it made the STW program again the central policy instrument to stabilize the labor market during the COVID-19 crisis. The current chapter discusses the economic consequences of the program. The analysis yields three main results.

First, the STW program successfully prevented a large increase in unemployment during the COVID-19 recession in Germany. Further, the program led to a net fiscal gain in the short run, if the fiscal cost of unemployment benefits is included in the analysis. Put differently, STW insurance proved to be a highly effective macroeconomic stabilization tool during the COVID-19 recession. There is, however, an unresolved question as to what extent the stabilization gain was due to the STW program itself or to what extent it was generated by the increase in the program's generosity and duration during the recession (i.e., automatic stabilizer versus countercyclical policy).

Second, there is little evidence that STW insurance caused a sluggish recovery by weakening companies' incentives to expand employees' working hours. However, as of June 2022, some of the special policy measures implemented at the start of the COVID-19 recession were still in place, and it is too early to assess the overall effect of the program extensions.

Further, the reduction in working hours due to STW is not only an economic cost but also an economic opportunity for retraining workers, thereby enhancing future growth potentials. The German government has already taken steps to combine STW insurance with public support for training programs, and these policy efforts should continue. In other words, the German government's commitment to reach climate neutrality by 2045 requires a fundamental transformation of the production process, and the recovery phase after the COVID-19 crisis is the right time to make the necessary human capital investments.

Third, the available evidence points toward a net positive effect of the STW program on productivity and long-run growth in Germany, though it is too early to draw firm conclusions. On one hand, the program avoided large productivity losses due to the loss of human capital associated with job displacement during recessions. On the other hand, the program might have reduced possible productivity gains by slowing the process of re-matching jobs to workers. However, it is doubtful that the negative productivity effect of STW has been substantial during the COVID-19 recession in Germany. Clearly, a combination of STW insurance with training programs for employed workers strengthens the positive productivity effects of the program.

In sum, the STW program has been an economic success story during the COVID-19 recession in Germany. This begs the question of why this policy instrument is not used more widely in other countries, such as the US. The answer most likely lies in the different institutional structures of the labor markets in Germany and the US.

The large-scale and efficient use of STW insurance during an economic crisis requires a certain level of cooperation between employers (capital owners) and employees (labor unions). In Germany, a certain balance of power and the idea of "social partnership" provide a solid foundation for such cooperation, whereas in the US, a cooperative approach is often impossible to achieve because bargaining power is asymmetrically distributed and parties distrust each other. A deeper analysis of the link between STW insurance and social partnership in the labor market is clearly an important topic—but beyond the scope of this chapter.

Figure 1. Quarterly Real GDP Growth Rates in Percentage, Not Annualized

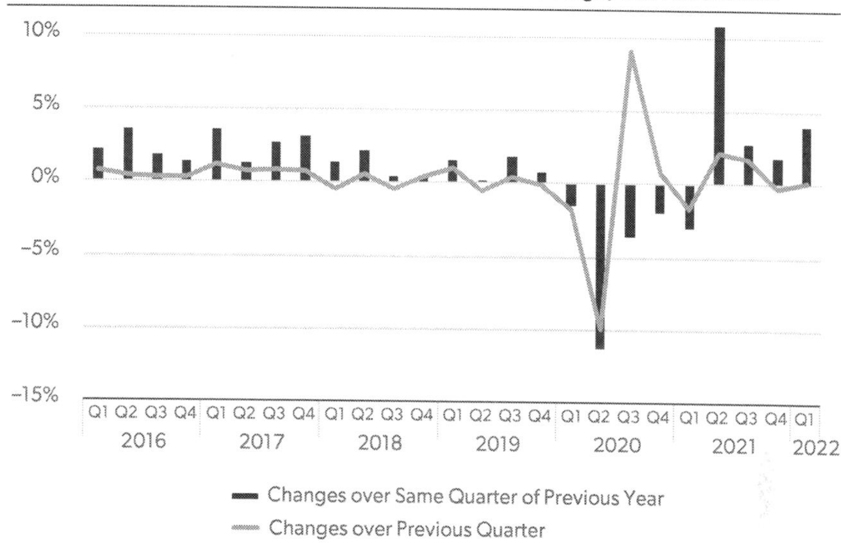

Note: Values for the first and third quarters in 2021 are estimates. Dark gray bars depict changes over the same quarter in the previous year, and the light gray line shows changes over the previous quarter.
Source: Statistisches Bundesamt [German Statistical Agency], https://www.destatis.de/DE/Home/_inhalt.html.

Background

The COVID-19 pandemic reached Germany in March 2020 with full force. In response to increasing infection rates, the German government restricted people's social interaction. In addition, many companies asked workers to stay home because of health concerns, though there was never a full lockdown. These events, in conjunction with the interruption of global supply chains, caused a dramatic drop in German aggregate economic activity.

Figure 1 shows the time series of real gross domestic product (GDP) and underscores the severity of the recession. Real GDP fell in the second quarter of 2020 by 10 percent compared to first-quarter GDP that year, and the total output loss was 5 percent relative to 2019. This decline in real GDP in 2020 is slightly smaller than the GDP decline of 5.7 percent in 2009, during the Great Recession, which makes it the second most severe one-year GDP drop in post–World War II Germany.

Figure 2 shows that the COVID-19 recession in Germany was, in a sense, a double-dip recession. After the dramatic drop in GDP in the second quarter of 2020, there followed a short recovery in the third quarter of 2020, but the recovery was short-lived, and another drop in GDP happened in the fourth quarter of 2020 and the first quarter of 2021. This second dip in economic activity was the result of a second wave of health restrictions imposed in the fall of 2020, after restrictions had been lifted in the summer of 2020. Finally, a second recovery started in the second quarter of 2021. These two economic waves correspond to the two waves in infection rates that were typical in many countries.[1]

Despite the dramatic drop in GDP during the economic crisis, the unemployment rate increased only mildly in 2020. The main reason for this positive labor market response is the heavy reliance on STW insurance, a policy tool that the German government had already used during the great financial crisis. STW provides incentives for companies to preserve existing employer-employee relationships in the face of production shortfalls so that most employers in Germany abstained from laying off or dismissing workers during the COVID-19 recession. Figure 2 depicts the development of the unemployment rate and STW rate (i.e., the fraction of workers in STW) before and during the crisis.

Figure 2 shows that the unemployment rate rose from 5 percent in February 2020 to 5.8 percent in April 2020 then reached its peak in June 2020 with 6.4 percent. The STW rate increased from 0.3 percent in February to 13.2 percent in April 2020 and then continued to decline. Figure 2 also shows that STW has quickly declined from its peak in April 2020 but remained at elevated levels in the summer of 2020; it then increased again in fall 2020 due to a second infection wave and corresponding health restrictions. The STW rate has been slowly falling since February 2021 and reached 1.5 percent in August 2021. In addition, by the summer of 2021, the unemployment rate had fallen almost to precrisis levels, reaching 5.5 percent in August 2021.

Figure 2 demonstrates that Germany did not experience an increase in unemployment comparable to the dramatic rise in unemployment in the US. However, the number of workers on STW increased substantially, leading to a large decline in total working hours. In other words, the German labor market adjusted to the recession shock mainly along the intensive

Figure 2. Unemployment Rate and STW Rate

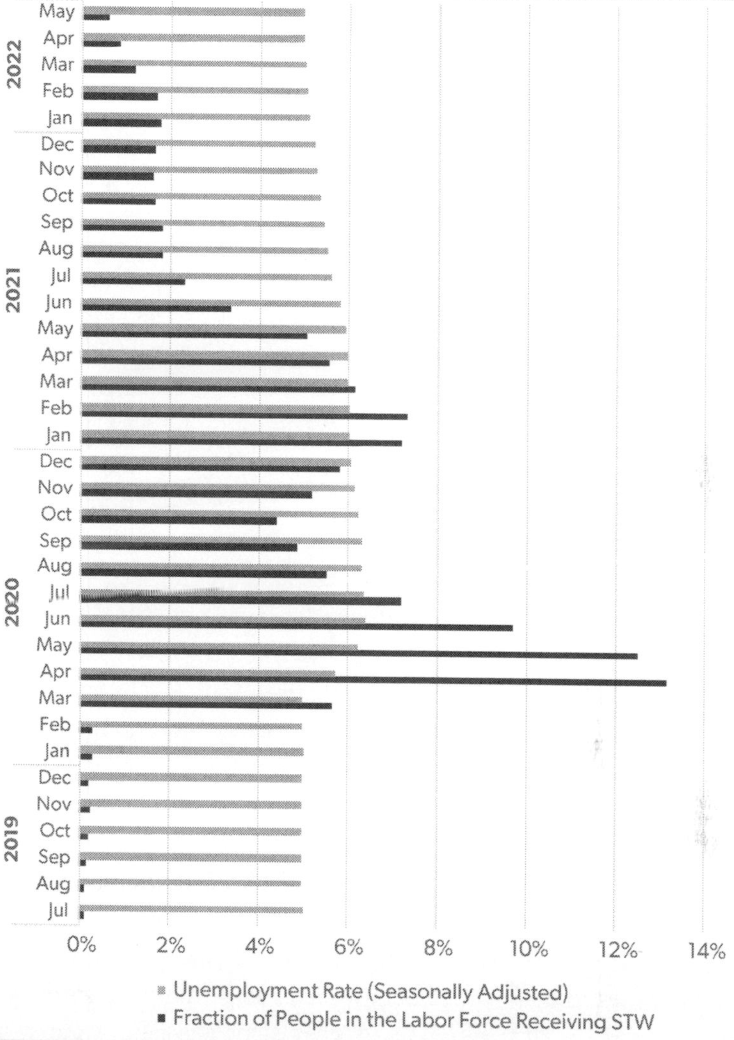

Note: Light gray bars depict the unemployment rate (i.e., the fraction of people in the labor force who are unemployed), and dark gray bars depict the STW rate (i.e., the fraction of people in the labor force who receive STW).

Source: Bundesagentur fuer Arbeit, Realisierte Kurzarbeit (hochgerechnet)—Deutschland, Länder, Regionaldirektionen, Agenturen für Arbeit und Kreise (Monatszahlen), https://statistik.arbeitsagentur.de/SiteGlobals/Forms/Suche/Einzelheftsuche_Formular.html?topic_f=kurzarbeit-hr; and Bundesagentur fuer Arbeit, Bezugsgrößen für Deutschland Zeitreihe, https://statistik.arbeitsagentur.de/DE/Navigation/Grundlagen/Definitionen/Berechnung-der-Arbeitslosenquote/Bezugsgroessen/Daten-Bezugsgroesse-Nav.html. Values for April and May 2022 are estimates from Ifo-Institute, "Kurzarbeit nach Branchen," https://www.ifo.de/sites/default/files/facts/ifo_Kurzarbeit_Branchen.pdf.

labor margin (i.e., employed workers reduced working time), preserving most employer-employee links, whereas the adjustment in the US labor market mainly took place along the extensive labor margin (i.e., employed workers were laid off), breaking a large number of employer-employee links.

Figure 3 underscores the point that the labor market adjustment in Germany was quite large during the COVID-19 recession despite an unemployment rate that barely moved. Figure 3 plots the underemployment rate (i.e., the sum of the unemployment rate and STW rate), underscoring that the adjustment in the German labor market was large during the COVID-19 recession.[2] This underemployment rate increased from 5.3 percent before the crisis to 19 percent at the peak of the crisis, in April 2020.

Two remarks regarding the labor market data shown in Figures 2 and 3 are important when drawing comparisons to the US experience. First, the unemployment rate depicted in Figure 2 is the unemployment rate reported by the German Labor Agency. This unemployment rate measures the number of people who have been registered unemployed at the Federal Employment Agency and receive unemployment benefits, including the long-term unemployed. It is usually higher than the unemployment rate according to the International Labor Organization (ILO) concept, which is based on surveys and comparable to the unemployment rate reported in the US. For example, in February 2020, the unemployment rate depicted in Figure 2 was 5 percent, whereas the internationally comparable ILO unemployment rate was 3.4 percent. However, changes in the ILO unemployment rate for Germany and changes in the official unemployment rate depicted in Figure 2 track each other quite closely.

Second, many employees receiving STW compensation still work a positive number of hours. Specifically, the average monthly working time among workers on STW is about one-third of their full-time working hours. Figure 4 depicts the aggregate reduction in working hours due to STW and shows that at its peak, the decline is 5.4 percent in the second quarter of 2020. If we use a Cobb-Douglas aggregate production function with a labor income share of two-thirds, then this corresponds to a GDP decline of 3.6 percent in the second quarter of 2020.

Figure 3. Underemployment Rate

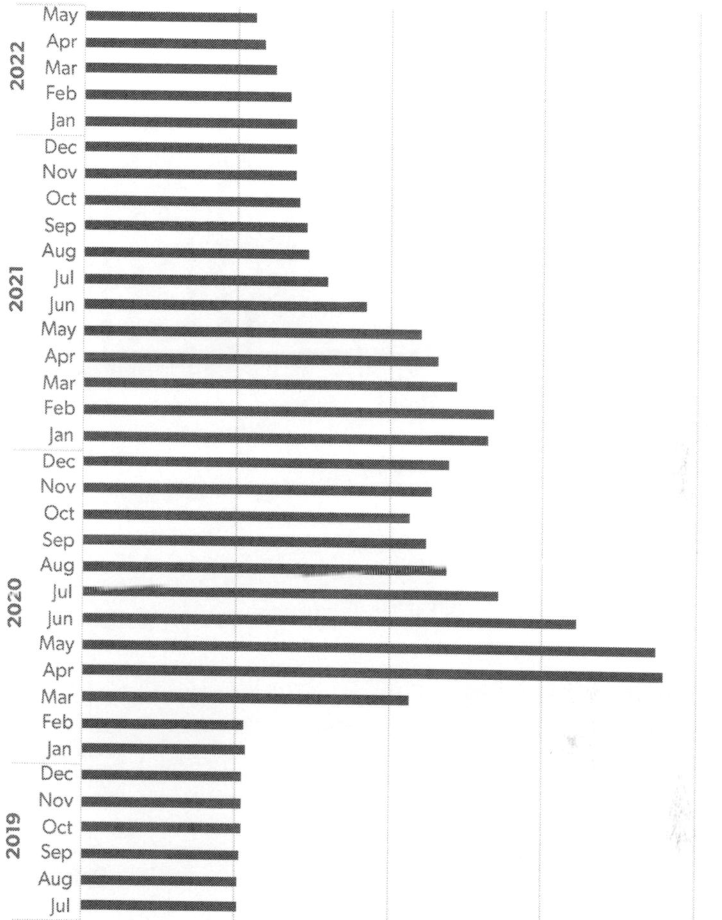

Note: The underemployment rate is the sum of the unemployment rate and STW rate, as depicted in Figure 2.

Source: Bundesagentur fuer Arbeit, Realisierte Kurzarbeit (hochgerechnet)—Deutschland, Länder, Regionaldirektionen, Agenturen für Arbeit und Kreise (Monatszahlen), https://statistik.arbeitsagentur.de/SiteGlobals/Forms/Suche/Einzelheftsuche_Formular.html?topic_f=kurzarbeit-hr; and Bundesagentur fuer Arbeit, Bezugsgrößen für Deutschland Zeitreihe, https://statistik.arbeitsagentur.de/DE/Navigation/Grundlagen/Definitionen/Berechnung-der-Arbeitslosenquote/Bezugsgroessen/Daten-Bezugsgroesse-Nav.html. Values for April and May 2022 are estimates from Ifo-Institute, "Kurzarbeit nach Branchen," https://www.ifo.de/sites/default/files/facts/ifo_Kurzarbeit_Branchen.pdf.

Figure 4. STW Hours Reduction

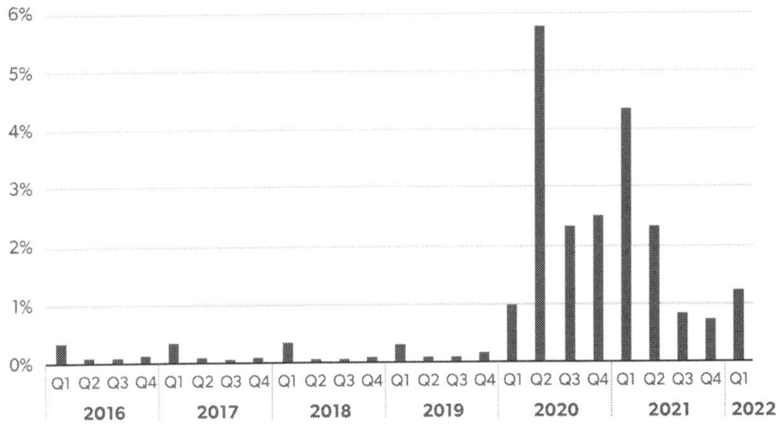

Note: The aggregate reduction in working hours for workers on STW is relative to aggregate working hours.
Source: Institut fuer Arbeitsmarkt-und Berufsforschung, https://iab.de/de/daten/iab-arbeitszeitrechnung.aspx.

STW Insurance

STW programs have a long tradition in Germany as a tool to reduce hours worked without layoffs. STW insurance is always available, but in "normal" times, pick-up rates are low. In contrast, during recessions the program is used extensively, and STW insurance constitutes an essential component of stabilization policy.

STW Insurance in Normal Times. STW compensation schemes provide insurance for workers against labor market risk. In this sense, this government program is similar to unemployment insurance. However, in contrast to unemployment insurance, STW insurance does not compensate income losses in case of job loss but insures workers against labor market risk by preventing job loss. In principle, all workers who pay social security contributions are entitled to STW compensation, including temporary agency workers and people on a fixed-term contract. Workers holding marginal jobs (so-called "mini jobs") and self-employed workers (e.g., entrepreneurs), who are usually exempt from social security contribution, do not receive STW compensation.

STW insurance programs have a long tradition in Germany. The systematic use of STW dates back to the oil crisis and the subsequent recession in 1975. The rules and regulations have changed over time, but the program's broad structure has not changed. The specific rules for STW in "normal" times—the years before the COVID-19 crisis—are as described below.[3]

A company can apply for STW compensation if it has to reduce working hours for economic reasons outside its direct control. At least one-third of the employees at a plant have to reduce working hours, and the corresponding reduction in salary must be at least 10 percent for all affected workers. The application for STW and the corresponding reduction in working time must be a joint decision of employers and employees—the German model of social partnership. In general, the company must have exhausted all alternative means of reducing working time, such as balancing working time accounts or granting leave days. A company receiving STW compensation can only recruit workers for plants that are not subject to the working hour reduction, and the possibility of dismissals is restricted.

The maximum duration of compensation in normal times is 12 months. However, a company can file again for STW after three months of not receiving any payments for workers in a particular plant. The net replacement rate is 60 percent of the salary loss due to the working hour reduction for workers without children and 67 percent for workers with children.

STW insurance is barely used in normal economic times. For example, in 2019, the STW rate varied between 0.1 percent and 0.3 percent. In contrast, during the COVID-19 recession, the STW rate increased quickly, from 0.3 percent in February 2020 to 13.2 percent in April 2020. This massive jump in take-up rates was caused by worsening economic conditions and a change in rules, which is discussed next.

STW Insurance During the COVID-19 Recession. During the great financial crisis and the COVID-19 crisis, the German government used STW insurance as one of its main policy tools to combat the economic crisis. Specifically, during the COVID-19 recession, the German government made the changes outlined below.

In March 2020, the German government decided to improve access to the insurance scheme by weakening the eligibility requirement. Specifically, in normal times, at least one-third of the workers at a plant need to be affected; this requirement was reduced to 10 percent of plant workers. In addition, the use of STW was made more attractive by reimbursing employers their social security contribution for the affected workers. These rule changes are expected to last until at least summer 2022.

The German government also increased the generosity of the scheme by raising the duration and level of STW compensation. Specifically, in April 2020, the maximum duration of STW compensation was extended to 21 months and in October 2020 to 24 months. In May 2020, the net replacement rate was increased for workers whose working hours have been reduced by more than 50 percent. For these workers, the net replacement rate was increased to 70 percent after three months of being on STW (77 percent for workers with children) and to 80 percent after six months on STW. Similar to the changes in unemployment benefit rules implemented in the US, these rule changes improved the insurance of workers' income during the crisis. In contrast to the US, these rule changes will last at least until summer 2022.[4]

In the US, a large number of workers laid off during the COVID-19 recession were recalled to their old job relatively quickly. This begs the question as to what extent temporary layoffs—the main margin of labor market adjustment in the US—are any different from STW—the main margin of labor market adjustment in Germany.

There are at least three fundamental economic differences between layoffs with the possibility of recall and STW that justify treating them as two distinct employment states. First, the majority of employees on STW work a substantial number of hours, and only a few reduce their working time to zero. Second, workers on STW have the same legal rights as employed workers do, including the right to receive unemployment benefits for the complete duration in case they should become unemployed after their time on STW. Third, for workers on STW, the unemployment risk is less than for laid-off workers on recall; that is, STW workers face less uncertainty than laid-off workers do.

Stabilization Policy During the COVID-19 Recession. At the onset of the COVID-19 recession in March 2020, the German federal government reacted quickly, with several policy measures. The main goal was to stabilize the economy by providing liquidity to companies and insurance to workers. This happened most prominently through low-interest loan programs of the German Development Bank, KfW, for companies affected by the COVID-19 recession and the STW program for workers. In addition, the maximal duration of unemployment benefit payments was increased, but this step was much less important in Germany than it was in the US, since most of the labor market adjustment in Germany took place through STW.

The German federal government quickly realized that the March 2020 emergency measures were not sufficient to prevent a downward spiral in the business sector, and it took further policy actions. Thus, the government established various crisis programs that compensated companies and small businesses for revenue losses incurred during the COVID-19 recession. In other words, these programs insured the business sector, including the self-employed, but not the employees of companies. In addition, the government took equity stakes in some larger companies that were at risk of bankruptcy (e.g., the German airline Lufthansa) and created a public equity program for small- and medium-sized companies in need of a capital injection.

In addition to these stabilization instruments, in June 2020 the German federal government implemented a fiscal stimulus package to help the German economy move out of recession as quickly as possible. This stimulus package included a temporary reduction in the value-added tax and several policy measures to boost private and public investment, with a focus on clean energy.[5] Overall, the German federal government went into the recession with a small budget surplus in 2019, which turned into a budget deficit of around 4 percent of GDP in 2020.[6] In addition, most state governments used debt-financed government spending to stimulate the economy.

Macroeconomic Effects of STW

The macroeconomic effects of STW insurance are best analyzed by distinguishing three different time frames: short run, medium run, and long run. In the short run, STW mainly stabilizes the economy during the crisis, and negative incentive effects play a minor role. In the medium run, STW still avoids unnecessary job losses but might slow the recovery, since companies have a disincentive to expand employees' hours worked. Finally, two countervailing forces determine the long-run growth implications of STW insurance. On the one hand, recessions leave permanent scars due to an increase in the human capital losses associated with job displacement, and STW reduces these losses. On the other hand, recessions can also raise long-run growth by improving productivity through re-matching jobs to workers, and STW reduces this positive "cleansing" effect.

Stabilization During the Crisis (Short Run). This subsection discusses the short-run effects of STW—that is, the effects during the economic crisis. For the COVID-19 crisis in Germany, this short-run period is split into two subperiods that run roughly from March 2020 to May 2020 and November 2021 to February 2022. As discussed above, we can think of the COVID-19 crisis in Germany as a double-dip recession, where two consecutive recessions were interrupted by a short-lived recovery in the summer of 2020.

The main policy goal of STW is to preserve the employer-employee link during recessions to avoid a steep rise in unemployment—or at least dampen the hike in unemployment during recessions. Figure 2 shows that the German unemployment rate moved up only modestly during the COVID-19 recession, whereas the STW rate moved up dramatically. The same pattern was observed during the great financial crisis. This suggests that STW insurance successfully reduced an increase in unemployment during the last two economic crises in Germany. Of course, we do not know the counterfactual; that is, we do not know how the German unemployment rate would have evolved without the policy. In other words, looking at only the aggregate time series evidence for Germany provides just two sample points.

Tito Boeri and Herbert Bruecker provide a more formal empirical analysis of the effect of STW on unemployment during the great financial crisis, based on a sample of Organisation for Economic Co-operation and Development countries. They find that STW benefit schemes reduced the rise in unemployment during the great financial crisis, but the number of jobs saved is substantially smaller than the reduction in hours worked (in full-time equivalents). Clearly, simple cross-country regressions with a limited set of data have to make strong assumptions and usually do not yield robust results.[7]

Boeri and Bruecker therefore also use German plant-level data to analyze the effect of STW insurance on German unemployment during the great financial crisis. They find that the program successfully prevented unemployment. Specifically, according to their empirical estimates, about 85 percent of the program's reduction in working hours would have led to unemployment without the program.[8]

In a recent empirical paper, Shekhar Aiyar and Mai Chi Dao study the employment effect of STW insurance during the COVID-19 crisis in Germany. The authors use state-level variation in the exposure to the COVID-19 shock and corresponding state-level variation in the share of workers who are eligible for STW insurance to estimate the extent the STW program dampens the employment response to the recession shock. They find that the STW program had substantial effects; without the program, the unemployment rate would have been 3 percentage points higher during the COVID-19 recession in Germany.[9]

Purely empirical studies are limited in dealing with the problem of the missing counterfactual. More specifically, empirical studies using micro-level data miss important aggregation and feedback effects, and empirical work using macro-level data cannot identify specific economic channels and suffers from the dataset's limited size. In other words, empirical work can only give a limited answer to the question of what would have happened to the German unemployment rate in the COVID-19 recession without the STW insurance system in place.

The common method in economics to address this issue is to use simulation analysis based on macroeconomic models that are theoretically sound (i.e., micro-founded) and empirically validated. Almut Balleer et al. conduct such an analysis of STW insurance for the great financial crisis in Germany based on a model with search and matching in the labor market, along the line of Dale Mortensen and Christopher Pissarides's work, which has become the workhorse structural model for labor market analysis.[10]

Balleer et al. find that the STW program effectively prevented a dramatic rise in the unemployment rate during the Great Recession of 2008–09 in Germany. They also find that STW insurance would have been effective without the program's extension during the crisis. Put differently, STW insurance has been an effective automatic stabilizer, but the discretionary measures taken—the weakening of the eligibility requirements and the extension of the eligibility duration—had less of an effect.

However, Balleer et al. consider only the weakening of the eligibility requirements, not the extension of the eligibility duration, in their analysis of discretionary policy. In addition, they assume that idiosyncratic shocks to firm productivity have no persistence over time. These two assumptions bias their results so that their analysis understates the importance of the discretionary policy. In line with this hypothesis, Britta Gehrke and Brigitte Hochmuth provide time series evidence that the discretionary STW program expansion during recessions in Germany had substantial employment effects.[11]

STW insurance affects the unemployment rate mainly through two economic channels. First, it provides an incentive for firms not to lay off or dismiss workers when a reduction in working time is necessary, which decreases the job separation rate and therefore unemployment. This channel was the focus of the analysis in Balleer et al. Second, as with any transfer scheme that insures workers' income, STW insurance stabilizes aggregate demand in a crisis and dampens hikes in the unemployment rate through this "Keynesian" demand channel. Research on New Keynesian models with a search-and-matching labor market suggests that transfer schemes such as the unemployment insurance system provide a powerful stabilization tool.[12] The same should apply to STW insurance, but there is no formal work at this stage that analyzes the stabilization effect of STW insurance using a New Keynesian model with a search-and-matching labor market.

We have seen that STW insurance successfully prevented a hike in unemployment during the COVID-19 recession in Germany. To assess the effectiveness of STW as a macroeconomic stabilization tool, we should compare this short-run benefit to the program's fiscal cost. A full-blown analysis of the issue requires a macroeconomic model of the type discussed, but a simple back-of-the-envelope calculation can provide some basic insights.

To a first approximation, the net fiscal cost of the program is equal to the outlays for STW benefits minus the outlays for unemployment benefits that would have been paid by the government without the STW program in place. For the 10-month period from March to December 2020, the average monthly outlay for STW was 2.2 billion euros for an average of 3.4 million workers on STW, which amounts to an average monthly STW benefit of 650 euros per worker. This is less than half the average monthly benefits an unemployed worker receives in Germany, so that the STW insurance system generated a net fiscal gain in 2020 as long as at least half the workers on STW would have become unemployed. As discussed above, the evidence suggests that up to 80 percent of the workers on STW would have become unemployed, pointing toward a substantial fiscal gain of STW.

Recovery After the Crisis (Medium Run). I now turn to a discussion of the STW program's medium-run effects, in the recovery phase. Clearly, the stabilization effect of STW analyzed above is still at work in the recovery period, but an additional economic channel gains importance at the recovery stage of the recession cycle. Specifically, STW insurance provides a disincentive for companies to expand employees' working hours, and this could lead to an unnecessarily sluggish recovery.[13] How important is this negative incentive effect?

There is no rigorous quantitative analysis of this question using the methods of modern macroeconomics as defined above. A glimpse at the aggregate data, however, shows that the German recovery after the Great Recession was swift, suggesting a relatively small impact of this STW disincentive effect on macroeconomic outcomes.

In the case of the COVID-19 recession, the results are less clear-cut. On one hand, the recession is dragging on longer than the Great Recession did, and in June 2021—16 months after the onset of the crisis—STW rates were still at elevated levels. (See Figure 2.) On the other hand, the German COVID-19 recession is really a double-dip recession, and STW rates declined relatively fast after each of the two peaks. In particular, the underemployment rate—the sum of the unemployment rate and the STW rate—decreased from 19 percent in April 2020 to 10.6 percent in October 2020 and from 13.3 percent in February 2021 to 7 percent in August 2021.

The reduction in working hours due to the incentive effect of STW can be economically efficient if STW programs are combined with training programs for employed workers using the program. This is even more the case in economic downturns, when the opportunity cost of worker training (i.e., human capital investment) is low and public support for training programs should expand. The German government has started to take steps toward expanding training programs by making it easier for workers on STW to enter them, but further steps should be taken, and additional funding should be provided.

Structural change is another economic reason for subsidizing training programs for particular professions and sectors. The economic transformation made necessary by digitalization and climate change has been a topic in policy debates for some time and requires a retooling of large parts of the workforce. In the past, such retraining of workers in the face of structural change has often taken place within firms in Germany,[14] and right after the COVID-19 recession seems to be a good time to enhance public support for these efforts. In other words, 2022 is when both structural and cyclical considerations suggest that the economic returns to retraining programs are high.

Economic Growth After the Crisis (Long Run). STW insurance affects productivity and therefore the long-run aggregate output. The productivity effect of STW is theoretically ambiguous, since the destruction of an existing employer-employee link (i.e., the firm-worker match) affects productivity in two opposing ways.

First, the destruction of an existing employer-employee link often leads to a loss of human capital, reducing productivity. Specifically, a large body of empirical work shows that job displacement is associated with substantial long-term earnings losses; that is, involuntary job loss leads to earnings losses that last even after a new job has been found. Moreover, these long-term earnings losses increase during recessions; it is always bad to lose a job but particularly bad to lose a job during a recession.

For the US, Steven Davis and Till von Wachter find that job displacement of high-tenure workers leads to large long-term earnings losses averaged over the business cycle and that these earning losses roughly doubled during the Great Recession.[15] Moreover, these long-term earnings losses are largely caused by the loss of occupation-specific human capital that occurs when workers are forced to switch occupations after job loss, which happens more often during recessions than in normal times.[16] For Germany, Johannes Schmieder, Till von Wachter, and Joerg Heining find similar results: Job displacement of high-tenure workers leads to large long-term earnings losses that almost double during recessions.[17]

Second, the breakup of existing employer-employee links allows for a re-matching of workers with firms, and this reallocation of resources can lead to new matches with better quality and higher productivity. The view that job separation is an essential feature of a dynamic labor market, leading to productivity gains, has a long tradition in economics. This view is often associated with the Schumpeter hypothesis of "creative destruction" and the "cleansing effect" of recessions.[18] Moreover, some economists have argued that the observed secular decline in productivity in the US has been driven by a corresponding decline in labor market fluidity.[19]

A study by Russell Cooper, Moritz Meyer, and Immo Schott uses simulation analysis based on a macroeconomic model of the German economy and shows that the negative effect of STW on long-run productivity can be substantial because it prevents efficient re-matching.[20] However, the analysis does not use empirical micro-level evidence on productivity to validate the model economy. Recent empirical evidence shows that most productivity gains in the US and Germany have happened within a firm, casting doubt on the hypothesis that job destruction is a main driver of innovation and long-run productivity growth through re-matching.[21]

These considerations suggest an intricate link among recessions, STW insurance, and long-run growth. On one hand, recessions leave permanent scars due to an increase in the human capital losses associated with job displacement, which reduces productivity and long-run growth. STW insurance and its expansion during recessions reduces recessions' negative hysteresis effect and therefore strengthens long-run productivity and economic growth. On the other hand, recessions can also raise long-run growth by improving productivity through re-matching jobs to workers. STW insurance reduces recessions' positive cleansing effect and therefore weakens long-run growth. The net effect of STW on productivity and economic growth depends on the relative strength of these two opposing effects. In other words, it depends on our view of recession: Do we view recessions as times of unnecessary human capital destruction or as times of economic cleansing?

The available evidence is not sufficient to give a final answer to this question. However, two reasons suggest an overall positive effect on long-run growth of using STW insurance as a stabilization tool during recessions. First, there is overwhelming empirical micro-level evidence for the view that recessions cause substantial human capital loss, whereas the empirical evidence for the cleansing view of recessions is slim. Second, there is convincing macroeconomic evidence that recessions cause long-run damage to an economy, though the extent of the damage varies across countries and recessions.[22]

The positive effect of STW insurance on long-run productivity is reenforced when STW programs are combined with training programs. In other words, the time workers on STW do not spend in production should be spent learning new skills, thereby enhancing their human capital and increasing worker productivity. More specifically, Germany and many other countries have made a commitment to reach climate neutrality by 2045, which requires a fundamental transformation of the production process and retraining of the workforce in various sectors: car manufacturing, the chemical industry, the steel industry, and many others. It makes economic sense for the government to increase its support of this transformation process at a time when there is an environmental need for economic transformation and the economic opportunity costs are low.

Conclusion

In this chapter, I argue that the STW program was a successful stabilization tool in Germany during the COVID-19 crisis. It helped the economy preserve valuable employer-employee links and prevented a large hike in unemployment. In addition, there is no evidence that STW insurance slowed down the economic recovery. Finally, available evidence suggests that the STW program positively affected productivity and growth by preventing large human capital losses during the recession.

The positive assessment of STW insurance in Germany begs the question of why countries such as the US do not use this policy instrument more extensively. The answer is most likely due to a difference in institutional settings. Specifically, the efficient and large-scale use of STW insurance requires a cooperative approach that presumes a certain level of trust between employers and employees. Absent this type of social partnership between employers and employees (i.e., unions), STW programs are likely to fail. A more formal analysis of the relationship between social partnership in the labor market and the effectiveness of STW programs is an important topic for future research.

Notes

1. Global supply-chain problems, rising energy prices, and health restrictions reimposed in fall 2021 slowed growth in quarters 3 and 4 of 2021 and prevented a strong recovery in 2021. The first two factors continue to weigh on the German economy in 2022. As of June 2022, the consensus forecast is around 2 percent gross domestic product growth in 2022.

2. The underemployment rate as defined by the German Statistical Labor Agency (*Bundesagentur fuer Arbeit*) differs from the definition used here. Specifically, the underemployment rate according to the official definition includes workers in training programs and on sick leave, but it does not include workers on short-time work (STW).

3. The STW program is administrated by the Federal Employment Agency (*Bundesagentur fuer Arbeit*). Employers must apply to the local employment agency (*Arbeitsagenturen*) if they want to introduce an STW scheme. To align the procedures among all local agencies, the Federal Employment Agency provides general rules and regulations, including a specification of the administrative process.

4. Additional agreements between employers and employees were made in particular sectors. For example, in the case of the hotel and restaurant sector, the German Food, Beverages, and Catering Industry Trade Union and its corresponding employer organization reached an agreement that raised the net replacement rate to up to 90 percent of the net monthly wage.

5. A detailed discussion and assessment of the stimulus package can be found in Tom Krebs, "Schriftliche Stellungnahme für die Anhörung im Haushaltsausschuss des Deutschen Bundestages zum Entwurf eines Gesetzes über die Feststellung eines Zweiten Nachtragshaushalts für das Haushaltsjahr 2020 und zum Entwurf eines Gesetzes über begleitende Maßnahmen zur Umsetzung des Konjunktur- und Krisenbewältigungspakets" [Expert Statement to the House and Means Committee of the German Congress Regarding the Fiscal Stimulus Package of June 2020], https://www.bundestag.de/resource/blob/703182/0d55a2147eec32a16a7381e8168bf03f/Prof-Tom-Krebs-Ph-D--data.pdf.

6. International Monetary Fund, European Department, "Germany: 2020 Article IV Consultation—Press Release; Staff Report; and Statement by the Executive Director for Germany," January 19, 2021, https://www.imf.org/en/Publications/CR/Issues/2021/01/15/

Germany-2020-Article-IV-Consultation-Press-Release-Staff-Report-and-Statement-by-the-50020.

7. Tito Boeri and Herbert Bruecker, "Short-Time Work Benefits Revisited: Some Lessons from the Great Recession," *Economic Policy* 26, no. 68 (October 2011): 697–765, https://ftp.iza.org/dp5635.pdf.

8. Boeri and Bruecker, "Short-Time Work Benefits Revisited."

9. Shekhar Aiyar and Mai Chi Dao, "The Effectiveness of Job-Retention Schemes: COVID-19 Evidence from the German States" (working paper, International Monetary Fund, Washington, DC, October 1, 2021), https://www.imf.org/en/Publications/WP/Issues/2021/10/01/The-Effectiveness-of-Job-Retention-Schemes-COVID-19-Evidence-From-the-German-States-474182.

10. Almut Balleer et al., "Does Short-Time Work Save Jobs? A Business Cycle Analysis," *European Economic Review* 84 (May 2016): 99–122, https://www.sciencedirect.com/science/article/abs/pii/S0014292115000720; and Dale T. Mortensen and Christopher A. Pissarides, "Job Creation and Job Destruction in the Theory of Unemployment," *Review of Economic Studies* 61 (1994): 397–415, https://www.jstor.org/stable/2297896.

11. Balleer et al., "Does Short-Time Work Save Jobs?"; and Britta Gehrke and Brigitte Hochmuth, "Counteracting Unemployment in Crises: Non-Linear Effects of Short-Time Work Policy," *Scandinavian Journal of Economics* 123, no. 1 (2021): 144–83, https://onlinelibrary.wiley.com/doi/pdf/10.1111/sjoe.12395.

12. Alisdair McKay and Ricardo Reis, "Optimal Automatic Stabilizers," *Review of Economic Studies* 88, no. 5 (March 16, 2021): 2375–406.

13. In a certain sense, this disincentive effect of STW on working hours is broadly similar to the disincentive effect of unemployment insurance on workers' job search, which has been extensively analyzed in the literature on unemployment insurance. Pierre Cahuc, "Short-Time Work Compensation Schemes and Employment," Institute for the Study of Labor, World of Labor, May 2019, https://wol.iza.org/uploads/articles/485/pdfs/short-time-work-compensations-and-employment.pdf.

14. Wolfgang Dauth et al., "The Adjustment of Labor Markets to Robots," *Journal of the European Economic Association* (May 12, 2021), https://www.eeassoc.org/journal/adjustment-labor-markets-robots.

15. Steven J. Davis and Till von Wachter, "Recessions and the Costs of Job Loss," Brookings Institution, September 2011, https://www.brookings.edu/wp-content/uploads/2011/09/2011b_bpea_davis.pdf.

16. Christopher Huckfeldt, "Understanding the Scarring Effect of Recessions," *American Economic Review* 112, no. 4 (April 2022): 1273–310, https://www.aeaweb.org/articles?id=10.1257/aer.20160449&&from=f.

17. Johannes F. Schmieder, Till von Wachter, and Joerg Heining, "The Costs of Job Displacement over the Business Cycle and Its Sources: Evidence from Germany" (working paper, National Bureau of Economic Research, Cambridge, MA, 2019), http://www.econ.ucla.edu/tvwachter/papers/Jobloss_wp_2019_11_10.pdf.

18. For "creative destruction," see Philippe Aghion and Peter Howitt, "A Model of Growth Through Creative Destruction," *Econometrica* 60, no. 2 (1992): 323–51, https://dash.harvard.edu/bitstream/handle/1/12490578/A%20Model%20of%20Growth%20through%20Creative%20Destruction.pdf. For "cleansing effect," see Ricardo J.

Caballero and Mohamad L. Hammour, "The Cleansing Effect of Recessions," *American Economic Review* 84 (December 1994): 1350–68.

19. Steven J. Davis and John Haltiwanger, "Labor Market Fluidity and Economic Performance" (working paper, National Bureau of Economic Research, Cambridge, MA, September 2014), https://www.nber.org/system/files/working_papers/w20479/w20479.pdf.

20. Russell Cooper, Moritz Meyer, and Immo Schott, "The Employment and Output Effects of Short-Time Work in Germany" (working paper, National Bureau of Economic Research, Cambridge, MA, August 2017), https://www.nber.org/system/files/working_papers/w23688/w23688.pdf.

21. For the US, see Daniel Garcia-Macia, Chang-Tai Hsieh, and Peter J. Klenow, "How Destructive Is Innovation?," *Econometrica* 87, no. 5 (September 2019): 1507–41, https://www.jstor.org/stable/45217218. For Germany, see Dauth et al., "The Adjustment of Labor Markets to Robots."

22. Laurence M. Ball, "Long-Term Damage from the Great Recession in OECD Countries" (working paper, National Bureau of Economic Research, Cambridge, MA, May 2014), https://www.nber.org/system/files/working_papers/w20185/w20185.pdf; and Antonio Fatás and Lawrence H. Summers, "The Permanent Effects of Fiscal Consolidations," *Journal of International Economics* 112 (2018): 238–50, https://faculty.insead.edu/fatas/Permanent%20Effects%20Fiscal%20Policy.pdf.

6

COVID-19: The Italian Job

RUSSELL COOPER AND IMMO SCHOTT

This chapter focuses on Italian labor market outcomes during the time of the COVID-19 shock. This experience reflects two factors: the exogenous shock affecting product demand and labor supply during this period and the policy response to the COVID-19 shock. The data reflect both factors. The model we construct allows us to take them apart.

Italy was one of the first European countries to feel the adverse social and economic effects of COVID-19. It was also one of the first to enact policies in an attempt to alleviate the economic consequences of the pandemic.

Not surprisingly, the Italian economy, like that of other countries, displayed a sharp reduction in economic activity as the COVID-19 shock took effect. This shock could not be seen through conventional models as it did not neatly fit into the common categories of a technology shock to production or banking, nor was it a monetary or fiscal-policy shock. Instead, it embodied elements of both supply and demand shocks with implications for labor market outcomes. The focus here is largely on how the reduced demand for labor was accommodated, whether through variations on the extensive margin (i.e., layoffs) or the intensive margin (i.e., hours reduction). As demonstrated below, the Italian experience was largely through adjustments in hours with little impact on unemployment compared to, say, the US.

There were a number of policy responses, to both supplement aggregate spending and directly intervene in the labor market. We focus primarily on two such interventions. One allowed for extended work sharing in that workers could receive a form of unemployment insurance even if they retained their job with a reduction in hours worked. The point of this policy was to reduce unemployment by spreading the total labor input across workers. A second policy essentially prohibited dismissals.

The data reflect both the shocks and the policy interventions. It takes a model to decompose the response into the part caused by the shock alone and the remainder that is policy induced. Our model, along the lines of one made by Russell Cooper, Moritz Myer, and Immo Schott,[1] studies worker flows in a search environment. In contrast to many other such models and appropriate for the questions at hand, the model features variations in worker hours and multi-worker firms.[2] This enables us to study the COVID-19 shock and the effects of the policy response. We can also use the model to predict the effects of relaxing the policy, particularly the prohibition on dismissals.

The model reproduces the labor market outcomes during the COVID-19 period. Given the policy interventions, the reduced demand for labor was met by reductions in hours rather than layoffs. From the estimated model, the key policy intervention was not subsidizing hours. Instead, the prohibition of firing induced the substitution toward hours reductions rather than layoffs.

Background

This section provides background to the Italian COVID-19 economic experience along two dimensions: (1) the basic facts about the Italian labor market and (2) some of the policy measures taken during the COVID-19 pandemic that directly affect worker-firm flows.[3]

The COVID-19-induced drop in economic activity was unlike previous experiences in a few important ways. First, the shock itself was uncommon, combining a reduction in spending with a reduction in available workers. Second, there were government policies that reduced economic activity through the isolation of workers from employment and buyers from stores. Further, there were direct labor market interventions, a focus of this study, that influenced the effects of these shocks on employment, hours, and worker attachment to firms.

Facts. The presentation of facts focuses on labor market outcomes, on both the extensive margin of employment and unemployment rates and the intensive margin of hours variation. For the most part, the comparison is among Italy, the European Union, and the US.[4]

Figure 1. Unemployment Rates

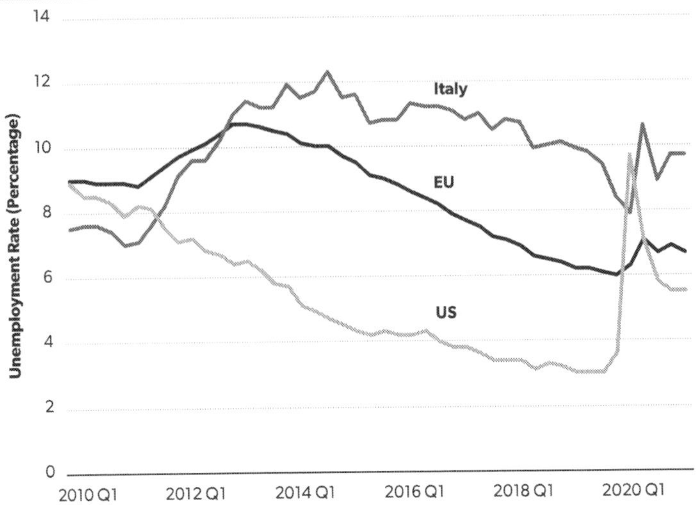

Note: The figure shows unemployment rates for prime-age individuals (25–54 years).
Source: Eurostat and FRED.

In the second quarter of 2020, real gross domestic product (GDP) in Italy contracted by 18.1 percent compared to the previous year and by nearly 9 percent for the entire year. For comparison, in 2020, real GDP fell by 7.9 percent in France, 4.8 percent in Germany, and 3.5 percent in the US.[5]

During this period, there were significant job losses: Employment in Italy fell by 3.6 percent in the second quarter of 2020 and by 2.6 percent in the third quarter compared to the same quarters in 2019. These losses were largely for self-employed individuals and those with temporary contracts. Individuals with permanent contracts were more protected from the economic conditions.[6]

Given the negative GDP growth, these employment losses are not surprising. What is of interest, though, is their composition. Overall, employment variations occur on the extensive (i.e., employed versus not employed) and intensive (i.e., hours worked) margins. This decomposition is important for evaluating the role of hours sharing through short-time work (STW).

From Figure 1, Italy experienced a drop in the unemployment rate in the first two quarters of 2020 relative to the end of 2019: from 9.4 to

Figure 2. Labor Force Participation Rates

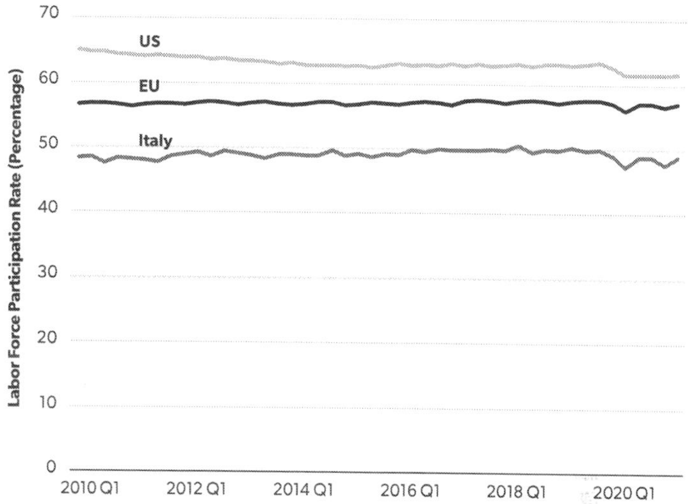

Source: Eurostat and FRED.

7.9 percent. In the United States, the unemployment rate rose from 3.0 to a high of 14.8 percent in April 2020.[7]

The drop in the unemployment rate is partly due to a change in labor force participation, sometimes called the activity rate, as shown in Figure 2. Between 2019 and 2020, almost 750,000 individuals left the Italian labor force. This is almost a 3 percent reduction over the year. As shown in the figure, the reduction in labor force participation was temporary in Italy and the EU but more permanent in the US.

Generally, a fall in the labor input during a recession includes extensive and intensive margins. Figure 3 shows average hours worked at a main job.[8] A number of countries experienced a reduction in hours worked, as did the entire EU. The drop in Italy was sizable, with hours falling almost 14 percent in the second quarter of 2020 before rebounding in the third quarter.

The nature of the employment adjustment is important partly due to the investment involved in worker-firm relationships. In contrast to the purchase of many goods and services, hiring and training workers is a dynamic decision reflecting the costs of hiring and training and frictions in job separations.

Figure 3. Hours Worked by Full-Time Employees

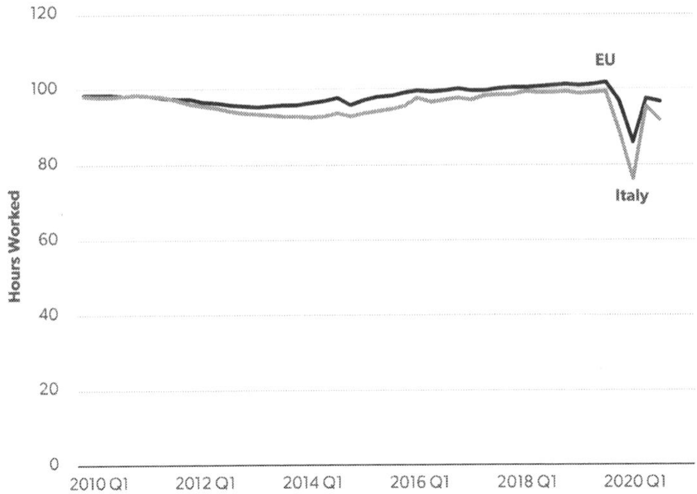

Note: The figure shows an index of total actual hours worked in the main job rates for full-time employees.
Source: Eurostat and FRED.

One measure of this is the rate at which employed workers lose their jobs and become unemployed. These flows are shown in Figure 4, Panel A. The start of the COVID-19 recession is almost impossible to discern. There was no rapid increase in the transition rate from employment to unemployment during this period. This is consistent with the relatively small movements in the unemployment rate in Italy.

Another measure of worker mobility is the pace of transitions from unemployment to employment, shown in Figure 4, Panel B. Normally during recessions, the exit from unemployment slows, and the figure indicates that indeed did occur during the COVID-19 crisis. But the reduction in this exit rate was much smaller in Italy compared to the EU overall.

Figure 5 shows job separations and hires on a quarterly basis from the start of 2011 to the third quarter of 2020. As expected, hires fell considerably in the second quarter of 2020—from 543,000 in the first quarter to only 406,000 in the second quarter. Hiring rebounded a bit but did not recover to the levels in previous years.[9]

Figure 4. Worker Transitions

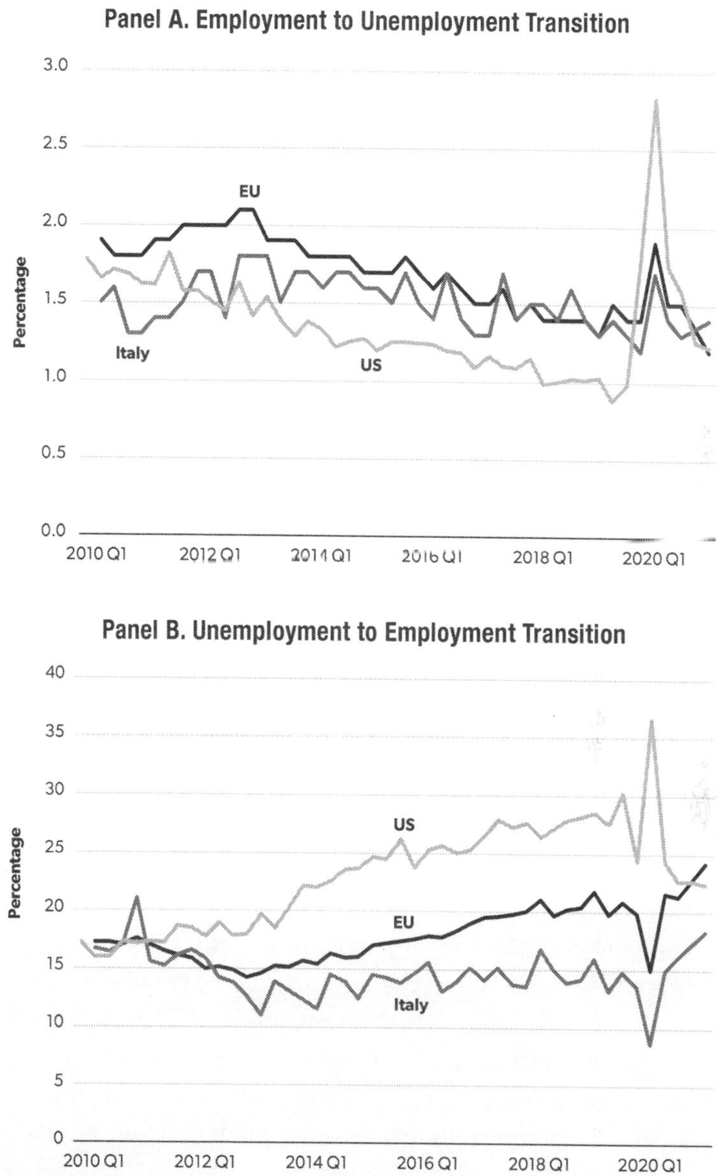

Note: Panel A shows transitions from employment to unemployment as a fraction of beginning-of-period employment. Panel B shows transitions from unemployment to employment as a fraction of beginning-of-period unemployment.
Source: Eurostat and FRED.

Separations followed a similar pattern, being about 150,000 lower than in the previous quarter. This is surprising given the large reduction in economic activity.

Figure 5 also shows these flows in the US. Job separations spiked in the US in the first quarter of 2020, remained high in the second quarter, and returned to normal afterward. At its peak, the separation rate was 6.1 percent. Hiring in the US remained relatively strong during the entire period. Interestingly, there was a quick rebound in hiring just after the burst of separations. This pattern's rapid increases in both separations and hires contrasts with the experience in Italy.

These flows matter, not just for individual firms and workers but for aggregate outcomes such as productivity. In economies with heterogeneous firms, worker reallocation is a necessary ingredient in maintaining high aggregate productivity. Policies that limit those flows, such as those related to the COVID-19 shock described next, can affect aggregate productivity.

Policies. The impact of COVID-19 on labor market outcomes in Italy must be considered together with the policies implemented during this period. That is, the data presented above show not just the impact of the COVID-19 shock but also the effects of policy interventions. One valuable contribution of the model presented below is that it allows us to distinguish between the outcome induced by the policies and the outcome from the COVID-19 shock alone.

There are two principal policies of interest. The first, called Cassa Integrazione Guadagni (CIG), facilitated work sharing.[10] Specifically, it provides compensation to workers for hours reductions below a contracted level. The extent of the support is influenced by firm size, the sector of activity, and the reason for the hours reduction. This ongoing program was enhanced during the COVID-19 period to broaden coverage and make COVID-19 a rationale for support. Between May and September 2020, about six million workers in Italy received support through this STW program, about 27 percent of the workforce.

These measures, originally taken by decree on March 17, 2020, were extended to the end of March 2021 and are still available to firms. But there is a new restriction that goes with participation in this program.

Figure 5. Job Flows: Separations and Hires

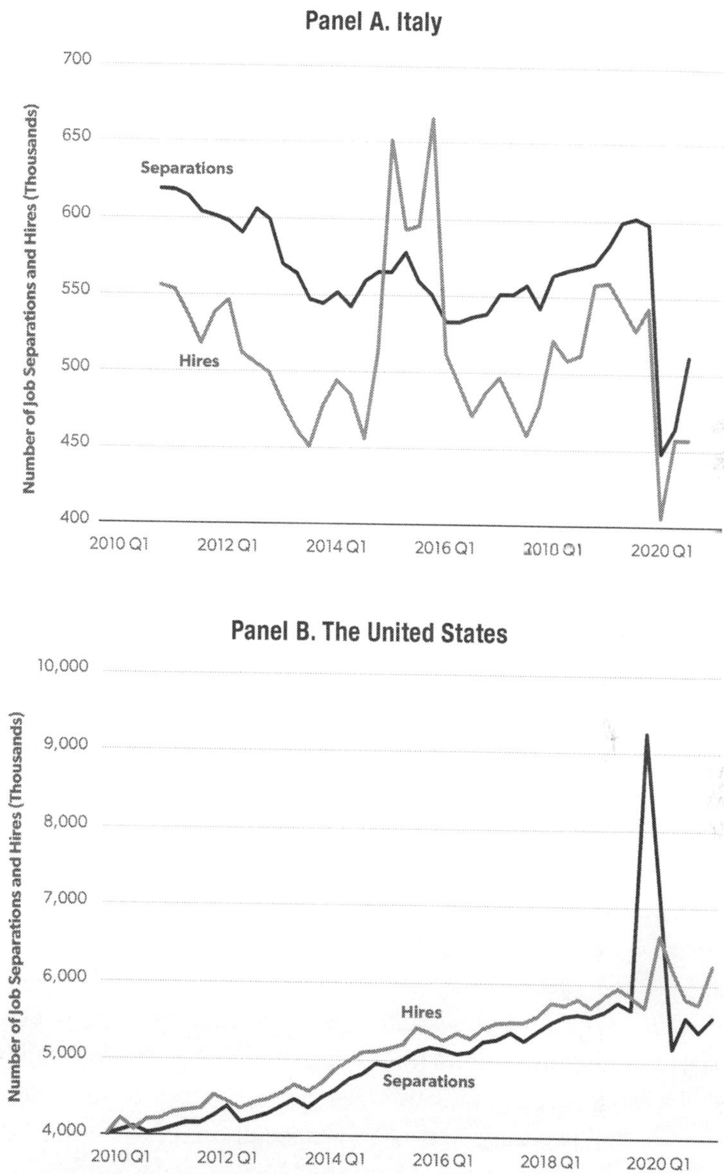

Note: Although the shock was severe, labor mobility did not completely shut down, even in Italy. Indeed, hires were lower, but the hiring rate was not zero. This will be part of our model economy as well, reflecting the combination of aggregate and firm-specific shocks to profitability.
Source: Comunicazioni Obbligatorie and JOLTS.

Firms accepting the payments for reduced hours are not allowed to lay off workers.

The second policy, also part of the March 17, 2020, decree, limited workers' mobility by imposing a ban on firing. Evidently this added friction was specific to Italy among European countries. Job separations were much lower in the second quarter of 2020 compared to the previous year despite the large reduction in economic activity.

These firing restrictions were eliminated on July 1, 2021. However, there are some exceptions. First, the measure remains in force in some industries, such as textiles, shoe manufacturing, and fashion. Second, the "no firing" restriction has been integrated into the work-sharing program, giving firms access to 13 extra weeks of CIG, provided they do not fire any workers.

The point of these policies is to alter the employment response to the reduction in profitability. Clearly firms with reduced demand for their products were induced to lower work hours but not fire workers. These firms received subsidies to help compensate workers for their reduced hours.

In analyzing these types of interventions, there are two elements to keep in mind. The first is the policy itself. Although these policies have details beyond the elements of the model, the crux of their intention, in hours sharing and no firing, is within the domain of the framework we construct.

The second is more subtle and involves expectations. Any specification of a government policy is incomplete without an accompanying statement of the conditions under which the intervention will be continued. In some cases, there are statements that the intervention will last a year, only to be continued or modified at that point in time.

In models of dynamic choice, such as employment by a firm, expectations matter. Thus, understanding the response to a policy partly depends on how the firms perceived the intervention in the future. As our analysis proceeds, we evaluate the power of this expectations effect.

Framework

The framework for the analysis is a dynamic contracting model, focusing on the employment relationship between a firm and its workers at a point in time and the evolution of those matches over time. The model is structured to highlight the effects of the COVID-19 shock and the policy measures taken in response.

A journal article by Kenneth Burdett and Randall Wright analyzes a static labor-contracting model that provides insights into the interaction of unemployment insurance and work-sharing schemes.[11] They dub the former the "US system" and the latter the "European system." In their analysis of the two systems, there are two key results of direct relevance. First, if benefits are sufficiently generous in the US system, then layoffs will occur. This is important since the layoffs, in their baseline model, would not have occurred without government-funded unemployment insurance. Second, layoffs do not occur in the European system, though the hours decision may be inefficient due to work-sharing subsidies.

Our analysis builds on Burdett and Wright's by studying the role of work sharing from the perspective of an optimal contracting problem.[12] One important difference, though, is that in our approach, the COVID-19 experience is not incorporated in the optimal labor contract and thus is treated as an unanticipated shock. We model the resulting policies, including the hours-sharing scheme, given a contract that was formulated without any expectation of these interventions.

The second component embeds a modified version of the contracting into a dynamic search-and-matching structure. This allows us to extend the analysis to study worker and job flows and the productivity implications of reallocation.[13] This model is the one ultimately taken to the data and is used for the policy analysis.

A Contracting Approach: Intuition

The point of this section is to make clear the contracting approach. The presentation starts with a contract that has no layoffs, just hours sharing. The work-sharing policy is introduced into this problem. The model is then extended to include layoffs. The more formal details are available in the appendix.

Hours Variation. Initially, consider the optimal labor contract between a worker and a firm.[14] The choice is a state-contingent contract that stipulates hours worked, $h(\varepsilon)$, and the compensation per hour worked, $\omega(\varepsilon)$, paid when profitability (i.e., productivity, output price) is ε. The contract is struck before the realization of ε but is allowed to depend on the realization of this random variable.

The optimal contract solves this problem:

$$max_{h(\varepsilon),\omega(\varepsilon)} E_{\varepsilon}[\varepsilon f(h(\varepsilon)) - \omega(\varepsilon)h(\varepsilon) + \lambda u(\omega(\varepsilon)h(\varepsilon) - g(h(\varepsilon)))]. \qquad (1)$$

Here $f(h)$ is output if the worker supplies h hours where $f(\cdot)$ is strictly increasing and strictly concave. The worker utility function is $u(c - g(h))$, where $u(\cdot)$ is strictly increasing and strictly concave and $g(h)$, the disutility of work, is strictly increasing and strictly convex.[15] The bargaining (i.e., welfare) weight for the worker is λ. As the model is static, consumption is simply the state-dependent level of compensation, $\omega(\varepsilon)h(\varepsilon)$.

At this point, there is no unemployment, and there is no government program to promote the sharing of hours. Further, there is no model of how a worker came to be attached to the firm. All these features are explored below and in the quantitative analysis once the basics are established.

The first-order conditions characterizing the optimal contract have two key elements.[16] First, the firm provides insurance to its workers. In principle, the worker's compensation and hours worked will vary with the productivity, ε. Since the function $u(\cdot)$ is strictly concave, the worker finds variation in consumption net of the disutility of work, $\omega(\varepsilon)h(\varepsilon) - g(h(\varepsilon))$, undesirable.

The firm, being risk neutral, profits by supplying this insurance to its workers. In the optimal contract, consumption less the disutility of work is independent of ε.

Second, hours are set efficiently so that the marginal benefit and marginal cost of additional time working are equated. Here the marginal benefit is the marginal product, $\varepsilon f'(h(\varepsilon))$. The marginal cost, reflecting worker preferences, is $g'(h(\varepsilon))$. Note that the determination of the optimal hours is independent of the wage and thus consumption of the workers.[17] As long as the marginal product of labor is higher relative to the disutility of work near zero hours, the firm will choose to operate for all realization of ε.

Hours Subsidy. Consider the occurrence of a low value of ε and the introduction of a subsidized hours-sharing program (i.e., a subsidy to worker hours). View the introduction of the subsidy as a complete surprise in that this possibility was not considered at the time the contract was determined.[18] At this point, the focus is on the consequences of this intervention rather than its rationale.

For this presentation, the hours-sharing scheme is simply modeled as a wage subsidy. For the purpose of exposition, we ignore nonlinearities in the scheme and restrictions imposed on the workers and firms that apply for the subsidies.[19]

Specifically, the hours-sharing scheme implies that consumption is given by $c = \tilde{\omega}\tilde{h}(1 + s)$. Here the workers receive a subsidy s from the government. Given this scheme, the worker and the firm reformulate the contract ex post. The optimization problem is given by:

$$max_{\tilde{\omega},\tilde{h}}[\varepsilon f(\tilde{h}) - \tilde{\omega}\tilde{h} + \lambda u(\tilde{c} - g(\tilde{h}))]. \qquad (2)$$

If there is no subsidy (i.e., $s = 0$), then the determination of hours is the same as in the optimal contract. That is, without a subsidy, the firm and the worker have no incentive to vary from the optimal contract. But, with $s > 0$, for firms with relatively low productivity, the subsidy paid to workers provides an incentive for an increase in hours.[20]

Here the subsidy is paid from tax revenues that are outside this contracting problem. But even if the taxes were paid, say, by this firm, the subsidy would still act to increase hours as long as the entire cost of the marginal subsidy is not internalized by the firm.

Layoffs. A key argument in favor of hours subsidies is that they reduce the incentive for firms to lay off workers. Accordingly, we add the possibility of layoffs to the model. Layoffs could occur in the ex ante contracting problem. Whether employment adjustment includes layoffs depends on the firm's ability to adjust hours and the presence and cost of unemployment insurance, as discussed by Burdett and Wright and in a journal article by Costas Azariadis.[21]

Our focus is on the ex post stage, with the occurrence of a large fall in profitability, through ε. In this case, the government intervention might entail a scheme to share hours and increase unemployment insurance.[22] The former was the response in Italy, while the latter was key in the US.

With a single-worker firm, the choice of laying off the worker and stopping production are the same. To add the potential for layoffs, suppose there is a fixed cost of operating, which here we take as the worker losing unemployment benefits. Specifically, if the firm operates in state ε, the worker obtains utility of $V^e(\varepsilon) = u(\omega^*(\varepsilon)h^*(\varepsilon)) - g(h^*(\varepsilon))$. If the firm does not operate, then worker utility is $V^u = u(b)$, where b is an unemployment benefit.[23] Further, let $\pi^*(\varepsilon) = \varepsilon f(h^*(\varepsilon)) - \omega^*(\varepsilon)h^*(\varepsilon)$ be the firm profit flow in state ε. Both the value for an employment worker and the value of the firm are calculated under the optimal contract, denoted $(\omega^*(\varepsilon), h^*(\varepsilon))$ without subsidy.

Finally, let $W(\varepsilon) = \pi(\varepsilon) + \lambda V^e(\varepsilon)$ be the joint surplus under this contract. Note that this joint surplus is increasing in ε.

Consider the choice of operating or not. If the firm and worker separate, then the joint surplus is simply $V^u(b)$. Thus the firm operates if

$$W(\varepsilon) \geq V^u(b). \tag{3}$$

The left side is increasing in ε, while the right side is constant. Thus, for b to be sufficiently large, there will exist a critical level of profitability, $\tilde{\varepsilon}(b)$, such that the firm operates if $\varepsilon \geq \tilde{\varepsilon}(b)$. Since $V^u(b)$ is increasing in b, the critical profitability such that the firm operates is increasing in b.

So in this model, layoffs and equivalently firm closures are more likely with higher unemployment insurance benefits. As emphasized by Burdett and Wright, unemployment insurance creates an incentive for layoffs when hours reduction would have arisen instead in response to low ε realizations.

Hours Subsidy with Unemployment Insurance. Having introduced unemployment insurance and thus the possibility of layoffs, we return to the policy analysis. Again, ex post, there is an adverse shock that creates low ε. In the COVID-19 case, this affected many firms. Some governments, such as the US, responded by increasing unemployment insurance, b. All else the same, this induces layoffs and thus creates unemployment.

One way to counter this would be to introduce a wage subsidy for continued operation. The introduction of such a subsidy would increase $W(\varepsilon)$. This is directly seen by the fact that this value increases with s holding fixed the contract and only increases more once there is re-optimization over wages and hours. As before, if a firm operates, then the hours subsidy leads to an increase in hours relative to the contracted hours without a subsidy.

Dynamic Matching

The model that forms the basis of the quantitative analysis embeds a version of this contracting problem into a search-and-matching structure. This subsection discusses that approach. The formal presentation is in the appendix.

The contracting problem explored above had no implications for the dynamics of worker flows and reallocation. The extension of the model to include a search-and-matching structure complements the contracting approach to characterizing the employment relationship between a stock of workers and a firm.[24] Further, the expanded model has implications for flows between heterogeneous firms and thus for aggregate productivity.

The key is the addition to the firm problem of adjustments on the extensive margin. This arises from the posting of vacancies and the ultimate matching of workers with job opportunities. Further adjustments occur through separations, with some additional dynamics created through a time cost of adjusting the workforce.[25]

The contracting problem, as written above, determines the compensation, hours, and employment status of the set of workers matched with the firm at the start of the period. The terms of that contract partly depend on the unemployment insurance and hours subsidy available to the contractants. In the model with dynamics, the additional features are the forward-looking values associated with an existing employment relationship.

To be clear, the contract is the result of a sequence of bargains between the firm and each worker, as in a journal article by Michael W. L. Elsby and Ryan Michaels.[26] The outcome is not the same as the bargain between a union, representing the n workers, and a single firm. When the hours-sharing policy is available, the firm—not the contractants—decide whether to participate in the program.

Firm Value. The value of a firm with profitability ε and n workers in state S is given by

$$V(\varepsilon, n; S) = \max_{h,n'} \{A\varepsilon\,(nh)^{\alpha} - \omega(\varepsilon, n, h; S)\,n - C(n', n, S) + \mathbb{E}_{S',\varepsilon'|S,\varepsilon}\beta V(\varepsilon', n'; S')\}, \tag{4}$$

where S includes all the aggregate variables that might affect the firm's value. Among these are A, representing aggregate profitability, and θ, labor market tightness.

Here the firm is choosing hours worked, h, given the state and given a state-contingent compensation function, $\omega(\varepsilon, n, h; S)$. This is a slightly different formulation of the contracting problem in which the negotiations establish a compensation function and the firm chooses hours ex post.

There are two important features of this compensation function, $\omega(\varepsilon, n, h; S)$.[27] First, it reflects the worker disutility of hours, $g(h)$, and the marginal product of labor, weighted by bargaining power. Bargaining with workers sequentially implies that the marginal product of the worker enters into the bargain. A consequence of this is that a decrease in hours worked increases the marginal product of labor and thus can increase the wage paid per hour. Second, compensation depends on S. This allows the aggregate state, including government policies, to affect this function.

Besides hours worked, the firm chooses future employment, denoted n'. There are various costs of adjusting the workforce embedded in $C(n', n, S)$. Here S can affect the cost of adjustment, say, due to labor market tightness affecting the costs of hiring. The last term in the formula, $(\varepsilon', n'; S')$, is the firm's discounted expected continuation value.

Worker Value. An employed worker in a firm in state (ε, n) has an expected lifetime utility of

$$W^{e}(\varepsilon, n; S) = \omega(\varepsilon, n, h; S) - g(h) + \beta E_{S',\varepsilon'|S,\varepsilon}\,[sW^{u}(S') + (1 - s)W^{e}(\varepsilon', n'; S')]. \tag{5}$$

Here the compensation and hours worked are as in the static contracting problem. The compensation of an employed worker can depend on S, say, through an STW program. The continuation values reflect the discounted expected value of losing a job, with probability s, or of continuing in employment. The value in the unemployment state, $W^u(S')$, includes the payment of unemployment insurance, similar to the structure in the static contracting problem.

Equilibrium. There is an equilibrium component to the search-and-matching structure that is absent from the simple contracting problem. In this setting, the probability that a firm that posts vacancies finds a worker depends on the unemployment and the vacancy rates; both are economy aggregates and determined in equilibrium. As in other studies, with constant returns to scale matching function, the likelihood of filling a vacancy depends on the tightness of labor markets, defined as the vacancy-to-unemployment-rate ratio and denoted θ. This is contained in S and affects the cost of labor adjustment, $C(n', n, S)$.

The search-and-matching model goes beyond the individual firm problem to focus on worker and job flows across heterogeneous firms. The heterogeneity across firms in the form of differences in demand or productivity creates a role for the reallocation of workers across firms. In this way, worker mobility becomes an important component of aggregate labor productivity. Importantly, this reallocation is limited by not only the frictions associated with the search-and-matching process but also government policies, such as firing costs.

The model incorporates these features and is estimated, as explained below, to match key features of employment-adjustment distributions at the firm level and labor market outcomes in Italy. The model provides insights not just about normal times but also in response to large unexpected events, such as COVID-19.

One feature of the model deserves some emphasis. There is a nondegenerate distribution of firms in the model, distinguished by their size and profitability. This is important for understanding aggregate productivity, which depends on the allocation of workers across these heterogeneous producers. This heterogeneity does not directly affect the design of the labor contracts but is key for the incentives underlying the worker flows in the search-and-matching dimension of the economy.

Policy Experiments. The policy analysis is conducted within the equilibrium of the model. Along with a large reduction in profitability, seen as a reduction in spending and disruptions in labor supply due to health considerations, we introduce the two policy tools mentioned earlier. The equilibrium outcome is determined through the estimated model.

Specifically, the shock is taken as a reduction in A in firm revenue. In addition, the firing prohibition is introduced into the adjustment cost function. Finally, and most importantly, compensation to workers for a reduction in income when hours are cut is introduced. This payment is given as $\tau \times \omega \times max\ ((\bar{h} - h), 0)$, where $\bar{h}$ represents "normal" hours (i.e., in the absence of the COVID-19 crisis), and τ is a policy parameter determining the replacement rate. For Italy, it was 80 percent from Organisation for Economic Co-operation and Development (OECD) data.[28]

Importantly, this compensation payment creates an incentive for firms to reduce hours. The reason is that from the firm's perspective, the hourly wage remains at the contracted level. Absent the policy, reducing hours would increase the marginal product of labor and hence the hourly wage. With the policy in place, the firm can reduce hours without triggering an increase in wages. Because of the fall in productivity, firms have an incentive to do so. This is discussed more formally in the appendix using the equilibrium-compensation function.

Imposing these features on the single-firm problem is relatively straightforward, and the responses are seen through the discussion in the "Layoffs" section of this chapter. But in the search-and-matching setting, the analysis is much richer along two lines.

First, the policies influence labor market tightness and thus the costs of hiring workers for all firms. This is important since not all firms experience reductions in profitability and some—say, a delivery service that expands during COVID-19—want to hire.

Second, beliefs matter in dynamic setting. Beliefs about the evolution of labor market tightness affect current hiring and firing. Further, there are beliefs about the policies themselves. Forward-looking firms make decisions based on expectations about future interventions. To take an extreme case, hiring and firing in the current period are quite different if the firm believes there are no firing restrictions in the future compared to the case with future firing restrictions. The same goes for the hours subsidies. And, of course, beliefs over future labor market tightness are not independent from beliefs about future policies.

These interactions are taken into account in the policy analysis. They are also of interest in decomposing policy into its direct effects and those acting through expectations.

Quantitative Analysis

This section presents the quantitative analysis.[29] The first subsection outlines the approach, and the second summarizes the parameterization of the steady state.

Approach. The equilibrium of the search-and-matching model is the basis for the quantitative analysis. The model is used in two ways.

First, it is used to understand labor market outcomes in Italy during normal times. These labor market outcomes are used to set the parameters of the model. To do so requires the solution of the model to find the equilibrium outcome given parameters.

Second, the model is used to study the COVID-19 experience. Initially, this is achieved by feeding into the model the direct effects of COVID-19 on product demand and worker supply and the indirect effects through Italian policies. The model is then used to produce counterfactuals, thus isolating the COVID-19 effects from the policy measures. Finally, the model is used to project labor market outcomes post-COVID-19.

Parameterization. The model parameters are chosen to match key moments, referred to as estimation through simulated method of moments. The moments for the steady state are shown in the top block of Table 1. They are chosen with two criteria in mind. First, they relate directly to the labor market outcomes of interest in Italy. Second, variations in the parameters lead to variations in the moments so that matching the moments is informative about the underlying parameters.

Table 1. Data and Model Moments

Moment	Data	Model
	Steady State	
Unemployment Rate	9.7%	9.7%
Replacement Rate	60%	59.4%
Average Hours	35.5	35.5
Median Firm Size	13.7	13.7
Employees in Inactive Firms	54.6%	65.3%
Employees in High Job-Creation Firms	16.1%	19.2%
	Hours Subsidies	
Workers in Firms Using STW	30.0%	30.5%
Aggregate Hours Change Under STW	–8.0%	–8.1%

Source: Cassa Integrazione Guadagni and Organisation for Economic Co-operation and Development.

The calibrated model matches the data moments well. Specifically, the model generates an unemployment rate, a length of the average workweek, the generosity of unemployment benefits, and a median firm size that are close to the Italian-data counterparts.[30] The model slightly overstates the fraction of workers in firms that do not adjust their workforce ("Employees in Inactive Firms") and the fraction of workers in firms with high job-creation rates (in excess of 10 percent). Both moments are responsive to the non-convex costs of adjusting the labor force.

The second block of moments concern the impact of the hours subsidies following the COVID-19 shock. These are explained below.

The parameters that generate these moments are shown in Table A1. A few of them are key for the policy experiments conducted with the model, as discussed in the following paragraphs.

The steady state of the model is matched to these aggregate averages in the top block. The bottom block has moments under STW.

Simulation. The effects of the shock and the policy are obtained by simulation of the estimated model. To do so requires additional elements as the model was parameterized in steady state to match economy averages, as listed in Table 1.

The COVID-19 shock is introduced as randomness in productivity: $A \in \{A^H, A^L\}$ with $A^H > A^L$ capturing aggregate fluctuations. Recall that in addition to these aggregate shocks, individual firm-productivity shocks are present as well.

Other variables co-move with A and need to be taken into account. First, there are the associated labor market policies that, in the baseline simulation, are present during a recession (i.e., $A = A^L$). Second, labor market tightness, θ, is an equilibrium object and thus depends on the current state.

Bringing together the states of aggregate productivity with the policies, we consider a three-state Markov process. In state A^H, the economy has relatively high productivity and no policy interventions. In state A^L, productivity is lower, as in a recession, but there are no policy interventions. Finally, state A^{LP} brings together low productivity and the two policy interventions, STW and no firing.

The transition matrix is given by Π:

$$\Pi = \begin{array}{c} \\ A^H \\ A^L \\ A^{LP} \end{array} \begin{array}{c} \begin{array}{ccc} A^H & A^L & A^{LP} \end{array} \\ \left[\begin{array}{ccc} \rho^H & (1-\rho^H)(1-\pi) & (1-\rho^H)\pi \\ 1-\rho^L & \rho^L & 0 \\ 1-\rho^L & 0 & \rho^L \end{array}\right] \end{array}. \tag{6}$$

In the high-productivity state, the probability of continuation is given by ρ^H. If the economy shifts to low productivity, then with probability $(1 - \pi)$ there is no policy, and with the complementary probability the state is A^{LP}, where productivity is low and the policies are in place. At this point, in this state there is STW, and no firing is allowed. Once the economy is in the recession state with these policies, the policy will continue with probability ρ^L. The probability of entering the high-productivity state, $(1 - \rho^L)$, is not affected by the STW policy. We calibrate (ρ^H, ρ^L) to generate average durations of expansions and recessions of three years and one year, respectively. The probability ϖ is chosen to generate an expected duration of STW of six months.[31]

Firms in the model need to be able to forecast future labor market tightness θ because its value determines the future vacancy-creation costs. With aggregate shocks, θ is a slow-moving variable. Firms form beliefs about future labor market tightness, and these beliefs need to be accurate.

Following a journal article by Per Krusell and Anthony A. Smith Jr.,[32] we assume that firms create forecasts of labor market tightness θ_{t+1} in period t using all available information about the aggregate state in period t.[33] Regarding the implementation of the no-firing restriction: In Italy, there are temporary and permanent workers. We assume that employers, while unable to fire workers, are not forced to renew the contracts of temporary workers. From OECD data, the fraction of temporary workers in Italy was 17 percent in 2019. In the simulation, we therefore allow firms to decrease employment by 17 percent per month during the COVID-19 shock.

Findings

This section presents our main quantitative findings using the parameterized model. The first part provides an assessment of the effects of the shock on key labor market outcomes and aggregate productivity. This part decomposes these overall effects into the response to the adverse shock per se and the part attributed to the policy response. The final section projects the effects of eliminating the policies.

Effects of the COVID-19 Shock. Figure 6 compares the reaction of the economy to a persistent adverse productivity shock in the case with and without the policy. The solid lines show recessions without STW and without a restriction on firing. The dashed lines correspond to the situation when STW is available. In line with the Italian response to the COVID-19 pandemic, we include a no-firing policy in addition to the STW policy for this case. Thus, all STW policies include a provision of no layoffs, regardless of whether the firm is in the STW program.

The main result is clear from this figure: Despite an identically sized exogenous drop in aggregate productivity, the unemployment rate increases without the STW policy but actually decreases when it is in place. As we shall see, this is mainly due to the no-firing restriction rather than the STW incentives. There are also significant differences in output effects, where the recession is deeper when the policies are in force.

In normal recessions, firms reduce both margins of labor demand. The solid lines in Figure 6 show that without STW and allowing layoffs, total

Figure 6. Impulse Response Functions

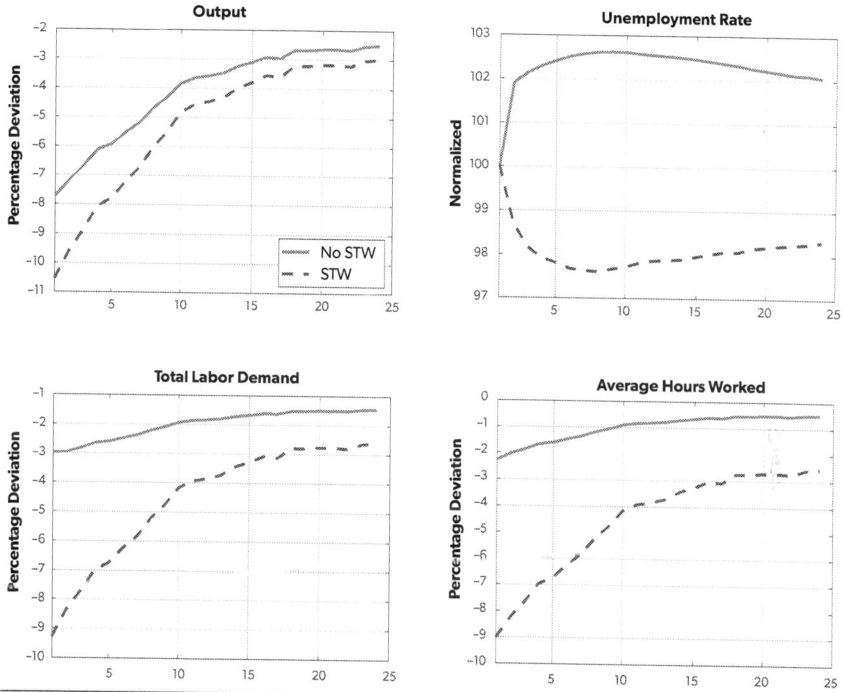

Note: The solid lines show a recession without the possibility of STW and a no-firing restriction, while the dashed lines show a recession with the same elements. Impulse-response functions were computed from a simulation of $T = 50{,}000$ periods.
Source: Authors' research using model simulation.

labor demand falls by around 3 percent in the recession, resulting from a 2 percent reduction in average hours worked and a sizable increase in the unemployment rate. Firms respond to the large, persistent change in profitability with employment adjustments because large deviations from "baseline hours" (i.e., hours worked absent aggregate shocks) are costly. Consequently, job destruction increases and the unemployment rate rises, while output falls.

At the onset of the recession, job-destruction rates spike from less than 4 percent to around 6 percent, while job-creation rates fall. As productivity rebounds, job-creation rates pick up, albeit slowly, bringing the unemployment rate back to its long-term average.

Table 2. Effect of the Policy on Unemployment

Scenario	Unemployment Rate
Recession Without Policy	+ 2.1%
Recession with Policy and No Firing	− 2.0%
Recession with Policy and Firing	+ 2.1%

Source: Authors' research using model simulation.

This picture drastically changes when the policy is in place. When STW is available, there is a larger reduction in total labor demand because firms are encouraged to decrease hours. In line with the Italian data, aggregate hours worked fell by about 8 percent with the policy in place. The decrease in labor demand leads to a larger reduction in aggregate output compared to recessions without STW.

The first two rows of Table 2 show the effect on the unemployment rate under the scenarios of the recession with and without the policy joint with the firing prohibition. The difference in unemployment rates is about 4 percentage points. So, if the policies had not been in place, the model predicts that the unemployment rate in Italy would have risen to over 13 percent.

As the dashed lines in Figure 6 show, if the policy includes a no-firing clause, the entire adjustment in labor demand stems from reductions in average hours worked. Firms cannot lay off workers, no jobs are destroyed, and the unemployment rate cannot increase. In fact, the unemployment rate decreases during the pandemic-induced recession. This is driven by firms that experience a high demand in spite of (or due to) the recession and wish to hire new workers.

The model simulation produces hiring and firing patterns that are very much in line with the data presented earlier in the section titled "Facts." Both job destruction and job creation fall when the policy is in place. Job destruction falls because of the no-firing clause and because firms can reduce labor demand via the hours margin. Job creation declines for two reasons. First, the deep recession leads to less labor demand from firms. Second, those firms that wish to expand face higher job-creation cost because of the artificially low unemployment rate.

There are two reasons for the differential response of the economy under STW. The first is a direct effect. Because hours reductions no longer entail an increase in compensation payments when a firm is using the policy, incentives are for firms not to fire workers and instead reduce hours. This is the intended effect of the policy, and it is clearly present in the model.

The second is an indirect effect coming through a lower vacancy-filling probability, denoted q. Higher job destruction during recessions leads to an increase in unemployment and consequently a higher vacancy-filling probability for firms. This incentivizes job creation. Under the STW policy, this channel is muted. Every time a firm decides to hold on to a worker instead of releasing him or her into the pool of unemployed, the firm inadvertently decreases the vacancy-filling probability for all other firms. An individual firm does not take this externality into account.

The vacancy-filling probability increases by much less under the policy, thereby generating less productivity-enhancing labor reallocation. The smaller increase in q reinforces the substitution away from the extensive margin of labor adjustment toward the intensive margin. Firms that were otherwise hiring are either refraining from doing so or hiring fewer employees when q is lower. Because the decrease in q effectively enlarges firms' region of employment inactivity, an increase in labor demand for some firms may lead them to increase average hours worked instead.

Using the model, we can decompose the composite policy into its components. Figure 7 shows the impulse responses in two cases: (1) without a firing prohibition and (2) with one. In both cases, STW is not an option. Interestingly, the output response is similar for the two cases. But with layoffs allowed, firms do fire, and this is seen in the total labor input and the unemployment rate. Hours worked actually rise in this case, and thus the fall in output is about the same regardless of the firing policy. This is in contrast with the baseline model, in which a firm that takes the STW policy and cannot fire reduces hours quite a lot given the subsidy.

The quantitative results of the economic model depend on the model parameters. The key parameters of the model are those that determine the trade-off between hours and workers. These include e_0 and e_1, which govern the worker disutility of hours worked, and b, which determines workers' outside option. These parameters were estimated to generate

Figure 7. Impulse Response Functions

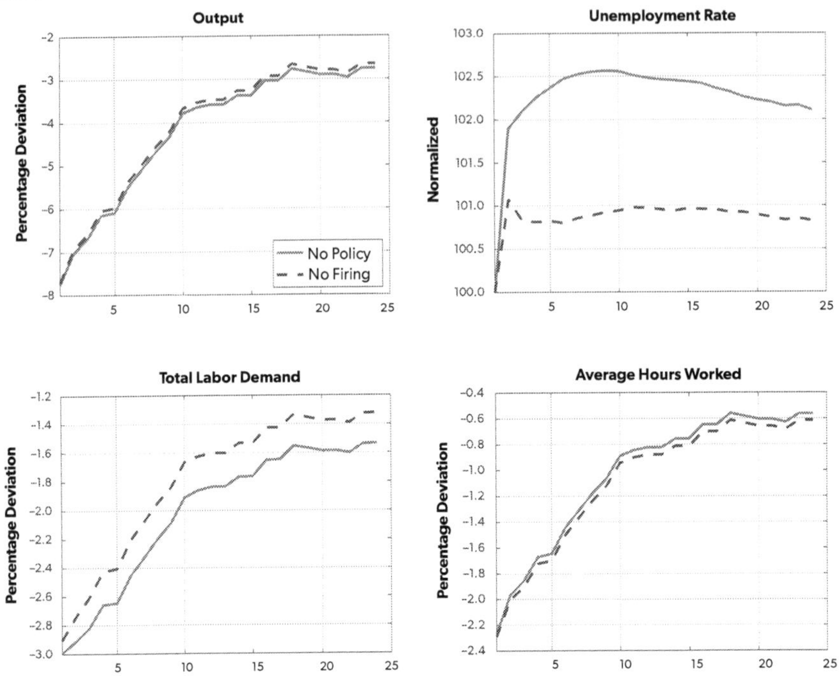

Note: The solid lines show a recession without a no-firing policy, while the dashed lines show a recession with the same policy. Impulse-response functions were computed from a simulation of $T = 50{,}000$ periods.
Source: Authors' research using model simulation.

the same average hours worked in the model as in the data, the same unemployment rate as in the data, and the same median firm size as in the Italian data.

Another important parameter is the expected duration of the STW policy. If firms expect the COVID-19 recession to be short-lived, firing workers will not be optimal because rehiring workers during a boom is costly. On the other hand, if market participants expect the pandemic to last for many periods, firing workers becomes more attractive. The Italian labor market policies of work sharing and no firing played an important role in preventing this adjustment, according to our simulations.

Figure 8. Impulse Response Functions: Productivity Implications

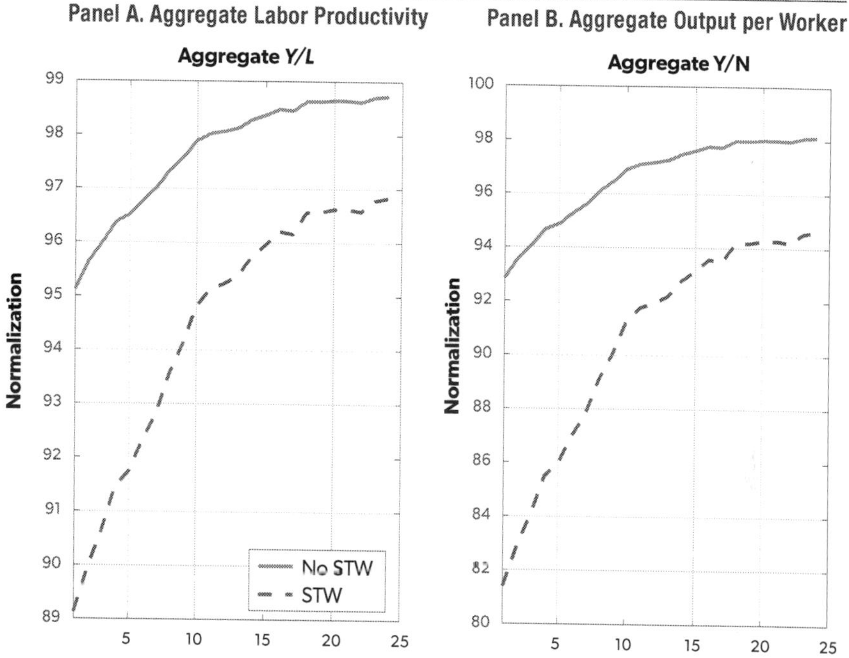

Note: The solid lines show a recession without the possibility of STW, while the dashed lines show a recession with the same possibility. Impulse response functions were computed from a simulation of $T = 50{,}000$ periods.
Source: Authors' research using model simulation.

Productivity. Figure 8 shows the productivity effects of the policy, measured either as labor productivity ($\frac{Y}{L}$) or output per worker ($\frac{Y}{N}$). To be clear, neither of these productivity measures are exogenous, as they reflect worker flows between heterogeneous firms.

The solid lines show that recessions cause both measures of labor productivity to fall. When the STW policy is active, there is an additional decrease in labor productivity because of the deviation from firms' optimal hours-employment mix. The fall in productivity per worker is exacerbated by the strong decrease in average hours worked.

Under the policy, the most productive firms find it most costly to hire labor as fewer workers are released into the unemployment pool. In market economies, the efficiency of the allocation of factors across production sites plays an important role for aggregate productivity. Firms whose product is in high demand during the COVID-19 pandemic or firms that have created new products or technologies see their hiring costs increased because of the policies. By intervening into the reallocation of factors across production sites (i.e., preventing labor from flowing toward the most productive firms), hours sharing and no-firing policies can generate adverse effects on aggregate output.

Projections

Economies have rebounded, including in Italy. Real GDP is projected to grow at around 5 percent in 2021.[34] As noted above, some though not all the Italian labor market interventions ended in July 2021. In particular, firms have a choice of layoffs or hours subsidies with layoffs prohibited. What will this imply for Italian labor market outcomes?

In our model, if nothing forces firms not to lay off workers, then they prefer layoffs to hours sharing. Thus, we predict that low-productivity firms, except those with low firm-specific profitability draws, will lay off workers.[35] Although there are benefits through the subsidies that flow to firms, these are not sufficient to offset the gains they accrue from reducing the workforce.

Note that in a model with search frictions, unemployment allows for the reallocation of workers. This benefit underlies the productivity differences with and without the policy in Figure 8.

Conclusion

This chapter explores the effects of Italian labor market policies during the COVID-19 period. The analysis focuses on work sharing and firing restrictions. The model economy highlights the importance of worker flows between heterogeneous firms. These flows are hampered by adjustment costs.

The COVID-19 shock is modeled as a substantial reduction in productivity. Without any policy interventions, firms would respond by laying off workers with relatively small reductions in average hours. The introduction of an STW program and a prohibition on firing alter the response so that average hours fall. In the model economy, unemployment falls as well. The reduction in job separations is consistent with the data from Italy.

Using the model, it is possible to decompose this response and thus isolate the effects of STW distinct from the prohibition on firing. For the estimated model, if firms would fire workers, they would prefer that form of adjustment to the STW program. Thus, in the case of Italy, it was important that STW was coupled with a prohibition on firing workers.

Acknowledgments

We thank Michael R. Strain for inviting us to participate in this project. Elia Moracci provided superb assistance in putting together the basic facts and summarizing the Italian policies.

Appendix

This appendix provides additional details on the models and the quantitative analysis.

A Contracting Approach: Formalizations

The first-order conditions characterizing the optimal contract in state ε are

$$1 = \lambda u'(\omega(\varepsilon)h(\varepsilon) - g(h(\varepsilon))) \tag{7}$$

and

$$\varepsilon f'(h(\varepsilon)) = g'(h(\varepsilon)). \tag{8}$$

Both these conditions hold for all ε. Denote the solution by the two functions of ε, $(\omega^*(\varepsilon), h^*(\varepsilon))$, prescribing the state-contingent wage rate and hours worked.

Equation 7 is an optimal insurance condition. As the firm is risk neutral, worker marginal utility of consumption less the disutility of work is independent of the state. Generally, this does not mean that consumption is constant as hours will vary with ε. But the constant marginal-utility result implies that $\omega(\varepsilon)h(\varepsilon) - g(h(\varepsilon))$ is state independent. With hours increasing in ε, this means that consumption, too, is increasing in ε.

The condition for efficient hours allocation is given by Equation 8. Given the assumptions on the technology and $g(h)$, $h(\varepsilon)$ is an increasing function. Note that as long as the marginal product of labor is higher relative to the disutility of work near zero hours, the firm will choose to operate for all realization of ε.

Impact of Hours Sharing

The first-order condition for the wage is:

$$1 = \lambda u'(\tilde{c} - g(\tilde{h}))(1 + s). \tag{9}$$

The first-order condition for hours is:

$$\varepsilon f'(\tilde{h}) - \tilde{\omega} = \lambda u'(\tilde{c} - g(\tilde{h}))[(\tilde{\omega}(1+s)) - g'(\tilde{h})]. \tag{10}$$

Simplifying using Equation 9 yields

$$\varepsilon f'(\tilde{h}) = \frac{g'(\tilde{h})}{1+s}. \tag{11}$$

Clearly $\tilde{h}(\varepsilon) > h^*(\varepsilon)$ when $s > 0$. Not surprisingly, an hours subsidy leads to an increase in hours worked.[36]

The Dynamic Model

This is a multi-worker environment with firms that compete for workers. The labor market has search frictions whereby workers and firms are randomly matched. For the labor input, there are two dimensions: the number of workers at a firm and the number of hours each worker works.

Because of the multi-worker setting, the model includes a richer bargaining structure in which the firm negotiates sequentially with workers, setting a compensation function. Given this function, the firm determines the hours worked and, over time, the number of workers.

From the perspective of this model, the COVID-19 shock affects the revenue earned from output produced and the availability of a healthy workforce. The policy remedies matter through the costs of varying worker hours and the ability to fire workers.

Firms. Firms produce output with labor following: $F(nh) = A\varepsilon(h \cdot n)^{\alpha}$. As in the static contracting framework, n is the number of workers, and h is average hours per worker. In this production function there are two shocks: (1) aggregate productivity given by A and (2) idiosyncratic productivity shock given by ε. Both follow $AR(1)$ processes.

Given a compensation function, described below, the timing of events is as follows:

1. The firm starts the period with n workers and knowing productivity, (A,ε).

2. There is a wage schedule negotiated before that stipulates the cost of varying worker hours, subject to government restrictions and subsidies.

3. Given this schedule, the firm chooses how many hours its workers will work.

4. Production takes place, and revenues are realized.

5. The firm then adjusts it workforce, by either posting vacancies or firing workers. Both adjustments can be costly.

Note that there is a fundamental asymmetry in the treatment of hours and employees. The hours decision is made after productivity in the current period is known, but the hiring decision is made ex ante. In this way, the model highlights the response of hours to shocks compared to the slower adjustment in the number of workers.

The firm's ability to hire workers through the posting of vacancies depends on labor market tightness. This is determined in equilibrium by the joint decisions of the firms.

Without a STW subsidy, a firm in state $(\varepsilon, n; S)$ solves

$$\begin{aligned} V(\varepsilon, n; S) = \max_{h,n'} \{ & A\varepsilon\,(nh)^{\alpha} - \omega(\varepsilon, n, h; S)\, n \\ & - C(n', n, S) + \mathbb{E}_{S',\varepsilon'|S,\varepsilon}\beta V(\varepsilon', n'; S) \} \end{aligned} \tag{12}$$

given the compensation function, $\omega(\varepsilon, n, h; S)$. This function is allowed to depend on whether there is a short-term subsidy. The cost of adjustment, $C(n', n, S)$, is given by:

$$C(n', n, S) = \frac{n' - n}{q} \cdot c_v \cdot \mathbb{1}^v + F^- \mathbb{1}^- \tag{13}$$

where $\mathbb{1}^v$ is indicator functions that take the value of one if a firm is posting vacancies (i.e., when $n' > n$), and $\mathbb{1}^-$ indicates a firm that is firing workers and thus incurring a fixed firing cost F^-. Here q indicates how quickly vacancies can be filled and is thus directly related to labor market tightness and included in S.

Workers. Workers are identical and have preferences over consumption and work given by $\omega(\varepsilon, n, h; S) - g(h)$. Here consumption is the same as compensation, so workers do not save directly. The function $g(h)$ captures the disutility of hours worked, and it is increasing and strictly convex.

An employed worker in a firm in state (ε, n) has an expected lifetime utility of

$$W^e(\varepsilon, n; S) = \omega(\varepsilon, n, h; S) - g(h) + \beta \mathbb{E}_{S', \varepsilon' | S, \varepsilon} [sW^u(S') \\ + (1 - s)W^e(\varepsilon', n'; S)]. \tag{14}$$

The current utility is supplemented with a discounted future value that includes a lottery over future employment, where a match ends with probability s. If the worker remains in the same firm, that firm will be in idiosyncratic state (ε', n').

The match shock s includes the usual effects of shocks that cause a firm to go out of business. It also may reflect the effects of a fall in productivity that would lead the firm to reduce its workforce.

In COVID-19 times, the shock to sales was large. Further, there was the prospect of a worker not being healthy enough to work, included in s, so that the match must end.

If unemployed, the worker obtains some value of leisure or unemployment insurance b and has a value of

$$W^u(S) = b + \beta \mathbb{E}_{S', \varepsilon', n' | S, \varepsilon, n} [(1 - \varphi)W^u(S') + \varphi W^e(\varepsilon', n'; S')]. \tag{15}$$

Here φ is the probability a worker will transit out of unemployment to a job with a firm in state $(\varepsilon', n'; S')$.

Compensation. The compensation function is a key element of the model. It affects the size of firms but more importantly how they respond to shocks. Since the immediate response to changes in productivity is through hours, the sensitivity of compensation to hours variation matters.

The compensation function reflects a (Nash) bargain between a firm and its workers, following Elsby and Michaels.[37] The result is a compensation function that is common to all workers. As above, the firm chooses hours ex post given this function. As presented in Cooper, Meyer, and Schott,[38]

$$\omega(\varepsilon, n, h; S) = (1-\eta)\left[g(h)+b\right] + \eta\left[\frac{A\varepsilon\alpha h^{\alpha}n^{\alpha-1}}{1-\eta(1-\alpha)}\right] + \eta\theta c_v. \qquad (16)$$

Here η is the bargaining weight of the worker, θ is labor market tightness, and c_v is the marginal cost of posting a vacancy.

Equilibrium. The optimization problems presented here apply to all workers and firms in this economy. They are not independent problems for a couple reasons. First, the ease at which a firm can fill a vacancy depends on labor market tightness, which itself depends on the fraction of workers unemployed and the total number of vacancies in the economy. While each firm takes labor market tightness as given, denoted θ, it is jointly determined by all of them.

Second, though not shown formally here, the bargaining problem includes an outside option for workers. That option is determined by the other employment opportunities in the economy, partly summarized by the joint distribution of firms over productivity and size. This, too, is an equilibrium object.

Quantitative Analysis

This subsection provides more detail on the quantitative analysis.

Parameter Values. The parameters are presented in Table A1. The first block is parameters taken from other studies. The second block is those set such that model and data moments align in normal times. The final block is the two parameters used to match the use of extended work sharing during the COVID-19 experience.

COVID-19 Shock and Policy Experiments. As noted above, the COVID-19 shock and the various policies were unexpected by firms. Once the shock occurred, firms' beliefs follow the process stipulated for normal recessions. The transition matrix for the COVID-19 shock along with the policy measures is given by Π in Equation 6.

Under short-term work (STW), the firm has the option of choosing hours worked, given its stock of workers. There are no layoffs allowed so that the reduction in demand is met by a reduction in hours. Compensation to workers is given by

$$\omega^{\Sigma}(\varepsilon, n, h; S) = h(\varepsilon, n; S) \cdot \left[\psi \cdot \frac{\omega(\varepsilon, n, \tilde{h}; S)}{\tilde{h}} + (1 - \psi) \cdot \omega_h(\varepsilon, n, \tilde{h}; S) \right]. \quad (17)$$

Table A1. Model Parameters

Parameter	Meaning	Value	Target
β	Discount Factor	0.9967	Annual $r = 4$ percent
α	Labor Elasticity	0.582	Cooper, Horn, and Indraccolo (2021)
Υ	Match Elasticity	0.650	Kohlbrecher, Merkl, and Nordmeier (2016)
η	Worker Bargaining Power	0.650	Same as match elasticity γ
μ	Matching Efficiency	0.054	
ρ_{ε}	Persistence of ε	0.966	Cooper, Horn, and Indraccolo (2021)
σ_{ε}	Standard Deviation of ε	0.059	Cooper, Horn, and Indraccolo (2021)
μ_{ε}	Mean of Log ε	0.290	
e_0	Disutility Scale Parameter	5.1 x 10^{-5}	
e_1	Disutility of Work	2.069	
b	Flow Value of Unemployment	1.736	
c_v	Vacancy Creation Cost	1.034	
κ	Fixed Cost of Using STW	0.565	
ψ	Convex Cost of Using STW	0.256	

Note: The parameters in the upper part of the table were preassigned. The parameters in the middle part were found using a simulated method of moments procedure using the stationary economy. The parameters in the bottom part were found using a simulated method of moments procedure using the economy with aggregate shocks.

Source: Authors' research; R. Cooper, W. Horn, and L. Indraccolo, "Covid-19 and Productivity in Europe: A Responsiveness Perspective," European University Institute, 2021; and Britta Kohlbrecher, Christian Merkl, and Daniela Nordmeier, "Revisiting the Matching Function," *Journal of Economic Dynamics and Control* 69 (August 2016): 350–74, https://www.sciencedirect.com/science/article/abs/pii/S0165188916300951.

From Equation 17, compensation under STW is a linear combination of the baseline marginal and average hourly compensation multiplied with the actual hours chosen by the firm. These marginal and average wages are taken from Equation 16. The parameter ψ, shown in Table A1, is chosen to match the average hours reduction in the data. Further, to match the take-up rate of STW, the model includes a fixed cost of using the policy given by κ, also shown in Table 3.

Notes

1. Russell Cooper, Moritz Meyer, and Immo Schott, "The Employment and Output Effects of Short-Time Work in Germany" (working paper, National Bureau of Economic Research, Cambridge, MA, August 2017), https://www.nber.org/papers/w23688.

2. The standard search-and-matching models contain neither feature.

3. This section draws on Instituto Nazionale di Statistica, *Il Mercato del Lavoro 2020*, 2020, https://www.istat.it/it/files//2021/02/Il-Mercato-del-lavoro-2020-1.pdf.

4. Unless otherwise stated, the data for Italy and the EU are from Eurostat. See Eurostat, "Labour Market Flow Statistics in the EU," October 13, 2021, https://ec.europa.eu/eurostat/statistics-explained/index.php?title=Labour_market_flow_statistics_in_the_EU&oldid=501936. The US data come from Federal Reserve Economic Data, Federal Reserve Bank of St. Louis, website, https://fred.stlouisfed.org.

5. These mask some large quarterly movements. For example, in the US the annual growth rate of real gross domestic product in Q2 of 2020 was −31 percent, and in Q3 of 2020, it was 33.8 percent.

6. This discussion draws on Eurostat, "Labour Market in the Light of the COVID-19 Pandemic—Quarterly Statistics," November 23, 2021, https://ec.europa.eu/eurostat/statistics-explained/index.php?title=Labour_market_in_the_light_of_the_COVID_19_pandemic_-_quarterly_statistics.

7. The focus here is on the changes in the unemployment rates within a country. As noted, for example, in Constance Sorrentino's report, there are differences in measurement of unemployment between the US and the EU. See Constance Sorrentino, "International Unemployment Rates: How Comparable Are They?," *Monthly Labor Review* 123, no. 6 (June 2000): 3–20, https://www.bls.gov/opub/mlr/2000/06/art1full.pdf.

8. For additional discussion and data links, see Eurostat, "Fall in Hours Worked in Q4 2020," April 21, 2021, https://ec.europa.eu/eurostat/en/web/products-eurostat-news/-/ddn-20210421-3.

9. Figure 2 of Tommaso Colussi's report *IZA COVID-19 Crisis Response Monitoring: Italy* provides annual evidence on hiring and separations from INPS-UniEmens, which shows comparable patterns. The spike in hires in 2015 reflects a jobs act intended to stimulate employment. See Tommaso Colussi, *IZA COVID-19 Crisis Response Monitoring:*

Italy, IZA Institute of Labor Economics, May 23, 2020, Figure 2, https://www.iza.org/wc/files/downloads/IZA_CrisisMonitoring_IT.pdf.

10. This is the basic scheme that was supplemented by others to broaden coverage during the COVID-19 period. See the presentation at INPS, "Cassa Integrazione Guadagni Ordinaria," April 30, 2017, https://www.inps.it/prestazioni-servizi/cassa-integrazione-guadagni-ordinaria.

11. Kenneth Burdett and Randall Wright, "Unemployment Insurance and Short-Time Compensation: The Effects on Layoffs, Hours per Worker, and Wages," *Journal of Political Economy* 97, no. 6 (December 1989): 1479–96, https://www.jstor.org/stable/1833249.

12. For an optimal contracting model into a search-and-matching framework, see Russell Cooper, John C. Haltiwanger, and Jonathan Willis, "Search Frictions: Matching Aggregate and Establishment Observations," *Journal of Monetary Economics* 54, Supplement 1 (September 2007): 56–78, https://www.sciencedirect.com/science/article/abs/pii/S0304393207000530.

13. The model is formally presented in the section of the appendix titled "The Dynamic Model," which highlights the main channels of interaction and policy impacts. The model builds on the study of work sharing in Cooper, Meyer, and Schott, "The Employment and Output Effects of Short-Time Work in Germany."

14. The quantitative model allows multiple workers.

15. This function form is chosen to illustrate results as it neatly separates risk sharing from the hours allocation.

16. These conditions are presented in the section of the appendix titled "A Contracting Approach: Formalizations."

17. This is what makes the specification of utility so attractive.

18. In contrast, the hours sharing is taken as given in determining the optimal contract in Burdett and Wright, "Unemployment Insurance and Short-Time Compensation."

19. In reality, some restrictions are imposed on the firms and workers. For Germany, see Cooper, Meyer, and Schott, "The Employment and Output Effects of Short-Time Work in Germany." As for Italy, Cassa Integrazione Guadagni Ordinaria returns about 80 percent of income lost for hours worked between zero and the contracted level. These restrictions are discussed in the context of the policy experiments for the quantitative model. See INPS, "Cassa Integrazione Guadagni Ordinaria," April 30, 2017, https://www.inps.it/prestazioni-servizi/cassa-integrazione-guadagni-ordinaria.

20. As we shall see, the actual extended work-sharing program had the opposite effect of subsidizing an hours reduction instead of firms laying off workers. The possibility of layoffs is introduced next.

21. Costas Azariadis, "Implicit Contracts and Underemployment Equilibria," *Journal of Political Economy* 83, no. 6 (December 1975): 1183–202, https://www.jstor.org/stable/1830855.

22. Since the ex ante problem allows state-specific choices without restrictions across states, this is the same as that problem if the policy were anticipated.

23. Here we use $g(0) = 0$.

24. The approach adds the multi-worker bargaining structure of a report by Michael W. L. Elsby and Ryan Michaels to the search-and-contracting framework of a report by Russell Cooper, Moritz Meyer, and Immo Schott. See Michael W. L. Elsby and Ryan Michaels, "Marginal Jobs, Heterogeneous Firms, and Unemployment Flows," *American Economic Journal: Macroeconomics* 5, no. 1 (January 2013): 1–48, https://www.aeaweb.org/articles?id=10.1257/mac.5.1.1; and Cooper, Meyer, and Schott, "The Employment and Output Effects of Short-Time Work in Germany." Also see Cooper, Meyer, and Schott, "The Employment and Output Effects of Short-Time Work in Germany" for a discussion of the appropriateness of the sequential bargaining model, particularly for Germany. For a related discussion of Germany versus Italy, see Tito Boeri et al., "Wage Equalization and Regional Misallocation: Evidence from Italian and German Provinces" (working paper, National Bureau of Economic Research, Cambridge, MA, February 2019), https://www.nber.org/papers/w25612.

25. Thus, in contrast to the presentation of layoffs above, hiring and firing have a one-period (i.e., month) lag.

26. Elsby and Michaels, "Marginal Jobs, Heterogeneous Firms, and Unemployment Flows."

27. This function is shown as Equation 16 and discussed in the subsection of the appendix titled "COVID-19 Shock and Policy Experiments."

28. Organisation for Economic Co-operation and Development, Benefits, Taxes, and Wages, 2021.

29. The section of the appendix titled "Quantitative Analysis" presents the approach more formally.

30. The generosity rate of unemployment benefits reflects an exogenous policy instrument and the average wages, which are endogenous.

31. This corresponds to $\pi = 0.8706$. The maximum duration of short-time work (STW) was six months before the 2009 episode. During 2009, the maximum duration was increased to 24 months.

32. Per Krusell and Anthony A. Smith Jr., "Income and Wealth Heterogeneity in the Macroeconomy," *Journal of Political Economy* 106, no. 5 (October 1998): 867–96, http://www.econ.yale.edu/smith/250034.pdf.

33. We assume that the COVID-19 shock and the implementation of the policies that followed were initially unexpected by firms. Once the shock occurred, we let firms believe that the COVID-19-induced recession has the same length as an average recession.

34. See the recent forecast from the Bank of Italy. ANSA English, "Bank of Italy Ups 2021 Growth Forecast to 5.1%," July 16, 2021, https://www.ansa.it/english/news/business/2021/07/16/bank-of-italy-ups-2021-growth-forecast-to-5.1_59fef8b8-fb84-404c-8ea0-f70ed2125edf.html.

35. As with the baseline simulations, these statements pertain to the outset of a recession.

36. As we shall see, the actual STW program had the opposite effect of subsidizing an hours reduction. In that case, it is as if $s < 0$. The point here is simply to see how a subsidy affects hours in a contracting problem.

37. Elsby and Michaels, "Marginal Jobs, Heterogeneous Firms, and Unemployment Flows."

38. Cooper, Meyer, and Schott, "The Employment and Output Effects of Short-Time Work in Germany."

7

The Dutch Experience with Job-Preserving Policy During the Coronavirus Pandemic

ROEL BEETSMA AND RAYMOND GRADUS

As with many countries, the Dutch economy was hit hard by the COVID-19 crisis. However, soon after the potential scale of economic devastation became clear, the Dutch government adopted a broad series of measures to protect the economy from an uncontrolled downward spiral. These measures primarily aimed at protecting jobs and avoiding bankruptcy by supporting the business sector.

Measures were also taken at the EU level. The EU provided 100 billion euros in loans as support for short-time work arrangements.[1] The European Stability Mechanism made 200 billion euros available for loans on health-related causes, a financing source that has so far remained unused, while the European Investment Bank (EIB) provided 40 billion euros of new investment. The EU also created a 25 billion euro Pan-European Guarantee Fund, to be managed by the EIB, and expected to mobilize 200 billion euros of additional financing for mostly small and medium-size enterprises (SME).[2]

Monetary policy also did its part to dampen the crisis. The European Central Bank's (ECB) asset-purchasing program, after having been paused for some time, had already been resumed. In addition, it started the so-called Pandemic Emergency Purchase Programme, a temporary asset-purchase program of private- and public-sector securities.[3]

At least partly due to the Dutch economy's high degree of digitalization, economic activity coped relatively well with the pandemic. There was an instant and widespread move to teleworking, implying that a substantial share of activity could continue as before. Moreover, some sectors benefited directly, such as those focused on online sales. However, there have also been sectors, in particular leisure activity–related sectors, that have suffered enormously, and they were still suffering in the summer of 2021.

Overall, though, it seems that the pandemic narrowly affected unemployment and bankruptcies and that the fall in output has been less severe than originally expected.

The purpose of this chapter is to learn from the measures taken in response to the COVID-19 crisis, which may be of use for future crises. The remainder of this chapter lays out the measures the Dutch government adopted in response to the pandemic—in particular, the measures to support employment. It looks back at how the economy has fared under these measures, it looks forward to the short- and long-term prospects for the Dutch economy, and it discusses what we can learn from our policy experience so far.

Measures Taken by the Dutch Government in Response to the Pandemic

The Dutch government has taken many measures in response to the pandemic. In contrast to the US, there has been relatively little direct support for families. Most of the Dutch government's support (and the support by most other EU governments) went to the business sector and was primarily aimed at preserving employment and preventing bankruptcies. This was to limit the potential for a downward economic spiral fueled by rising unemployment and widespread business failure, which in turn could lead to short-term demand fallout and longer-term economic scarring through write-offs of human and physical capital. The government supported individual companies, established sector-specific support schemes, and set up general arrangements for the entire business sector.

Priority was given to simple and generally applicable arrangements that could provide rapid financial support. In the Netherlands, the closing of restaurants, bars, and schools was announced on the evening of March 15, 2020. The Dutch government reacted promptly by announcing several business support packages. At the end of March 2020, the general arrangements for the entire business sector were published, and on April 6 that year, the first wage subsidy was paid to businesses. In July 2021, the wage supplementation program was extended for the fifth and last time.

General Business Support to Preserve Employment and Cover Fixed Costs. Most support during the coronavirus crisis has gone to businesses, mainly through generic arrangements but also support of several major individual firms.

The NOW and TVL Programs. The main general business support arrangements introduced by the Dutch government were the Temporary Emergency Bridging Measure to Preserve Employment (NOW) and the Reimbursement of Fixed Costs of SMEs (TVL). The first is based on a wage supplementation arrangement due to loss of income. Employers with at least a 20 percent revenue fall could apply for this support, which then covers 90 percent of x percent of their wage cost, where x is the drop in firm revenue. The firm's annual 2019 revenue is used as a benchmark for establishing income loss during the pandemic. Starting April 6, 2020, applicants received an 80 percent advance payment of the wage costs associated with the estimated revenue loss. As a consequence of NOW's simplicity requirement, until October 2021, startup firms (i.e., those without an income in 2019) were not allowed to apply for financial support. From November 2021 to March 2022, startup firms were allowed to make use of NOW, and their reference period was July through October 2021, as this was a period with relatively mild coronavirus-related restrictions.

Started in June 2020, the TVL is based on an estimate of the average fixed cost of a firm's sector (rather than its actual fixed costs, which would be impossible to calculate for each firm given the scale of the operation).[4] Due to the protracted nature of the coronavirus crisis, the maximum compensation and number of sectors covered by the scheme have risen over time. Starting in April 2021, reimbursement was 100 percent of this average cost, conditional on a revenue fall of at least 30 percent (lowered to 20 percent in November–December 2021 and January–March 2022). In principle, these NOW and TVL arrangements were available until October 1, 2021. However, due to omicron curfew measures, the government reintroduced NOW and TVL from November 2021 until March 2022. As this curfew came unexpectedly, the conditions for this period are relatively mild, although the number of firms using these arrangements is expected to be smaller.

Table 1. Conditions for Different Rounds of NOW and TVL

	Period	Maximum Reimbursement Wage	Range of Revenue Fall Eligible for Support	Maximum Wage Bill Reduction	Maximum Support Fixed Costs (in Euros)
2020	March–May	90%	> 20%		4,000
	June–September	90%	> 20%		50,000
	October–December	80%	> 20%	10%	90,000
2021	January–March	85%	> 20%	10%	550,000 (600,000*)
	April–June	85%	> 20%	10%	550,000 (1,200,000*)
	July–September	85%	20–80%	10%	550,000 (600,000*)
	November–December	85%	20–90%	15%	550,000 (600,000*)
2022	January–March	85%	20–90%	15%	550,000 (600,000*)

Note: * The higher numbers given for maximum support fixed costs in the January–March 2021, April–June 2021, July–September 2021, November–December 2021, and January–March 2022 periods are for large companies with more than 250 employees. The lower numbers are for SMEs.
Source: Netherlands Employee Insurance Agency, "Tijdelijke Noodmaatregel Overbrugging Werkgelegenheid (NOW)," https://www.uwv.nl/werkgevers/overige-onderwerpen/now/index.aspx; and Netherlands Ministry of Economic Affairs and Climate, "Aanvullende aanpassingen in het steunpakket in het vierde kwartaal," November 26, 2021, https://www.rijksoverheid.nl/documenten/kamerstukken/2021/11/26/kamerbrief-over-anvullende-aanpassingen-in-het-steunpakket-in-het-vierde-kwartaal.

Table 1 reports the main conditions of the different rounds of NOW and TVL. The first two reimbursed up to 90 percent of the wage bill—conditional on a revenue fall of at least 20 percent—and were accompanied by a maximum support to cover fixed costs of 4,000 euros in the first three months and 50,000 euros per firm during the second three months.[5] In subsequent rounds, the threshold for revenue fall was maintained, while the maximum reimbursement of the wage bill went down slightly and the maximum support of fixed costs for SMEs went up to 550,000 euros.

Starting in 2021, large companies with more than 250 employees could get a maximum of 550,000 euros in the first quarter and 1,200,000 euros in the second quarter. Due to EU restrictions on state aid,[6] the total amount of wage and fixed-cost support in 2021 could not exceed 1,800,000 euros, while the maximum support fell to 600,000 euros in the third quarter. In addition, in the last three rounds, firms were allowed to marginally cut wage costs while maintaining the right to subsidies.[7]

How well have NOW and TVL worked? Judged by the moderate increase in unemployment and low number of bankruptcies during the coronavirus period, the measures seem to have worked well. However, any type of support measure will produce collateral damage. We discuss this below.

Other Support Programs. Further arrangements include (1) temporary financial support for self-employed persons (TOZO), which were also available until October 1, 2021, and were intended to provide some minimum financial security for the self-employed; (2) temporary support for essential costs of households (frequently self-employed) that have lost a substantial part of their income (known as "TONK"); and (3) an inventory allowance for restaurants and nonfood retail (during the lockdown of Christmas 2020).[8] These arrangements were available until October 2022.

Also, the government has made liquidity support available through guaranteeing bank credits, and it has alleviated firms' tax obligations. In January 2021, the total alleviation or respite amounted to 36 billion euros, of which 16 billion had already been paid and four billion spent on tax reduction, leaving 16 billion euros of claims to still be paid. In fact, the government extended the maximum payment term from 36 to 60 months. So far, the government has refrained from a generic partial or complete cancellation of tax obligations, as this would lead to arbitrariness and disrupt competition. It would, moreover, only alleviate the burden of the business sector toward the government if other creditors do not also come forward.

As a result of the coronavirus crisis, firms have seen their debt grow. So far, this has not resulted in additional bankruptcies. However, at some point these debts need to be dealt with. Recently, the so-called Wet Homologatie Onderhands Akkoord came into existence—a law intended to prevent bankruptcy through debt restructuring, allowing firms to continue operating their viable parts—a solution that may in the end make creditors better off. Therefore, a maximum of 100,000 euros for debt restructuring per SME was announced.[9]

The Netherlands Bureau for Economic Policy Analysis analyzes the possibilities of public-private collaboration in the debt restructuring of viable firms.[10] The government (i.e., the tax authorities) typically is a large creditor, while the bank typically has more information about the specific firm under consideration. If private creditors are prepared to write off part of the debt, the government could do the same, allowing the firm to continue operating and thereby preventing the loss of knowledge and knock-on effects to the rest of the economy. This may be in the interest of those private creditors, because in the case of bankruptcy, the tax authorities are the first creditors to be honored.

Finally, a 1.4 billion euro package is in the pipeline to help people find new jobs or new gainful activities. Measures consist of developing intensive support and coaching, providing schooling and development, combating unemployment, and fighting poverty and household debt. In the Netherlands, municipalities are responsible for social assistance and combating long-term unemployment and poverty. Recently, the government announced that the municipal role would continue in 2022.

Overall Figures for General Business Support. The budgetary consequences of the coronavirus support are summarized in Table 2. Total discretionary support raising the public deficit was 35.4 billion euros—4.4 percent of gross domestic product (GDP)—in 2020 and estimated at almost 35.1 billion euros—4.1 percent of GDP—in 2021. Most of the support comes from the spending side, with the main items being NOW (15.9 and 9.5 billion euros in 2020 and 2021, respectively), TVL (2.0 and 6.0 billion, respectively), and TOZO (2.3 and 0.9 billion, respectively). Support relating to the costs of vaccination, infection source and contact investigation, and coronavirus testing amounted to five billion euros in 2020 and 6.7 billion euros in 2021. For 2022, the various amounts are smaller, presumably in anticipation of the coronavirus's receding impact on the economy.

Furthermore, a number of other spending items are not explicitly listed in Table 2, such as support to special arrangements for childcare, culture, and media; lower-level government; and the education and transportation

Table 2. Support in Billions of Euros

	2020	2021	2022
Aggregate Discretionary Support			
Total	**35.4**	**35.1**	**4.5**
Discretionary Expenditure Support Package			
Total	**31.0**	**34.6**	**5.1**
NOW	15.9	9.5	0.1
TVL	2.0	6.0	1.0
TOZO	2.3	0.9	—
Vaccination, Testing, Medical Support, and Related	5.0	8.2	3.8
Other Supporting Measures	5.7	11.5	0.3
Discretionary Tax Support Package			
Total	**4.4**	**0.7**	**–0.6**
Fiscal Corona-Reserve Corporation Tax	3.0	—	—
Guarantees			
Total	**50.3**	**41.6**	**41.1**
Next Generation EU	27.4	27.9	27.9
EIB—Pan-European Guarantee Fund	1.3	1.3	1.3
Support to Mitigate Unemployment Risks in an Emergency	6.1	6.1	6.1
Guarantee KLM	2.2	2.2	2.2
Reinsurance Supplier Credits	12.0	0.065	0.065
Other Items	1.3	4.0	3.6

Note: Positive numbers raise the deficit relevant for EU fiscal surveillance, the so-called "EMU deficit" of a country, while negative numbers reduce it. Guarantees are the amounts on September 26, 2021. It should be noticed that the figures for 2022 are estimates.

Source: Measures are taken from Netherlands Bureau for Economic Policy Analysis, *Projections September 2021*, September 2021, 44, https://www.cpb.nl/en/macro-economic-outlook-mev-2022; Netherlands Ministry of Economic Affairs and Climate, "Aanpassingen van het steunpakket in het vierde kwartaal," November 16, 2021, https://www.rijksoverheid.nl/documenten/kamerstukken/2021/11/16/kamerbrief-aanpassingen-steunpakket-4e-kwartaal-2021; Netherlands Ministry of Economic Affairs and Climate, "Aanvullende aanpassingen in het steunpakket in het vierde kwartaal," November 26, 2021, https://www.rijksoverheid.nl/documenten/kamerstukken/2021/11/26/kamerbrief-over-anvullende-aanpassingen-in-het-steunpakket-in-het-vierde-kwartaal; Netherlands Ministry of Economic Affairs and Climate, "Kamerbrief over aanpassing steunmaatregelen na directe lockdown december 2021," December 21, 2021, https://www.rijksoverheid.nl/documenten/kamerstukken/2021/12/21/kamerbrief-over-aanpassing-steunmaatregelen; and Netherlands Ministry of Finance, *Corona garanties*, January 20, 2022, https://www.rijksfinancien.nl/overheidsfinancien-coronatijd/corona-garanties.

sectors. Remarkably, the total amount of this support for these items increased from 5.7 billion euros to 11.5 billion euros in 2021. Overall tax support amounted to 4.4 billion euros in 2020, with the largest part made up by the "fiscal corona-reserve" corporation tax, a postponement of the corporation tax payments. In December 2021, also due to the omicron curfew, a new postponement was given.

Support through NOW, TVL, and TOZO decreased from 20.2 billion euros in 2020 to 15.5 billion euros in 2021, due to some relaxation of the pandemic restrictions in the spring of 2021 and the strong economic recovery that year. In May 2021, the government extended the NOW wage supplementation program to the third quarter of 2021. It was terminated in October but reopened again in November. Further, the fixed-cost TVL subsidy is no longer included in the eventual calculation of the revenues relevant for NOW. Notably, the budgetary cost of TVL in 2021 was three times higher than it was in 2020.

Finally, guarantees amounted to about 50 billion euros in 2020 and almost 42 billion in 2021. The largest item by far was the guarantee associated with Next Generation EU, which is mainly composed of the Recovery and Resilience Facility. Reinsurance of supplier credits, at 12 billion euros in 2020, fell to close to zero in 2021.

Support to Individual Firms. Between March and August 2020, the government committed 3.5 billion euros of support to individual firms. The Netherlands Court of Audit (*Algemene Rekenkamer*) analyzes the support programs and explores whether lessons from past support operations have been learned.[11] Overall, the court is critical about the COVID-19-related support.[12] While the government tends to claim that each individual case is exceptional, unique, and urgent, the court views the COVID-19-related support operations as fundamentally similar to past support operations, so that it should have been possible to learn useful lessons from them for the current operations.

The most high-profile rescues were those of Koninklijke Luchtvaart Maatschappij (KLM) Royal Dutch Airlines and Royal IHC, a Dutch shipbuilding company. Apart from these rescues of individual firms, the government also provided support to firms with a public function—in particular, public transportation.

KLM Royal Dutch Airlines. KLM falls under the Air France–KLM holding, in which the French and Dutch governments have a substantial equity stake. The rescue of KLM is described in a letter to the Dutch parliament.[13] The motivation for the rescue is the importance of KLM for the national airport Schiphol's network of international connections. Schiphol's high degree of connectivity is considered of great importance for high-end business activity in the Netherlands.

The rescue consists of two main components: One is a 90 percent guarantee of a 2.4 billion euro private-creditor loan to KLM, while the other is a direct, junior loan of one billion euros by the Dutch government to KLM. The loans are designed to incentivize KLM to repay them as soon as possible. KLM pays the Dutch state a fee for its guarantee toward private creditors. The fee increases over time. The same is true for the interest rate on the direct loan to KLM. The rescue of KLM took place under several conditions aimed at improving the airline's competitive position by cutting costs, in particular salaries; reducing the airline's environmental footprint; and reducing its effects on the livability of the neighborhood where it is located.

The Netherlands Court of Audit is critical about KLM's rescue. It sees the cabinet's public announcement, before any agreement had been reached, that it would be prepared to rescue KLM as a mistake.[14] The bail-in of the private sector was limited, and by far most of the risk (93 percent) resides with the state. Finally, there is a conflict of interest in that ABN AMRO, one of the banks involved in the rescue, is partially owned by the state. In addition, KLM received wage support of more than one billion euros from NOW. Despite this support, which is conditional on the absence of forced layoffs, more than 5,000 employees have left the company.

Royal IHC. Royal IHC received almost 400 million euros from the government while receiving debt relief from a few creditor banks. The motivation for the government's support was the strategic importance of IHC in the form of specialized, high-tech knowledge and the large number of employees in the firm and its suppliers. Another argument was the fact that through an export guarantee, the government was a major creditor of IHC. However, as the government's letter to the parliament also makes clear,[15] IHC's troubles began before the pandemic, in production losses on ships.

In return for its help, the state required an improvement in the governance structure and replacement of the current management. Again, the Court of Audit is critical in its evaluation, claiming that the maximum risk associated with this rescue operation (895 million euros) is substantially higher than the direct damage of almost 400 million euros.[16]

How Has the Economy Fared During the Coronavirus Pandemic?

Table 3 reports the Dutch economy's main macroeconomic figures for 2019–22, taken from the Bureau for Economic Policy Analysis.[17] Obviously, the figures for 2021 and 2022 are projections, while those for 2020 may still be subject to some revision, in view of the high degree of economic uncertainty at the moment of writing (summer 2021).

The Dutch economy has taken a major hit from the coronavirus pandemic. However, with a growth of –3.8 percent in 2020, the economy's shrinkage was smaller than expected and smaller than in most other EU countries. Among the reasons for this relatively limited damage are the Dutch economy's high degree of digitalization, making it relatively easy to work from home, and the government's generous economic support, effectively causing the government to largely absorb the coronavirus's economic shock.

Economic activity will exceed the pre-pandemic level in 2022. Other figures depict a rather benign picture, given the magnitude of the shock and the ensuing lockdowns. Unemployment remained rather low at 3.8 percent in 2020 and 3.4 percent in 2021, and it is expected to rise mildly to 3.5 percent in 2022. It is not unusual for unemployment to continue to rise for a while after the economy has started growing again.

While the effect on unemployment was rather small, the reduction in hours worked was larger (–2.7 percent in 2020). This is a better measure of the reduction in activity for a situation in which many firms sent their workers home while keeping them on the payroll. Indeed, the limited increase in unemployment suggests that the business support measures have effectively protected employment. Hence, the internal margin became the margin through which the deployment of personnel was adjusted (i.e., by adjusting the average number of hours worked by employees).

In 2020, inflation remained stuck at a low level. However, in 2021 it rose to a relatively high level in recent historic terms, driven by temporary effects and constrained supply meeting unleashed pent-up demand. In turn, the latter is the result of a (partially forced) steep increase in individual saving as measured in percentage of disposable income, from 4.5 percent in 2019 to 11.6 percent in 2020, though it is expected to have stayed at the same level (11.4 percent) in 2021.

The anticipated strong increase in consumption once lockdowns have been lifted can be expected to spur new business investment. The investment response will depend on the extent to which firm balance sheets have been damaged, and the inevitable build-down of business support will be followed by an increase in bankruptcies in sectors that suffered from the pandemic. The rapidly improving economic outlook has also led to a strong positive update of investment growth, from 2.3 percent in March 2021 to 5.3 percent in June.[18]

The public budget balance deteriorated by 6 percentage points, to −4.2 percent of GDP, from 2019 to 2020 and was set to deteriorate further, to −5.4 percent, in 2021. On the back of the unwinding of the support measures, the estimated deficit for 2022 is 1.8 percent, hence comfortably below the Stability and Growth Pact (SGP) limit of 3 percent. Public debt exhibited a substantial increase between 2019 and 2020, driven by increases in spending, reductions in tax revenues, and a fall in GDP (the "denominator effect"). Debt rose further in 2021, substantially driven by strong growth in government consumption (6.0 percent), including extra education spending to make up for learning deficits caused by the pandemic. But it remains below the SGP's 60 percent limit and will fall again slightly in 2022.

Individual sectors have been hit by the crisis to substantially different degrees. In particular, business services; trade, transportation, and hospitality; and culture, recreation, and other services have been severely hit. The latter was hurt by a drop in value added of more than 30 percent between the end of 2019 and the end of 2020. This is different from previous crises, in which the export sector was disproportionately hurt. Sectors that have done relatively well are information and communication, agriculture, and industry. For the former, this should not be surprising, as people massively shifted to working at home and communicating via electronic devices.

Table 3. Macroeconomic Realizations and Projections for the Dutch Economy

	2019	2020	2021	2022
Real GDP Growth	2.0%	–3.8%	3.9%	3.5%
Unemployment Level	3.4%	3.8%	3.4%	3.5%
Employment Change (Hours)	2.1%	–2.7%	2.3%	1.8%
Inflation	2.7%	1.1%	1.9%	1.8%
Budget Balance (Percentage of GDP)	1.7%	–4.2%	–5.4%	–2.3%
Debt Level (Percentage of GDP)	48.5%	54.3%	57.5%	56.5%
Individual Savings (Percentage of Disposable Income)	4.5%	11.6%	11.4%	6.8%

Source: Netherlands Bureau for Economic Policy Analysis, *Macro Economische Verkenning 2022*, September 2021, https://www.cpb.nl/sites/default/files/omnidownload/CPB-Raming-Macro-Economische-Verkenning-MEV-2022.pdf.

The coronavirus crisis has been unusual compared with other crises. As already pointed out, unemployment and bankruptcies have been hardly affected, while house price increases accelerated in 2020 (in the Netherlands as in other countries) on the back of lagging construction, low financing costs, and substantial cash balances in search of a higher yield. Moreover, policy idiosyncrasies appear to have contributed to the 2020 housing inflation.

The announcement of an increase in buyer taxes from 2 to 8 percent on second houses at the start of 2021 boosted housing demand by investors in the fall of 2020. At the same moment, the transaction tax for first-time buyers under age 35 went to zero, boosting demand (at the lower end of the price range) in the first months of 2021. The relatively mild trajectory of the Dutch economy compared to other EU economies is all the more remarkable in view of Brexit. Of course, 2020 was still a transition year, with the UK still part of the internal market, but the UK has since left. As a share of GDP, Dutch exports to the UK are some of the highest in the EU, and the estimated long-term value-added loss due to Brexit is about 0.4 percent of GDP.[19]

Simplicity and a generally applicable package of business support programs can give rise to negative side effects, as the Dutch case shows. Firms that do not actually deserve support, because their revenue loss is a consequence of economic dynamics unrelated to the pandemic, receive it anyway. Menno Schellekens, Anne Li Cnossen, and Rianne 't Jong provide suggestive evidence for this.[20] For March–September 2020, they have data for individual companies on their support received for wages and fixed costs and their actual revenues in 2019 and 2020. They show that more than 80 percent of the companies receiving an advance payment overestimated their fall in revenues.

Moreover, companies in the Netherlands from sectors that did well during the crisis received support. In total, the information and communications technologies sector received 0.4 billion euros, of which only an estimated 29 percent can be related to the pandemic.[21] Also, large amounts of wage support were given to other business and technical services, with the relationship to the pandemic even weaker.

Outlook and Policy for the Coming Years and the Longer Run

The combination of ultra-loose monetary and fiscal policies has dampened the economic fallout from the pandemic. As a result, the economic scarring associated with the destruction of physical and human capital has been comparatively limited. Still, by 2025, GDP is expected to fall short of its pre-coronavirus projection by 1.5 percent, due to weaker growth trends in labor productivity associated with investments forgone during the pandemic.

Outlook. In the short to medium run, positive effects will be felt from the massive government support in the US, which will drive up imports from the Netherlands. However, over the longer run, some sectors will likely need to shrink compared to the pre-pandemic situation, simply because demand has shifted. For example, a substantial fraction of brick-and-mortar shops will see their business replaced by web shopping, while traveling may be partially replaced by teleconferencing, and construction of office space will likely suffer from a permanent shift toward working from home.

However, an increasingly important negative side effect of the massive support is that it hinders the efficient allocation of resources over activities. Inefficient firms are kept afloat, distorting the level playing field and hoarding scarce labor that would otherwise flow to more-efficient firms, where it could be put to more-productive use. This is particularly costly in a situation of increasing labor scarcity. Before the pandemic, the Netherlands' unemployment rate was the lowest among Organisation for Economic Co-operation and Development countries.

Second, support undermines the incentive to innovate, thereby hampering the "creative destruction" mechanism by which inefficient activities are replaced by more innovative and productive ones—undermining growth in the longer run. Now that economic growth is expected to improve strongly, it is necessary and possible to replace financial support to businesses with policies aimed at recovery and restoring normal market functions. This was an important argument to end the support on October 1, 2021.[22]

A relevant, though hard to measure, negative effect will come from the reduced learning achievements of children and students who have received little and ineffective schooling during the crisis. These effects will be long-lasting, because they are likely to be felt during a person's entire work career. The focus of policymakers in the Netherlands and elsewhere was on containing the health crisis rather than containing such long-term damages.

There is also mounting evidence that the crisis has disproportionately affected schooling achievements of weaker pupils and those from disadvantaged backgrounds, which likely increases future inequality, ceteris paribus. To mend the resulting learning deficits, the government has set up an 8.5 billion euro national educational program over 2021–23, although it is not clear yet how this extra money will be spent.

To what extent could the coronavirus crisis have positive economic side effects? The main one would be the faster adoption of digital technologies, especially in relation to teleworking and teaching. These effects cannot yet be estimated; in the longer run, we will see how large they are.

Running through all these developments are the consequences of Brexit. The COVID-19 shock has clouded these consequences over the shorter run. However, they will come to the fore in the longer run and take the form of lower Dutch exports to the UK and lower Dutch direct investment in the UK, although some compensation in terms of employment and output can be expected from firms that relocate from the UK to the Netherlands.

Policies. What should be the policy priorities in the coming years? First, while there may be microeconomic arguments to alleviate coronavirus-induced misery at the individual level, there is no longer a macroeconomic reason to stimulate demand and protect jobs. The government should shape policy and invest with an eye on long-run challenges. This implies setting the right conditions to incentivize the climate transition.

The best way to have firms reduce emissions is to price them (and plow the revenues back to the firms, to avoid competitive disadvantage).[23] Spending on infrastructure should be a priority. Transport of durably generated electricity runs into bottlenecks, and hydrogen production cannot get off the ground without proper infrastructure. Once the right infrastructure is there, firms will be attracted. Such investments not only pose costs but also provide business opportunities for firms shaping the energy transition.

The second major economic challenge is the future shrinkage of the workforce and, related, the continued shift to a knowledge economy. There is already a shortage of skilled labor, and this shortage is set to increase. During the pandemic, additional retraining opportunities have been introduced, and these should be continued both during the current economic restructuring and in the longer run. In fact, increasing life expectancy and rising retirement ages make it worthwhile for firms to invest more in training their employees—including the older ones.

There is further a substantial mismatch between the skills and knowledge students deliver on entry to the labor market and what is demanded by employers. Subjects such as psychology, communication, and festival organization are hugely popular, while the largest shortages are (and will remain) in the technical areas. When choosing their studies, prospective students often fail to internalize future labor market prospects, while institutions offering these programs often have an incentive to lure as many students as possible. Government intervention may be justified in this case, by limiting the numbers of seats in academic programs with bleak labor market prospects.

The third challenge concerns the public budget's sustainability, which, in the case of the Netherlands, did not receive much attention—partly because of low borrowing costs. The coronavirus crisis caused public debt-to-GDP ratios to rise, directly through the issuance of extra debt to finance additional spending and reduced revenues and indirectly through the fall in GDP. These effects have been limited for the Netherlands, although compared to the counterfactual of no coronavirus crisis, debt would still be higher by about 7 percentage points of the GDP.[24] Still, it is important to avoid placing additional structural burdens on the public budget. New, yet-unknown shocks may hit the Dutch economy (and others), while the costs of the climate transition are so uncertain (though likely to be large) that maintaining sufficient budgetary buffers is advisable.

The fourth challenge concerns the EU policy arena. The countries with the highest levels of pre-coronavirus debt have seen the largest debt increases.[25] This seems to be no problem as long as interest rates are low. However, financial stability will be put at risk if inflation rises and the ECB is forced to raise the interest rate. The ability of the most indebted countries to absorb the additional interest costs is limited. Moreover, rising interest spreads would then soon also put banks that hold a substantial amount of this debt under pressure. In turn, the lack of fiscal space and the impaired credit channel would undermine public and private investment and job creation. No EU economy, including that of the Netherlands, would be sheltered from the eruption of a debt-cum-banking crisis. Hence, the Netherlands, together with the other EU member states, must exert pressure on countries with large public debt to build down their excessive debts.

Lessons from the Response to the COVID-19 Crisis

A number of lessons can be drawn from the COVID-19 crisis. Some are general and relevant in any crisis. Several are more specifically coronavirus related.

First, a crisis of this size almost inevitably increases the government's presence in the economy. Expenses are raised, new spending items are added, the government may acquire stakes in private companies, and new arrangements are installed. These decisions are taken at taxpayers' expense. However, their interests tend to be subordinated to the need to face the urgency at hand.

The government's larger role also changes views on the economic model. This was the case after World War II, after the global financial crisis, and now toward the end of the coronavirus crisis. In all three cases, the public's expectations about the government's role in solving societal problems were raised while the public became more suspicious about the role of the free market. However, once the government starts to directly support business, it becomes difficult to scale its role back, even if such support is no longer necessary. The NOW facility, which up to the time of writing in summer 2021 had been prolonged for a fifth time, despite the strong pickup of the Dutch economy, seems to be a good example. There is a political-economic logic to this: The political cost of cutting subsidies is larger than the political gain from the resulting tax reduction.

In normal circumstances, government stakes in private companies are outright harmful. Politicians meddle with the day-to-day business of these firms. Parliament expects the government to intervene in strategic decisions, such as reorganizations of these firms or their potential takeover by foreign companies. As a result, politics easily gets in the way of effective management. Bankruptcy is often unthinkable, because of the loss of jobs. This creates moral hazard, as it encourages the firm to take more risks in the expectation that the taxpayer acts as a backstop.

The most telling examples of this are the rescues of the airlines during the coronavirus crisis and banks during the 2008 financial crisis. The need for these rescues is not often questioned, even though the place of disappearing and (partly) publicly held airlines could be taken by private airlines. The counterargument is then that Air France–KLM avails of an excellent network of connections, but again, no one points out that other airlines can take over these connections.[26] It was clear from the outset that it would have been politically unacceptable for KLM to go bankrupt, which strengthened the position of management in the rescue deal's negotiations.

Second, emergencies expose weaknesses in the way policymaking is organized and force governments to take potentially suboptimal decisions. In the case of the coronavirus crisis, national decisions to lock down economies were uncoordinated with other countries, giving the virus more opportunities to spread. Initially, each EU country individually tried to secure the medical supplies it needed, sometimes violating the operation of the internal market by closing its borders to the export of such supplies.

Governments also find it difficult to be decisive when it might hurt specific interests. For example, when it became clear that new and more-contagious virus mutations had developed and were raging through the UK and India, the Dutch government did not immediately close the border. Such a move would have been difficult to justify after the fact because, had it been successful, the counterfactual would have been a situation in which the decision would have appeared unnecessary.

Third, as mentioned, an emergency prompts governments to spend almost without regard to the cost and efficiency of the expenditures. This makes design of the spending arrangement almost necessarily suboptimal. Business support during the pandemic is based on advance payments and after-the-fact auditing. Especially in the beginning of the coronavirus crisis, many employers overestimated the fall in their revenues. Schellekens et al. show that more than 80 percent of the companies receiving an advance payment projected a too-large drop in revenues. Nevertheless, the cabinet decided that the support for fixed costs should not be part of the revenue calculation for NOW.

The support package's design also made it susceptible to inefficiencies and abuse. Interestingly, a substantial number of firms received advance payments for TVL, but they turned out not to have any sales activity at all.[27] There were also firms that used the support to purchase real estate. Estimates of the total excess NOW support in 2020 by Schellekens et al. range from four to seven billion euros.[28] Obviously, advance payments obtained via too-high revenues or fraud will need to be reclaimed. The question is how successful that will be.

In addition, Schellekens et al. estimate that one-sixth of companies have to pay back TVL, which for 2020 will be approximately 0.2 billion euros. There is a strong case for limiting support to certain sectors or providing a lower coverage rate than 100 percent for TVL. In such a case, the administrative burden of reclaiming support would be avoided. This is why the European Commission advised a maximum coverage rate of 90 percent for SME fixed costs and 70 percent for other firms.

Fourth, the regular budgetary rules, both for the EU and nationally, have effectively been cast aside during the crisis. While this may be perceived as a natural response, it reduces respect for the rules and the transparency of the budget. One example was an increase of spending on the judiciary.[29] Since 1994, Dutch budgetary rules have imposed limits on spending growth by each broad spending category during a government's tenure. Also, the coalition agreement of Rutte III (2017–21) included ceilings for the overall government budget for health, social security, and normal government expenditure.[30]

Normally, excess spending on some item would need to be compensated by a reduction in spending elsewhere. However, this has not happened during the pandemic. It would have been more transparent to maintain the regular ceilings on spending growth unrelated to the pandemic and use an escape clause for COVID-19-specific expenditures, such as the wage subsidies. Such an approach would have implied that the extra spending on the judiciary, unrelated to COVID-19, should have been compensated elsewhere in the budget.

Fifth, the deferral of tax payments on the one hand helps stabilize an economy by preventing basically viable companies from collapsing due to acute liquidity problems. However, it also creates expectations of forfeit. Deferring taxes keeps firms that would otherwise go under afloat, thereby reducing the size of the market for their more-efficient competitors. Tax deferral may lead to more risk-taking and filing for bankruptcy to avoid having to repay the taxes. Tax forgiveness undermines further the shakeout of weaker businesses and would be unfair toward those firms that do not get this relief—and the ordinary taxpayer who has to plug the gap. Even more so, tax forgiveness may lead to expectations of future forgiveness and therefore has adverse incentive effects. One way to make tax forgiveness more palatable is to provide relief only if private creditors also provide relief.

Sixth, providing financial support to firms struggling with a large external shock mitigates the destruction of physical and human capital, thereby reducing long-run scars on the economy. Equally important, it softens the human misery associated with firms going bankrupt. However, these benefits need to be traded off against the weakening of the dynamic reallocation of production factors toward more productive use.[31] This trade-off shifts when economic conditions improve.

Support also creates zombie firms that are not fundamentally viable and only survive thanks to that support. Zombie firms are more than merely useless. They hamper their more-efficient competition and thus obstruct the creative destruction process. Indirect evidence suggests that zombie firms have been created: During the current pandemic, the number of bankruptcies has been lower even than during the period before 2020.[32]

Seventh, the way support was designed is also responsible for a missed opportunity to improve the matching of the labor force with labor demand after the crisis. Substantial numbers of workers were sent home while still receiving their full salary. Rather than allowing them to sit idle, they could have been required to beef up their human capital, for example by improving their digital and computer skills or training for work in other sectors. It is telling that quite a few personnel from KLM—for example, stewardesses—left the company and went into the health care sector. The country would benefit from systematic training and schooling plans for its workforce that can be intensified in circumstances such as the COVID-19 pandemic.

Eighth, and related to the previous point, the COVID-19 crisis should prompt policymakers to assess how the Netherlands has organized its employment structure. During previous crises, a substantial part of the labor force was driven into self-employment. Self-employment used to be an active choice, but for many self-employed, this is no longer the case. A large fraction earns barely enough to stay above the social minimum. Clearly this group is at great risk when the economy is hit by a large shock, as the current crisis shows.

"Self-employment" often stands for work with limited content in terms of skills and schooling. The so-called "social partners" (trade unions and employer organizations) have recently advised a minimum hourly compensation for self-employed people who are hired by a firm.[33] However, this does not solve the fundamental problem with a substantial fraction of the self-employed: They provide low-skilled services for which there is limited demand relative to the supply. The best solution would be more investment in the workforce's knowledge and skills, both in firms and among the self-employed. Tax incentives could play an important role in this regard.

Conclusion

This chapter has laid out the Dutch government's economic measures in response to the coronavirus crisis. The government responded fast, with massive business support, thereby preventing, on the one hand, a lot of harm and long-term scarring of the economy and, on the other hand, substantial misery at the individual level. Policies were adjusted along the way according to what was needed, and parliament was frequently informed.

This does not preclude that, with hindsight, some policies could have been improved. For this reason, this chapter also discusses some potential policy lessons about the current crisis response. For example, even though a major shock may come totally unexpectedly and be of a nature that has not been seen before, it is worthwhile to have a crisis plan ready that allows for fast-tracking spending and spells out potential conditions for such spending. Because a crisis generally requires sectoral reallocation, such conditions should be designed with a specific eye toward the need for maintaining human capital and retraining personnel to ease the unavoidable eventual sectoral reallocations.

Acknowledgments

The authors thank Tjerk Budding, Michael R. Strain, and Stan Veuger for their helpful comments on an earlier version of this chapter. All remaining errors are our sole responsibility. The views expressed in this chapter are those of the authors and do not necessarily represent those of the institutions with which they are affiliated.

Notes

1. Frank Vandenbroucke et al., "The European Commission's SURE Initiative and Euro Area Unemployment Re-Insurance," Centre for Economic Policy Research, VoxEU, April 6, 2020, https://voxeu.org/article/european-commission-s-sure-initiative-and-euro-area-unemployment-re-insurance.

2. European Commission, "State Aid: Commission Gives Green Light to the Pan-European Guarantee Fund to Enable up to €200 Billion Financing for Companies Affected by the Coronavirus Outbreak in 21 Member States," press release, December 14, 2020, https://ec.europa.eu/commission/presscorner/detail/en/ip_20_2407.

3. European Central Bank, "Pandemic Emergency Purchase Programme (PEPP)," December 7, 2021, https://www.ecb.europa.eu/mopo/implement/pepp/html/index.en.html.

4. Depending on the Standaard Bedrijfsindeling (SBI) codes, the percentage fixed costs of revenue range from 7 percent (for employment agencies) to 62 percent (for airlines) and even 72 percent (for film production). For example, restaurants with at least a 30 percent revenue fall could apply for this support, which, in the beginning, then covered 50 percent of the estimated fixed cost of their *x* percent drop in revenue. In the fourth quarter (Q4) of October 2020, the coverage rate was raised to 50–70 percent; in January 2021 it was raised to 85 percent; and since April 2021 it has been 100 percent. It is likely practically impossible to base the Reimbursement of Fixed Costs of Small and Medium-Size Enterprises (TVL) on firm-specific fixed costs. It may also be undesirable: By benchmarking on the average in the sector, an advantage is given to the most efficient firms, and a disincentive effect for increasing efficiency (i.e., a "moral hazard") is mitigated.

5. In the first round, this TVL was equal for all firms and thus not dependent on SBI codes.

6. EU Publications Office, EUR-Lex, "Communication from the Commission: Temporary Framework for State Aid Measures to Support the Economy in the Current COVID-19 Outbreak," 2020, https://eur-lex.europa.eu/legal-content/EN/TXT/?uri=OJ%3AJOC_2020_091_I_0001.

7. Initially, the reimbursement of fixed costs was included in small and medium-size enterprises' (SME) revenue calculation, thereby affecting the eligibility for and amount received from the Temporary Emergency Bridging Measure to Preserve Employment (NOW). This was corrected, starting with the third round of the NOW.

8. This inventory allowance was based on a higher coverage rate for TVL. For restaurants, it was raised by 2.8 percentage points in 2020 Q4 and 2021 Q1. For nonfood retail, it was raised by 5.6 percentage points in Q4 and 21 percentage points in Q1. Consequently, the compensation of fixed costs for nonfood retail was 106 percent in Q1 (i.e., 85 percent plus 21 percent).

9. Netherlands Ministry of Economic Affairs and Climate, "Kamerbrief over het steun- en herstelpakket vanaf het vierde kwartaal van 2021," August 30, 2021, 8, https://www.rijksoverheid.nl/documenten/kamerstukken/2021/08/30/kamerbrief-steun--en-herstelpakket-vanaf-het-4e-kwartaal-van-2021.

10. Netherlands Bureau for Economic Policy Analysis, *Balansherstel bedrijven na corona*, May 2021, https://www.cpb.nl/sites/default/files/omnidownload/CPB-Corona-publicatie-Balansherstel-bedrijven-na-corona.pdf.

11. Netherlands Court of Audit, "Individual Support to Companies During the Corona Crisis: Lessons Learned from the Past Often Applied," November 12, 2020, https://english.rekenkamer.nl/latest/news/2020/11/12/individual-support-for-companies-during-the-corona-crisis-lessons-learned-from-the-past-often-applied.

12. Netherlands Court of Audit, "Individual Support to Companies During the Corona Crisis."

13. Netherlands Ministry of Finance, *Kamerbrief Steunmaatregelen KLM*, June 26, 2020, https://www.rijksoverheid.nl/documenten/kamerstukken/2020/06/26/kamerbrief-steunmaatregelen-klm.

14. Netherlands Court of Audit, "Individual Support to Companies During the Corona Crisis."

15. Netherlands Ministry of Economic Affairs and Climate, *Kamerbrief over de bijdrage van de Staat aan de continuïteit van het bedrijf IHC*, April 30, 2020, https://www.rijksoverheid.nl/documenten/kamerstukken/2020/04/30/kamerbrief-over-de-bijdrage-van-de-staat-aan-de-continuiteit-van-het-bedrijf-ihc.

16. Netherlands Court of Audit, "Individual Support to Companies During the Corona Crisis," 6.

17. Netherlands Bureau for Economic Policy Analysis, "Macro Economic Outlook 2022," September 2021, https://www.cpb.nl/sites/default/files/omnidownload/CPB-Projections-Macro-Economic-Outlook-MEV-2022.pdf.

18. Netherlands Bureau for Economic Policy Analysis, *June Projections 2021*, June 2021, https://www.cpb.nl/sites/default/files/omnidownload/CPB-June-Projections-2021.pdf.

19. The UK's loss is estimated at 5.4 percent, in terms of value added. The UK's larger loss is a logical result of the fact that its exports to the EU are substantially higher as a share of total UK exports than exports to the UK as a share of individual EU countries' total exports. Netherlands Bureau for Economic Policy Analysis, "Projections March 2021 (CEP 2021)," March 31, 2021, https://www.cpb.nl/en/projections-march-2021-cep-2021.

20. Menno Schellekens, Anne Li Cnossen, and Rianne 't Jong, "Terugvordering coronasteun wordt miljardenoperatie," *Economisch Statistische Berichten* 106, no. 4799 (July 7, 2021): 309–11.

21. Therefore, Menno Schellekens, Jeroen Wijnen, and Anne Li Cnossen compare the number of full-time equivalents in firms with more than 20 percent loss of revenue in 2019 and 2020. In 2019, this was 29,600, and in 2020, this was 41,500. See Menno Schellekens, Jeroen Wijnen, and Anne Li Cnossen, "Coronasteun compenseerde flink deel reguliere omzetverliezen," *Economisch Statistische Berichten* 106, no. 4799 (2021): 309–11.

22. Netherlands Ministry of Economic Affairs and Climate, "Kamerbrief over het steun- en herstelpakket vanaf het vierde kwartaal van 2021," August 30, 2021, https://www.rijksoverheid.nl/documenten/kamerstukken/2021/08/30/kamerbrief-steun--en-herstelpakket-vanaf-het-4e-kwartaal-van-2021.

23. Roel Beetsma and Sylvester C. W. Eijffinger, "Wet CO2-heffing voor industrie vatbaar voor verbetering," *Reformatorisch Dagblad*, August 26, 2020, https://www.digibron.nl/viewer/collectie/Digibron/id/tag:RD.nl,20200826:newsml_pr16124345. The revenues generated from a given sector's emissions could be distributed back to the firms in the sector—for example, giving back the same amount for each euro of revenue generated. Those firms that produce this euro with a high amount of emission compared to their sectoral peers will be at a relative disadvantage and, hence, induced to invest in cleaner technology.

24. The public debt predicted in the 2020 budget (presented in September 2019) was 47.7 percent of gross domestic product. The latest estimate for 2020 was 54.3 percent. (See Table 3 of this chapter.) Netherlands Bureau for Economic Policy Analysis, *Macro Economische Verkenning 2022*, September 2021, https://www.cpb.nl/sites/default/files/omnidownload/CPB-Raming-Macro-Economische-Verkenning-MEV-2022.pdf.

25. Roel Beetsma et al., *Consistent Paths Towards a Stable and Resilient European Economy*, Dutch European Economy Expert Group, June 30, 2021, Figure 2.11, https://www.rijksoverheid.nl/documenten/kamerstukken/2021/07/08/management-summary-of-the-report-showing-our-colours-for-a-stable-and-resilient-european-economy.

26. Roel Beetsma and Raymond Gradus, "Moet KLM gered worden?," Me Judice, June 11, 2020, https://www.mejudice.nl/artikelen/detail/moet-klm-gered-worden.

27. As Jan van Helden et al. write, "Accountability to parliament focused on the applicability of arrangements for specific groups, such as season sensitive businesses." However, causal links between the resources made available and the outcomes in terms of avoiding bankruptcies and unemployment were difficult to establish. See Jan van Helden et al., "COVID-19 Business Support Packages in the Netherlands; Governance and Accountability in Times of Turbulence," University of Groningen, *Mimeo*, 2021.

28. Mark Koster and Remy Koens, "7 miljard NOW-subsidies ging naar vastgoed, overnames en de spaarpot," *Follow the Money*, August 9, 2021, https://www.ftm.nl/artikelen/zeven-miljard-now-subsidies-te-veel-coronatijd.

29. Raymond Gradus, "Doelmatigheid: het kind van de rekening," *Tijdschrift voor Public Governance, Audit & Control*, 2020, 12, https://www.rvo.nl/octrooiportal/catalogus/tijdschrift-voor-public-governance-audit-en-control-tpc.

30. See VVD, CDA, D66 en ChristenUnie, *Vertrouwen in de toekomst, Regeerakkoord 2017–2021*, October 10, 2017, https://www.rijksoverheid.nl/documenten/publicaties/2017/10/10/regeerakkoord-2017-vertrouwen-in-de-toekomst.

31. The longer the support lasts, the more firms will adjust their behavior accordingly, as they come to expect government rescue when things go wrong. Arnoud W. A. Boot calls this "sunflower capitalism": Analogous to sunflowers turning toward the sun, firms turn their activities and expectations toward the government. Arnoud W. A. Boot, "De dominantie van de overheid in het economisch proces moet stoppen," *Economisch Statistische Berichten* 106, no. 4799 (2021): 314–17.

32. See Figure 13 in Hugo Erken and Nic Vrieselaar, *Waarom de werkloosheid ondanks de coronacrisis amper opliep*, July 16, 2021, https://economie.rabobank.com/publicaties/2021/juli/waarom-de-werkloosheid-ondanks-de-coronacrisis-amper-opliep.

33. If the hired person is paid less, they would be considered part of the firm's workforce, implying that the firm has to pay social contributions.

8

Labor Hoarding and Employment Protection During the COVID-19 Crisis in a Dual Labor Market: Spain

JUAN F. JIMENO

The COVID-19 pandemic provides a big natural experiment to assess the costs and benefits of labor hoarding. Being a transitory shock (although of uncertain duration) and given that its main transmission to economic activity was through short-term confinement of populations, forced lockdowns, and shutdown of firms, the incentives of all agents involved (employers, workers, and government) were aligned to favor labor hoarding. Hence, not surprisingly, in many countries, job-retention schemes (JRSs) were, quantitatively and qualitatively, the main instrument to protect employment and workers' rents during the pandemic.[1]

Nevertheless, JRS design and its effectiveness at protecting employment during a temporary crisis depend on the labor market's institutional and structural characteristics. Interactions with employment protection legislation (EPL), unemployment benefits, and hiring and firing patterns are key in assessing the potential contribution of JRSs to keep employer-worker links during the pandemic.

The Spanish labor market has a dual structure, with about three-fourths of workers employed under permanent contracts that give entitlements to high employment protection, while the rest are employed under short-term determined-duration employment contracts that employers can terminate at low cost. More than 90 percent of new hires take place under temporary contracts, the conversion rate of temporary into permanent employment is low, and the incidence of temporary employment is significantly higher in sectors that the pandemic harmed most (tourism, construction, hotels and restaurants, and recreation activities). Moreover, because unemployment insurance is designed under a contributory scheme, the protection provided by unemployment benefits in case of dismissal is also unequal between permanent and temporary workers.

Additionally, the Spanish labor market has experienced successive reforms since the mid-2000s and, after a big reshuffling of employment following the bursting of a housing bubble and the Great Recession, was coping with the polarization, population-aging, and automation trends that call for a big reallocation of labor across sectors and occupations. If anything, the COVID-19 shock has accelerated these trends, worsening wage and earning inequalities; widening the scope for automation, robotization, and digitalization; and, hence, increasing the scope of labor reallocation.[2]

Under these premises, the first section of this chapter briefly reviews EPL and other institutional and structural characteristics of the Spanish labor market that are relevant when discussing JRSs. The next section describes JRS design, implementation, and incidence in Spain during the pandemic. The third section assesses the cost-effectiveness of Spanish JRSs and distills lessons for the future, both during normal and exceptional times. A final section remarks on the future prospect for JRSs in Spain.

The Spanish Labor Market: Some Structural and Institutional Background

Certain institutional and structural features of the Spanish labor market are relevant for analyzing the impact of the COVID-19 crisis.

Employment, Sectoral, and Occupational Compositions and the Incidence of Teleworking. The Spanish labor market is well-known for displaying a persistently high (and volatile) unemployment rate and a huge incidence of atypical (e.g., temporary, seasonal, and part-time) employment (Figure 1, Panels A and B). In the past two big recessions (1992–93 and 2008–14), the unemployment rate almost reached 25 percent, and even after recovery from the Great Recession, it was about 15 percent just before the pandemic hit. Nonpermanent employment (employees not employed under the regular open-ended contract entitled to full EPL protection) was above 30 percent and declined to only 25 percent after the Great Recession.[3]

Figure 1. Unemployment, Nonpermanent Employment, and Worker Flows

Panel A. Unemployment Rate (Percentage of the Labor Force)

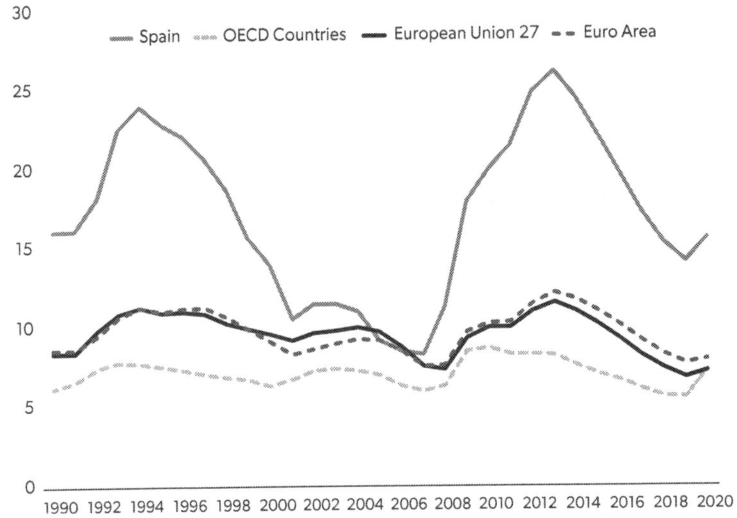

Panel B. Nonpermanent Employment (Percentage of Dependent Employment)

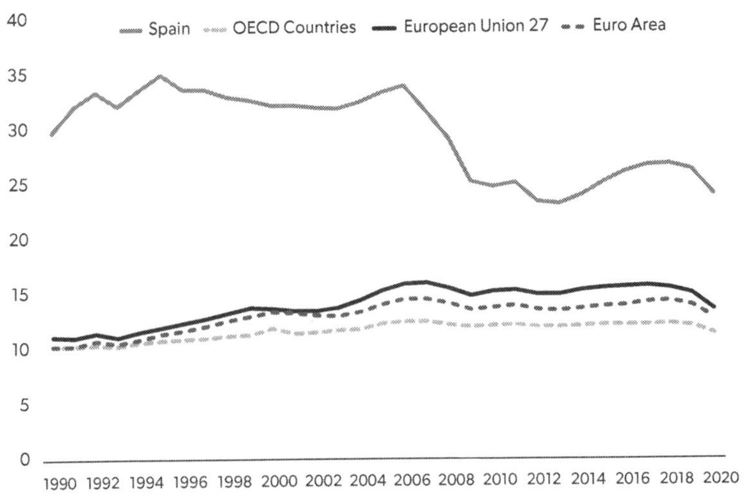

(continued on the next page)

Figure 1. Unemployment, Nonpermanent Employment, and Worker Flows (*continued*)

Panel C. Worker Flows (Percentage of Origin Status)

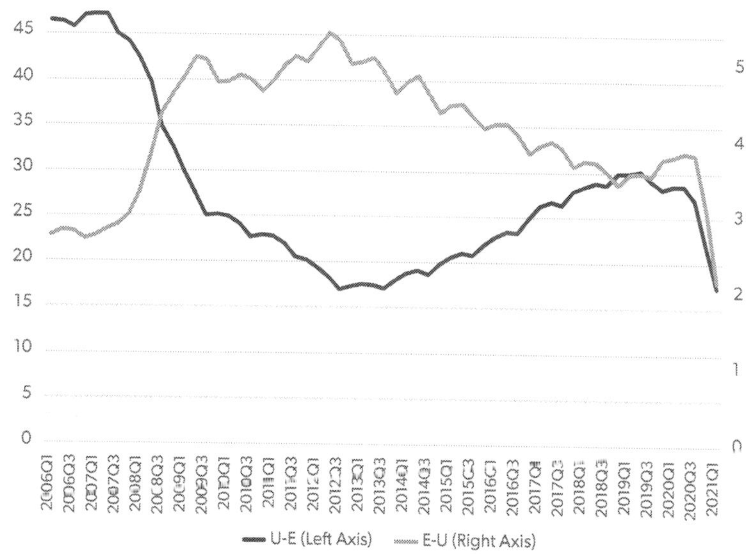

Note: "U-E" is the unemployment to employment transitions as a percentage of past-quarter unemployed; "E-U" is the employment to unemployment transitions as a percentage of past-quarter employed. Source: Organisation for Economic Co-operation and Development, *OECD Employment Outlook 2021: Navigating the COVID-19 Crisis and Recovery*, July 7, 2021, https://www.oecd-ilibrary.org/employment/oecd-employment-outlook-2021_5a700c4b-en; and Spanish National Statistics Institute, Labor Force Survey, Q3 2021, October 28, 2021, https://www.ine.es/dyngs/INEbase/es/operacion.htm?c=Estadistica_C&cid=1254736176918&menu=ultiDatos&idp=1254735976595.

The short duration of nonpermanent employment contracts and the high unemployment rate generate a labor market with large worker flows in and out of employment, with marked seasonal patterns (Figure 1, Panel C). Every quarter, about 3 percent of employees (up to 5 percent in recessionary periods) lose their jobs and enter into unemployment, while about 25 percent of the unemployed find new jobs. This suggests that, when adjusting their labor forces to varying economic conditions, Spanish firms considered labor hoarding as the main alternative only for a restricted set of high-skilled workers in specific occupations.[4]

Figure 2. Composition of Employment (Circa 2019)

Panel A. By Sector of Activity (Selected)

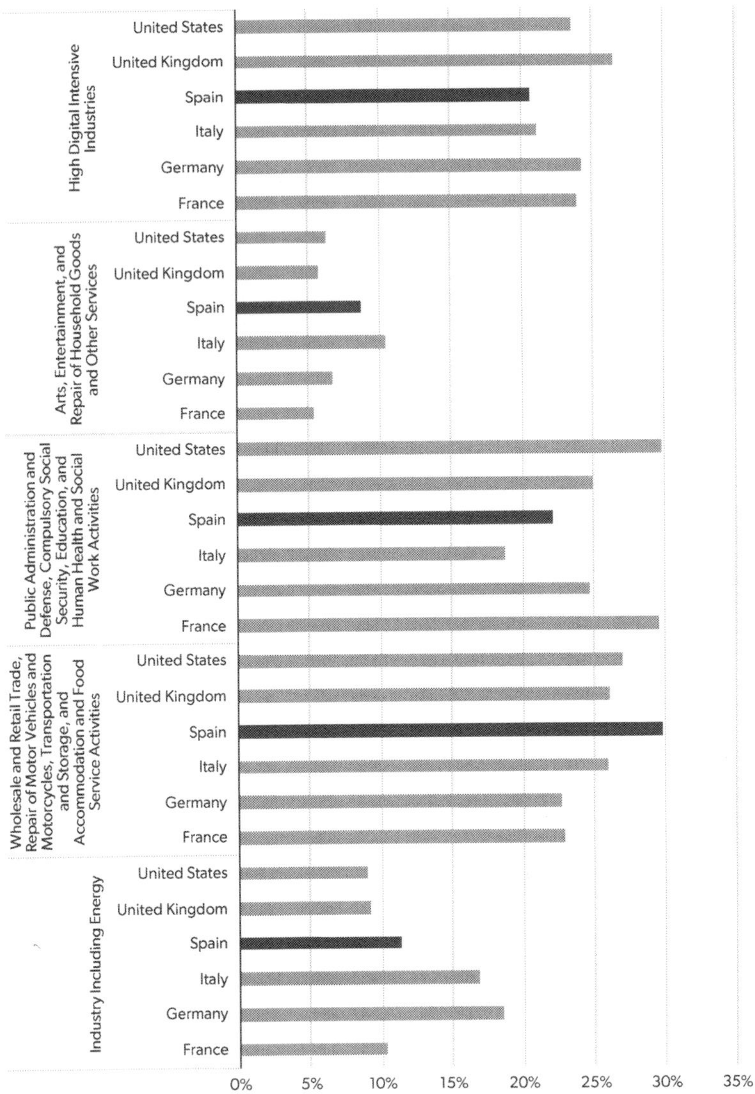

(*continued on the next page*)

Figure 2. Composition of Employment (Circa 2019) (*continued*)

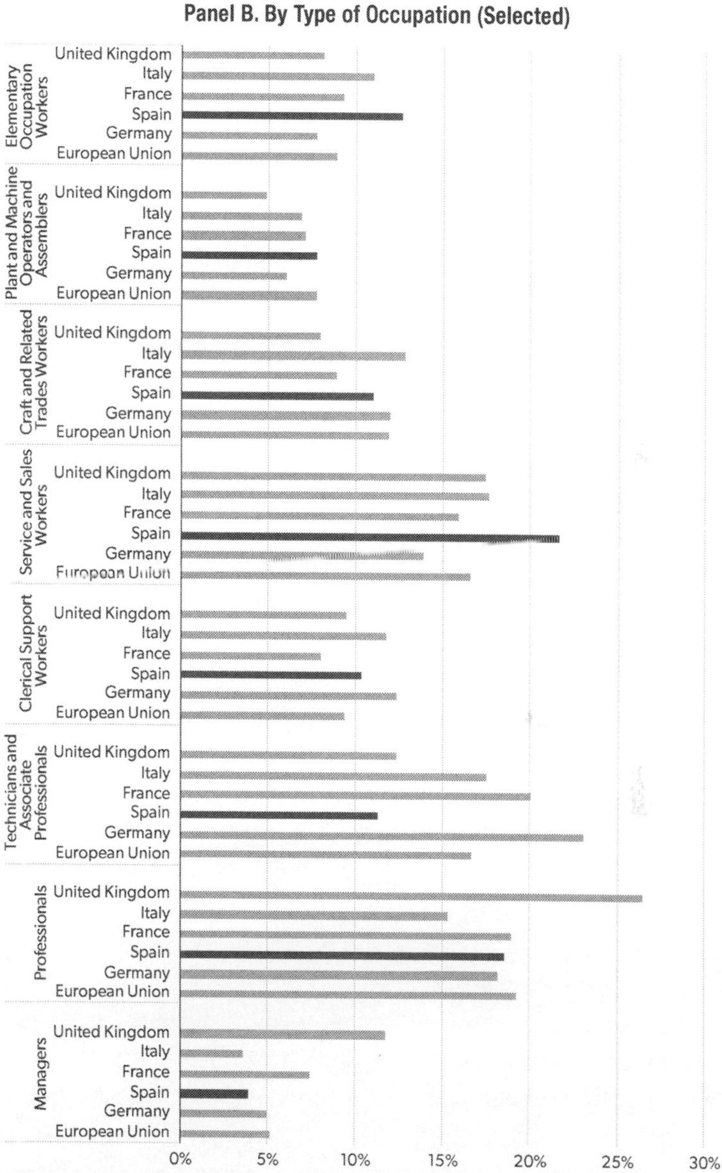

Source: Organisation for Economic Co-operation and Development, *OECD Employment Outlook 2021: Navigating the COVID-19 Crisis and Recovery*, July 7, 2021, https://www.oecd-ilibrary.org/employment/oecd-employment-outlook-2021_5a700c4b-en; and European Commission, Eurostat, https://ec.europa.eu/eurostat/data/database.

As for the sectoral composition of employment, Spain used to have a large share of employment in activities related to the construction sector (close to 15 percent). After the bursting of the housing bubble and the European debt crises during the early 2010s, the share of employment in construction decreased significantly, while it continued growing in market services—mostly tourism, restaurants, and cultural and recreation activities—sectors that have significantly larger employment shares than they do in other European countries. In contrast, there is a small share of workers in highly digital-intensive industries, which suggests a low scope for teleworking (Figure 2, Panel A). The composition of employment by occupations, which partly reflects the sectoral composition, shows large shares of service and sales workers and workers employed in elementary occupations and a small share in digital industries (Figure 2, Panel B).[5]

With this sectoral and occupational composition of employment, Spain was ill prepared to cope with the pandemic's labor market consequences. Figures 3 and 4 display, respectively, the COVID-19 crisis's impact on teleworking and the suspension of work while keeping the employer-employee link.[6] First, there was a substantial increase of teleworking in 2020, but it was smaller (7 percentage points) and from a lower level (2.5 percent) than it was in Germany, France, and Italy and for the EU average. Secondly, there was a substantial increase in the proportion of employees who did not work for several reasons: absenteeism, sickness leave, paternity and maternity leave, holidays and vacations, and, mostly, JRSs (as documented below).

Thus, the proportion of private-sector workers not working while occupied reached 16 percent in 2020, doubling its usual incidence (even during the Great Recession of the early 2010s) and closing the gap with the proportion of public-sector workers not working while occupied, which increased only from around 14 to 16 percent. In sum, the pandemic's impact on employment was somehow lessened by teleworking (to a minor extent compared to other countries and with large differences across sectors of activity[7]) and various forms of suspending work (mostly JRSs).

EPL, Unemployment Benefits, and JRSs. Spanish EPL, which used to be one of the most restrictive in Europe, now allows different routes for terminating employment contracts, with alternative firing costs depending on the cause of the firing and the nature of the contract. First, there

Figure 3. Share of Employees Usually Working from Home (Percentage)

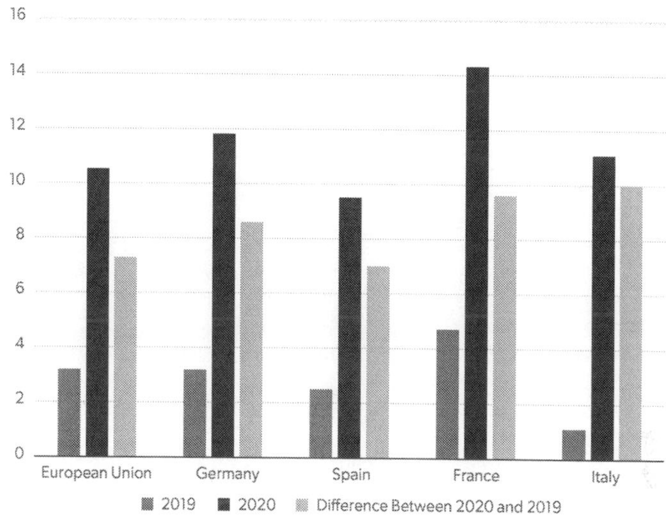

Source: European Commission, Eurostat, https://ec.europa.eu/eurostat/data/database.

Figure 4. Occupied Persons Who Did Not Work (Percentage)

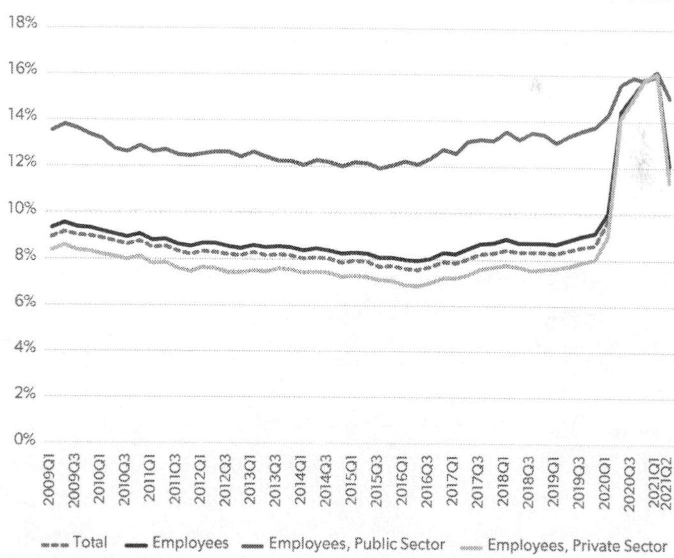

Source: Spanish National Statistics Institute, Labor Force Survey, Q3 2021, October 28, 2021, https://www.ine.es/dyngs/INEbase/es/operacion.htm?c=Estadistica_C&cid=1254736176918&menu=ultiDatos&idp=1254735976595.

is the distinction between disciplinary layoffs (caused by the employee's low performance) and economic dismissals for economic, technological, or organizational reasons. Secondly, when affecting more than 10 percent of the firm labor force, economic dismissals follow a different procedure subject to negotiations with worker representatives and administrative control (called *expediente de regulación de empleo*).

Thirdly, severance payments vary depending on negotiations and court rulings about the "fairness" of the cause of the firing. Employees dismissed under fair economic reasons are entitled to a severance pay of 20 days' wages per year of seniority, with a maximum of 12 months' wages. Employees laid off because of a fair disciplinary cause do not receive severance pay. If either the economic dismissal or the disciplinary layoff is ruled unfair, severance pay is 33 days' wages per year of seniority, with a maximum of 24 months' wages. When the firing is ruled null (if there is either discrimination, violation of the employee's fundamental rights, or breach of union rights), the worker is entitled to choose between reinstatement and the severance payments of an unfair dismissal.

All the above applies to workers under the regular permanent employment contracts. Workers employed under "atypical" contracts are typically dismissed, not by firings, but upon termination of the contract (with much lower severance pay, if any), and these terminations are rarely appealed to labor courts. Hence, employers use fixed-term contracts and other kinds of temporary contracts to buffer against negative shocks leading to downsizing of their labor forces, which leaves small scope for labor hoarding and generates unusually high employment volatility.[8]

Unemployment insurance provides (contributory) benefits to employees who, having worked for more than a year, become unemployed or have working-hours reduction between 10 and 70 percent of the normal working hours. (If the reduction is larger than 70 percent, there is full coverage as if the worker were unemployed; if the reduction is smaller than 10 percent, there is no coverage.) These benefits last for four months for each year worked in the past six years. Entitled workers receive 70 percent of wages during the first six months and 50 percent of the wage afterward. Benefits are capped depending on family situation. Additionally, there is a means-tested subsidy for workers who exhausted the contributory unemployment benefits or are above age 52.

A second pillar of unemployment subsidies covers workers whose previous employment spells were below one year but above six months. These subsidies amount to around 450 euros per month for six months. Workers with family dependents are entitled to the unemployment subsidy if the previous employment spell was larger than three months, and they can receive it for up to 21 months. The unemployment subsidy is means-tested, covering only individuals with total income below 75 percent of the minimum wage (which was about 1,100 euros per month in 2020).

JRSs, called *expedientes de regulación temporal del empleo* (ERTEs) in Spain's case, were already contemplated in the Spanish labor legislation before the pandemic. Employers could either suspend or reduce working hours due to economic, technological, organizational, or productive causes or unforeseeable circumstances that prevent fulfilling the employment contract (i.e., force majeure). Economic causes are the existence of losses, either actual or expected, and permanent reductions in sales or revenues. Technological and organizational causes are changes in the means, instruments, systems, and methods of production. Productive causes are changes in demand of the goods and services the firm produced.

To implement an ERTE, the employer has to communicate it to the labor administrative office in charge and open a period of negotiations (maximum 15 days) with worker representatives. In the case of agreement between employer and worker representatives, the existence of legal causes is accepted. The administrative office in charge of unemployment benefits can appeal the agreement if it implies undue benefits for the workers. During either suspensions or working-hours reductions, training activities should be promoted to increase worker employability. Salaries are reduced accordingly, and workers receive unemployment benefits for 70 percent of the salary reduction.

During the duration of the ERTE, a worker's entitlement to unemployment benefits (contributory system) is reduced accordingly. That is, for each month under the ERTE, the duration of entitlements to future unemployment benefits is diminished by one month, as if the worker were unemployed. Employers continue paying social security contributions for workers under ERTEs but could be entitled to reductions of social security contributions in case of force majeure if approved by the labor administrative office.

Figure 5. Workers Affected by Collective Dismissals and ERTEs, Spain, January 1977–February 2020

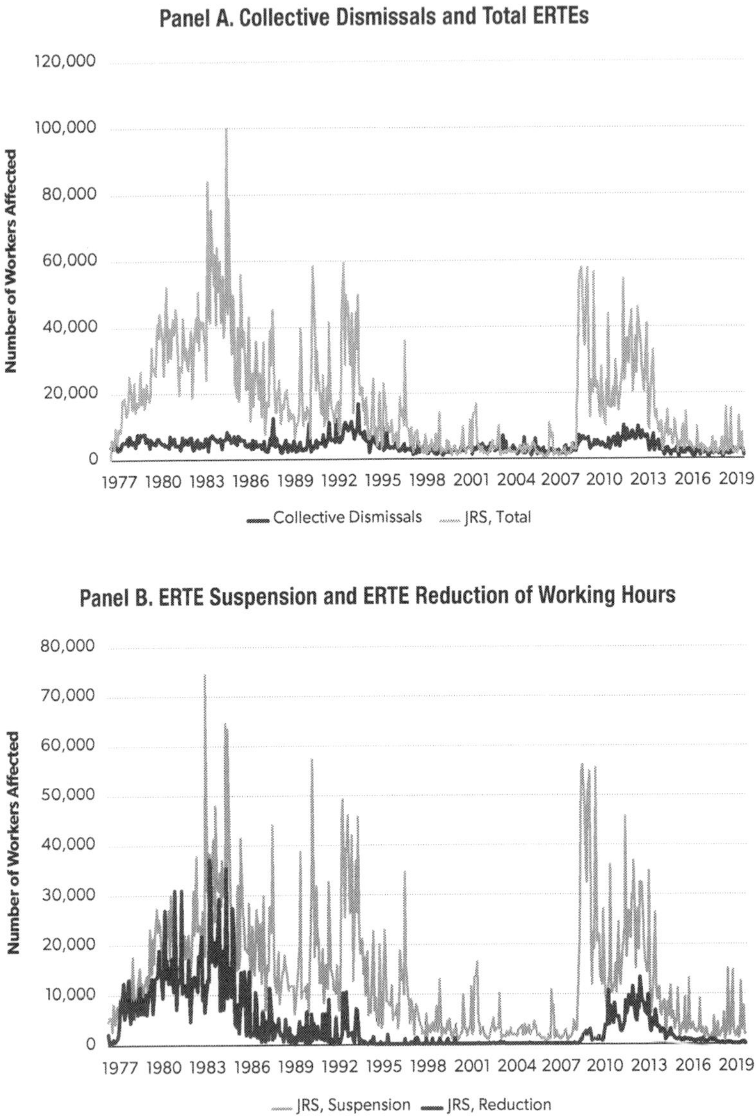

Source: Spanish Ministry of Labor and Social Economy, "Estadísticas" [Statistics], https://www.mites.gob.es/es/estadisticas/index.htm.

During the pre-pandemic period, the number of workers affected by ERTEs (either by total suspension of work or reduced working hours) was relatively low. Even during deep recessions (the beginning of the 1980s, 1992–93, and 2008–14), ERTEs did not play a significant role as an alternative to employment adjustments: The number of workers affected never surpassed 1 percent of the labor force. ERTEs were mostly implemented to suspend the employment relationship rather than reduce working hours. However, in both cases the incidence was low, although it was significantly higher than was the incidence of collective dismissals—that is, firings due to economic, technological, or organizational reasons involving more than 10 percent of the firm labor force. (See Figure 5.)

Employment Policies During the COVID-19 Crisis

As in other countries, the Spanish government announced and implemented a plethora of mechanisms to support businesses during the pandemic.[9] These measures include income support for households, provision of liquidity and easing of credits (through government-backed loans and tax deferrals), and direct grants to businesses. Nevertheless, the most important intervention for smoothing out the economic impact of the COVID-19 economic crisis has been the "flexibilization" and extension of JRSs (which in Spain's case are implemented as ERTEs). Since March 2020, there have been several changes in the definition of causes that justify an ERTE, and there has been an easing of procedures, rules of implementation, and economic incentives to entry and exit from an ERTE. These changes have been continuously reconsidered in accordance with the pandemic's evolution and the confinement and lockdown measures implemented to control the health crisis.

What follows is a brief summary of the lockdown and confinement measures in place since March 2020 and the changes in JRS regulation between March 2020 and the time of writing and an account of the substantial increase in JRS incidence.

Pandemic Containment Measures and Economic Activity. Data from international sources illustrate Spain's high COVID-19 caseload and the extensive scope of the restrictions adopted to contain it. (See appendix.) During the second quarter of 2020, there was a nationwide, restrictive confinement of the population with only "vital" activities and those performed under telepresence non-suspended. Measures were relaxed during summer 2020, making Spain among the countries with the least restrictive COVID-19 containment measures. Since then, it has also been more relaxed than other European countries have been.

However, keeping track of the pandemic containment measures implemented in Spain since March 2020 is a daring task, mostly because, after the initial state of alert[10] and the "great confinement" of March–May 2020, the measures were differentially implemented across time and regions, with lots of variability in intensity, scope, and effective implementation. Textual analysis of press reports delivers indicators of the restrictions imposed because of the pandemic that correlate well with Google mobility indicators for retail and recreation outlets, transit stations, and workplaces and with indicators of economic activity (measured with a broad set of regional indicators).[11]

Overall, results confirm the insights from international data: The restriction indicator was about three times higher at the beginning of the pandemic than it was during summer and autumn 2020, but displays find substantial regional variability since mid-2020. This regional variability in the restriction indicator is closely related to the regional variability of Google mobility indicators (with an R-squared of 60 percent), which in turn is also related to the observed regional variability in economic activity (with an R-squared also close to 60 percent).

In sum, after a few months of restrictive measures that led to the almost full lockdown of most activities, especially those in which Spain has a larger share of employment, restrictions have been relaxed since mid-2020, leading to a lower incidence of lockdowns and a rise in mobility and economic activity. Despite wide regional variability in restrictions, COVID-19's effect on economic activity somehow lessened since the beginning of summer 2020.

JRS Regulation During the Pandemic. JRSs have been the main instrument to cope with the labor market impact of the COVID-19 crisis in many countries.[12] However, their designs and implementations varied intensively and extensively, mostly because of differences in the initial situations and institutional configurations of each country's labor market. Their effects in protecting jobs and reducing the risks of unemployment also differed across countries. Rather than the traditional short-term work schemes that directly subsidize hours not worked (such as the German Kurzarbeit program) or furlough schemes, which restrict support to jobs that were temporarily suspended, in Spain the changes in JRS regulation extended and made more flexible the previous ERTE.

As soon as March 17, 2020, the Spanish government opted for making ERTEs the main employment policy instrument to cope with the labor market consequences of the COVID-19 crisis. On that date, it urgently approved an easing of ERTE procedures related to force majeure and COVID-19, and it extended the coverage of unemployment benefits to all workers affected by them, including those who had employment spells below the requirement for contributory benefits (without reducing entitlement to future unemployment benefits). The ERTE flexibilization also granted rebates of social security contributions paid by employers for affected workers—by 100 percent in firms below 50 employees and by 75 percent in the rest.

Initially, the duration of ERTEs justified by either force majeure or COVID-19-related causes was linked to the duration of the state of alert. Later, the link between ERTE duration and the duration of the state of alert was eliminated, so that the flexibilization and extension of ERTEs were extended, first until June 30, 2020, and then several more times (under different conditions) until February 28, 2022.

In June 2020, a mechanism to promote the exit of workers from ERTEs was introduced. This was implemented by extending and conditioning rebates of social security contributions to workers returning to "normal activity." Thus, for workers reactivated (returning to work in firms with partial activity), the rebate was 60 percent in firms below 50 workers and 40 percent in the rest, while, for workers not reactivated, the rebate was reduced to only 35 percent and 25 percent, respectively. For firms with ongoing ERTEs and still total suspension of work but that were not directly affected by lockdowns or restrictions of economic activity, the rebates were also modified to make them decrease over time: 70 percent in July 2020, 60 percent in August 2020, and 35 percent in September 2020.

ERTEs still linked to COVID-19 restriction measures kept the same rebates as for ERTEs by force majeure. However, new ERTE rebates, even those by COVID-19 causes, were established at 80 percent and 60 percent for workers suspended and reactivated, respectively, in firms below 50 employees; they were established at 60 percent and 40 percent, respectively, in firms above 50 employees.

Another way in which ERTEs were made more flexible was the possibility of transforming ERTEs by force majeure into ERTEs justified by economic, technological, organizational, or productive causes, with the same rebates in social security contributions paid by the employers. The regulation of unemployment benefits under the ERTEs mentioned above was also maintained until September 30, 2020, but since then the duration of worker entitlements to unemployment benefits has been reduced one-to-one with ERTE duration (excluding workers with entitlements starting in 2021).

In sum, the flexibilization and extension of ERTEs during the pandemic were based on three pillars: (1) the definition of new justified causes to implement ERTEs related to the lockdowns and confinement measures, first linked to the state of alert and later to restrictions of economic activity due to pandemic containment measures; (2) an extension of unemployment benefits by not reducing entitlements of workers affected by ERTEs (in 2020); and (3) a gradual return to work with incentives aimed at accelerating the return by increasing the social security contributions rebates for returning versus non-returning workers and by decreasing these contributions over time.

These measures were complemented by others that made firings more restrictive. Thus, initially, in the case of ERTEs of force majeure, firms were obliged to maintain the same level of employment during the first six months after finalizing the ERTE. Later, this obligation was extended to workers returning to work under the incentive schemes that provide social security contribution rebates. (If breached, firms were obliged to reimburse all the rebates enjoyed during the ERTE, not only those enjoyed by the worker being reactivated.) There were also extensions of unemployment benefits to extend the coverage of household employees and temporary workers, workers fired under the trial period, workers with job offers that did not materialize because of the pandemic, workers with seasonal employment contracts in firms under ERTEs, and workers who exhausted entitlements to benefits during the state of alert.

The flexibilization and extension of ERTEs and the complementary measures mentioned above were in effect until September 30, 2021. As of today, another extension until February 28, 2022, has been implemented.

Incidence of ERTEs During the COVID-19 Crisis. The flexibilization and extension of ERTEs paved the way for a rapid increase of workers affected by either suspended employment relationships or reduced working hours. Figure 6 shows the proportion of wage earners in the private sector who have been affected by COVID-19-related ERTEs in each sector of activity. As soon as the state of alert and the strict confinement measures began, ERTEs were initiated to cover almost 30 percent of the wage earners in the private sector (roughly 3.5 percent by suspended employment relationships and the rest by reduced working hours). This incidence was, as could be expected, much higher in services than in manufacturing and construction and almost nonexistent in the primary sector.

After confinement measures ended, ERTE incidence rapidly decreased, and since July 2020, the proportion of workers affected fluctuated around 1.5 percent and 5 percent, respectively, for suspended employment relationships and reduced working hours. Preliminary data from the most recent months (June–July 2021) signal a new but slow decrease of ERTE incidence, to around 2.5 percent of wage earners in the private sector. However, as of August 2021, some sectors of activities still have significant proportions of workers under ERTEs: bars and restaurants (6.5 percent), hotels (19.5 percent), travel agencies and tour operators (29.1 percent), air transportation (23.6 percent), and sport and cultural activities (6.2 percent), with most of them affected by suspended employment relationships rather than reduced working hours.

Figure 7 illustrates the importance of ERTEs at maintaining employment during the COVID-19 crisis, by plotting the evolution of the stock of wage earners in the private sector (registered at the social security administration). Given the significant decline of economic activity—around 11 percent of gross domestic product (GDP) in 2020—the employment stock was only slightly affected: It decreased by 5 percent between February and April 2020 and then gradually recovered, with an impasse in the

Figure 6. Wage Earners Affected by ERTEs During the Pandemic

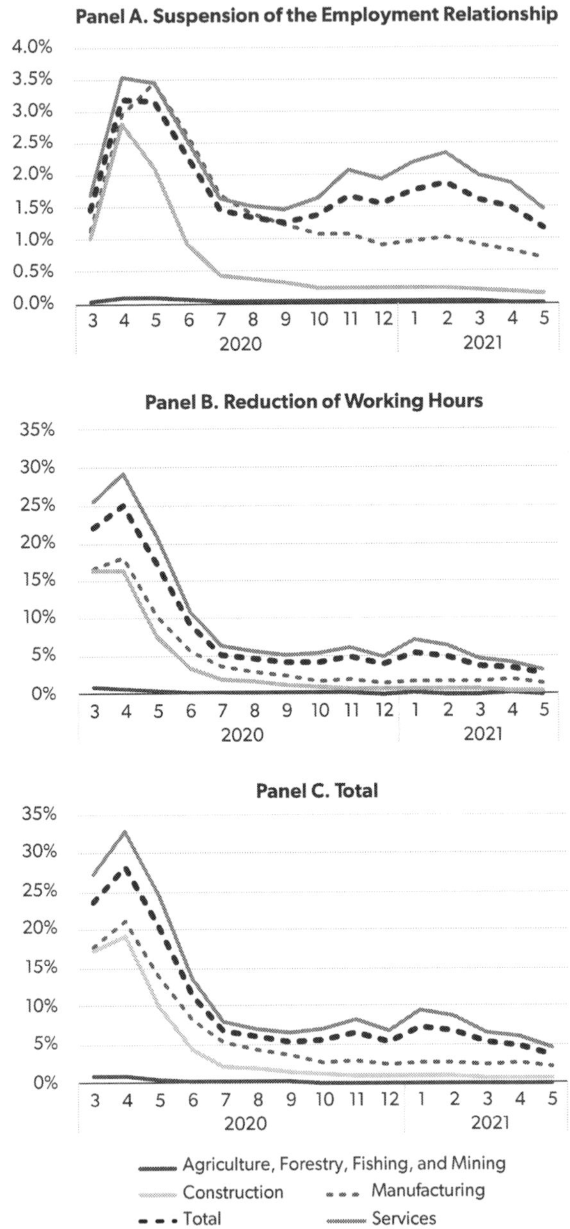

Source: Spanish Ministry of Inclusion, Social Security, and Migration, "Estadísticas" [Statistics], https://www.inclusion.gob.es/es/estadisticas/index.htm.

first quarter of 2021, until surpassing in July 2021 the level reached immediately before the pandemic began. (See Figure 7, Panel A.) Although the decrease of employment in the construction sector was largest initially, the decline of employment has been most acute and persistent in the service sector. Overall, the elasticity of employment to GDP was abnormally low.

The main reason for the break between the evolution of employment and GDP is, of course, the exceptionally high incidence of ERTEs. (See Figure 7, Panels B and C.) When taking account of the number of workers affected by either suspended employment relationships or reduced working hours, the decrease in employment in actual work was consistent with the decrease in economic activity. Thus, during the first months of the pandemic, employment (excluding ERTEs) decreased by almost 10 percent, with an additional 20 percent with reduced working hours.

Although the recovery took place almost immediately after the end of the confinement in the second quarter of 2020 (up to 95 percent of employment in February 2020, with an additional 5 percent of workers with reduced hours), the evolution of employment in actual work since then has been sluggish and is picking up only since the second quarter of 2021. Not surprisingly, the service sector, where ERTE coverage was highest, witnessed the slowest recovery of employment and was where ERTEs provided the biggest cushion at smoothing out the impact of the decrease of economic activity on employment.

As ERTEs increased their coverage and unemployment benefits were extended, the fiscal cost of these measures significantly increased. Its most evident manifestation is in the financial position of the unemployment benefits system. Revenues of this system come from a payroll tax rate of 7.05 percent of the wage bill of permanent employees and 8.3 percent of the wage bill of temporary employees. Expenditures, as described above, cover the contributory scheme for unemployed workers with previous employment spells longer than one year and subsidies, mostly for workers under special circumstances who exhausted the contributory benefits and workers with previous employment spells between three months and one year. In a typical year, revenues were about five billion euros larger than expenditures were.

Because the pandemic slowed down the increase in revenues and greatly increased expenditures (which will be permanent as workers covered

Figure 7. Wage Earners in the Private Sector

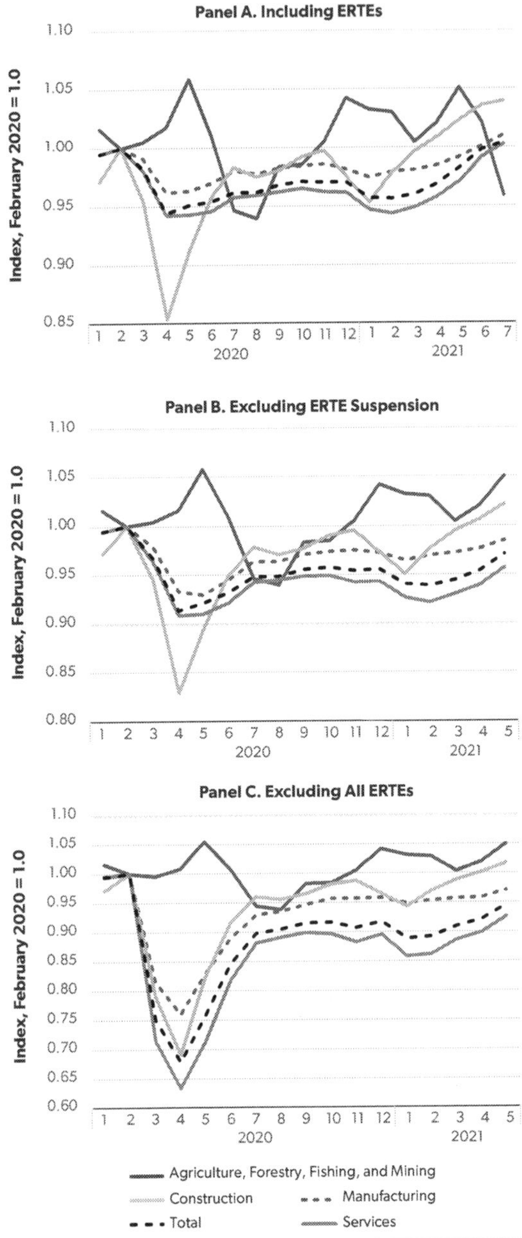

Note: February 2020 = 1.
Source: Spanish Ministry of Inclusion, Social Security, and Migration, "Estadísticas" [Statistics], https://www.inclusion.gob.es/es/estadisticas/index.htm.

Figure 8. Expenditures in Unemployment Benefits

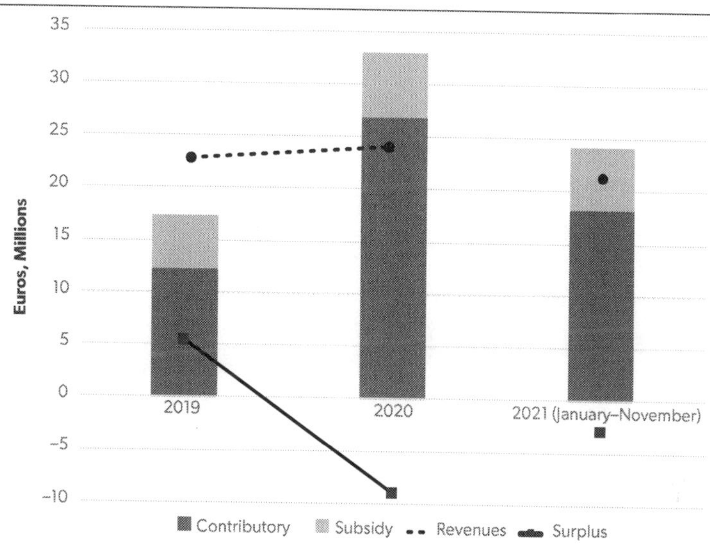

Source: Spanish Ministry of Labor and Social Economy, State Public Employment Service, "Statistics," https://www.sepe.es/HomeSepe/en/que-es-el-sepe/estadisticas.html.

under ERTEs did not fully exhaust entitlements to unemployment benefits), the deficit in 2020 reached nine billion euros, which implies the unemployment benefit system's financial position worsened by 14 billion euros (about 1.25 percent of GDP). Also, in the first half of 2021, the deficit was about 3.5 billion, so that for the whole year the deficit could be around 1 percent of GDP. (See Figure 8.) Although not all the increases in expenditures are ERTE related, the fiscal cost of ERTEs will eventually be significant.

Taking Stock: An Assessment of JRSs and Lessons for the Future

The economic rationale for JRSs is well-known. Firms may prefer to hoard labor during a temporary decrease of demand to reduce firing and hiring costs. Additionally, there are social costs to labor turnover, such as unemployment benefits, the costs of hysteresis (caused by either the depreciation of human capital in periods of unemployment or insider-outsider effects in wage determination), the consumption losses derived from lower income and uncertainty about future employment, and the psychological and health effects of uncertainty due to the unemployment situation. Thus, government and firms may find common ground to implement JRSs in situations when the decline in economic activity is expected to be temporary and short. During these periods, workers under JRSs receive wages above their productivity, employers save in destruction costs (severance pay, etc.) and job creation costs (search, selection, training, etc.), and the government helps provide a substitute for the unemployment benefits that workers would receive in case of layoffs. Hence, JRSs become an attractive measure to smooth out temporary recessions, especially in countries with high firing costs and inefficient job matching.[13]

Whether JRSs take the form of suspended employment relationships or are implemented by reducing working hours depends on the nature and size of the shock causing the decline of production and, mostly, on technological constraints of the firm affected by the shock and institutional restrictions related to the EPL. In principle, when labor is more homogenous and technology implies that the costs of fully stopping the activity are high, reducing hours seems superior to suspending employment relationships. When there is a high degree of heterogeneity among the employees and technology is more flexible, suspensions may be preferred over reduced working hours, similarly affecting the whole labor force. Other factors are also relevant; for example, given that the advantages of labor hoarding and the costs of hysteresis are greater the longer the employment relationships are at risk, JRSs are mostly targeted at more-experienced workers with longer job seniority, leaving young workers less protected and more prone to sectoral and occupational reallocation.[14]

The empirical evidence on JRS cost-effectiveness in European countries suggests that short-time JRSs saved jobs at significantly lower costs than other employment policies did, especially during the Great Recession.[15] Regarding Spain, given the low incidence of JRSs in the pre-pandemic period, no studies are available evaluating how JRSs affected employment. Moreover, it is still early for analyzing available data since March 2020, as information on the use of alternative margins of adjustment by Spanish firms is still lacking. Hence, after recognizing, as documented above, that ERTEs were instrumental at sustaining employment during the COVID-19 crisis in Spain, one can only conjecture on their costs and elements that need to be reconsidered for future improvements.

In the case of countries with a dual labor market structure such as Spain, where the main margins of adjustment are terminating temporary employment contracts and hiring new temporary employees, an important concern is the limitation of JRSs to cover workers with low attachment to firms because of the temporary employment relationship. A second source of inefficiency arises from the excessive legal complexity and the difficult management of JRSs, which create scope for significant deadweight losses (coverage of employment relationships that are bound to disappear anyway because they were not viable even before the arrival of the negative shocks causing the temporary crisis) and for distortions at choosing how many jobs in the firms need coverage and how many will be suspended versus affected by hours reductions.

The incentive schemes to reactivate workers under JRSs by rebates to social security contributions might have also generated significant deadweight losses, since in some cases workers would have been reactivated anyway as demand was increasing. The basic idea underpinning those incentives is that employers would reactivate workers more quickly if their nonwage labor costs were diminished relative to those of workers with suspended employment relationships. Although this might have played a role in the evolution of employment since mid-2020, the close connection between the recovery of demand and aggregate activity and the exit of workers from JRSs and the fact that these incentives do not significantly affect total labor costs cast doubts on their effectiveness. Still, with a longer perspective and more-detailed data, this feature of Spanish JRSs deserves closer scrutiny.

Moreover, JRS effectiveness depends crucially on duration: JRSs are more effective when the duration of the negative disturbance that caused them is shorter. At the beginning of the pandemic, it was highly uncertain how long the confinements and other restrictive measures of economic activity that were needed to contain the pandemic would last. Hence, it was a good decision to set JRS conditions for a few months and fine-tune them as the pandemic and economic uncertainty were resolved. As of today, which consequences of the pandemic on each sector of activity will be temporary and which will be permanent is still uncertain, and hence, a different approach than maintaining employment by JRSs is necessary.

JRS effectiveness also depends on companies being able to tackle other measures of internal and external flexibility of employment that complement JRSs. On this front, the Spanish experience should not be regarded as best practice. First, there were strict restrictions regarding firing workers during the pandemic: Employers were obliged to reimburse all the rebates to social security contributions if only one worker were fired within the six months before the JRS ended, and any firing justified on COVID-19-related causes was declared nil, although most labor courts end up declaring them unfair (that is, subject to higher severance payments than for fair dismissals but not requiring obligatory reinstatement of the worker as in the case of nil dismissals). Secondly, the incentives to provide training to workers under JRSs were minor (even though these workers have priority access to training courses versus those not affected by JRSs). These two drawbacks may have slowed down the adjustment of the labor force needed in the new economic environment and the reactivation of workers under JRSs.

Concluding Remarks

JRSs have become the star of employment policies during the pandemic. Having been implemented under special circumstances and with some innovations justified by the nature of this crisis, their benefits and costs need close evaluation. Time and new data will tell whether JRS cost-effectiveness was the same as in previous crises, whether the Spanish dual labor market structure and the sectoral and occupational composition of employment increased or decreased it, and whether the innovations embedded in JRS regulation worked as planned.

Judging preliminarily by the Spanish experience, JRSs were instrumental to smooth out employment during the pandemic. They reduced the hysteresis effects associated with a big decrease of employment after a temporary shock (due to unemployed worker loss of skills or to insider effects in wage determination) and saved a significant amount of firing and rehiring costs to firms, although at the cost of a significant increase in government expenditures in unemployment benefits (above and beyond those that would have occurred without JRSs). In the Spanish case, a drop of 11 percent of GDP in 2020 took place only with a decrease of employment lower than 5 percent and a rise in unemployment of only 1.5 percent (between the third quarter of 2019 and the second quarter of 2021), which is unprecedented for a country where the elasticity of employment to GDP has been historically close to one.

Nevertheless, in addition to assessing cost-effectiveness, other elements require consideration. Deadweight losses (of the JRSs and other incentives embedded in them) and the slowing down of the labor reallocation process should be closely monitored. In the case of the pandemic, even under the assumption that it will not permanently affect the sectoral and occupational structure of employment (a daring assumption), these losses may have been significant. Since the pandemic hit a dysfunctional labor market, which was already subject to the rapid aging of the labor force and automation and digitalization, JRSs may have increased wage and earning inequalities and retarded the adjustments needed to face these structural trends.

A first conclusion from this exercise is that, while JRSs can be an effective policy tool to help the labor market weather an economic downturn, they ought to be well designed, effectively implemented, and closely monitored and managed to minimize harming job creation, efficient labor reallocation, and growth. Given the nature of the problem that they could solve, timeliness, targeting, and temporary duration should be essential ingredients of well-designed JRSs.

As of today, the Spanish government's assessment of COVID-19-related JRSs has been positive. Thus, there are labor market reform proposals to make JRSs the main adjustment mechanism in economic downturns by creating a new "sustainable employment mechanism." Its goal is to make employment suspensions and reduced working hours the first response to any unexpected factors, whatever the cause, that either prevent or reduce firm activity.

However, the peculiar institutional configuration of the Spanish labor market (with its marked dual structure) and the exceptional nature of the shock caused by the COVID-19 crisis do not provide a strong basis for such a mechanism. Future and more detailed analyses of how JRSs worked during the pandemic and additional EPL reforms seem necessary for that mechanism to efficiently deal with negative economic shocks, even those that are temporary and short term.

Acknowledgments

The opinions and analyses in this chapter are the responsibility of the author and therefore do not necessarily coincide with those of the Bank of Spain or the Eurosystem.

Notes

1. See Marta Fana et al., *The COVID Confinement Measures and EU Labour Markets*, European Commission, EU Science Hub, Joint Research Centre, 2020, https://publications.jrc.ec.europa.eu/repository/handle/JRC120578.

2. See Juan J. Dolado, Florentino Felgueroso, and Juan F. Jimeno, "Past, Present and Future of the Spanish Labour Market: When the Pandemic Meets the Megatrends," *Applied Economic Analysis* 29, no. 85 (2021): 21–41, https://www.emerald.com/insight/content/doi/10.1108/AEA-11-2020-0154/full/pdf.

3. Employment is defined as salaried employment and wage earners, both under permanent contracts (open-ended and subject to firing constraints as regulated by employment protection legislation) and temporary contracts (of determined duration that can be terminated when special circumstances occur). As for unemployment, I follow the standard definition (participants in the labor market without a job and searching for one).

4. For a more detailed description of the institutional configuration of the Spanish labor market, see Samuel Bentolila, Juan J. Dolado, and Juan F. Jimeno, "Reforming an Insider-Outsider Labor Market: The Spanish Experience," *IZA Journal of European Labor Studies* 1, no. 4 (2012), https://izajoels.springeropen.com/articles/10.1186/2193-9012-1-4. For an analysis of the functioning of dual labor markets, see Samuel Bentolila, Juan J. Dolado, and Juan F. Jimeno, "Dual Labour Markets Revisited," *Oxford Research Encyclopedia of Economics and Finance* (February 28, 2020), https://oxfordre.com/economics/view/10.1093/acrefore/9780190625979.001.0001/acrefore-9780190625979-e-502?rskey=RtIFyO&result=165.

5. Elementary occupations are those that involve the performance of simple and routine tasks that may require the use of handheld tools and considerable physical effort. Most occupations in this group require skills at the first International Standard Classification of Occupations skill level.

6. As measured by Spanish National Statistics Institute, Labor Force Survey, Q3 2021, October 28, 2021, https://www.ine.es/dyngs/INEbase/es/operacion.htm?c=Estadistica_C&cid=1254736176918&menu=ultiDatos&idp=1254735976595.

7. See Juan C. Palomino, Juan G. Rodríguez, and Raquel Sebastian, "Wage Inequality and Poverty Effects of Lockdown and Social Distancing in Europe," *European Economic Review* 129 (October 2020), https://www.sciencedirect.com/science/article/pii/S001429212030194X.

8. See James Costain, Juan F. Jimeno, and Carlos Thomas, "Employment Fluctuations in a Dual Labor Market" (working paper, Banco de España, Madrid, Spain, 2010), https://repositorio.bde.es/bitstream/123456789/7011/1/dt1013e.pdf.

9. For a good taxonomy of measures to support businesses during the pandemic and an international comparison (Spain not included) of how they were implemented, see Gemma Tetlow and Grant Dalton, *Support for Business During the Coronavirus Crisis: An International Comparison*, Institute for Government, October 6, 2020, https://www.instituteforgovernment.org.uk/sites/default/files/publications/support-business-coronavirus-crisis.pdf.

10. The state of alert was first approved until June 21, 2020, but then was extended twice until November 9, 2020, and May 9, 2021.

11. Corinna Ghirelli et al., *The Relationship Between Pandemic Containment Measures, Mobility and Economic Activity*, Banco de España, March 2021, https://www.bde.es/f/webbde/SES/Secciones/Publicaciones/PublicacionesSeriadas/DocumentosOcasionales/21/Files/do2109e.pdf.

12. See Organisation for Economic Co-operation and Development, *OECD Employment Outlook 2021: Navigating the COVID-19 Crisis and Recovery*, July 7, 2021, https://www.oecd-ilibrary.org/employment/oecd-employment-outlook-2021_5a700c4b-en.

13. See, for instance, Pierre Cahuc and Stéphane Carcillo, "Is Short-Time Work a Good Method to Keep Unemployment Down?," *Nordic Economic Policy Review* 1, no. 1 (2011): 133–64.

14. Shigeru Fujita, Giuseppe Moscarini, and Fabien Postel-Vinay, "Measuring Employer-to-Employer Reallocation" (working paper, National Bureau of Economic Research, Cambridge, MA, September 17, 2021), https://papers.ssrn.com/sol3/papers.cfm?abstract_id=3649889.

15. See, for instance, Pierre Cahuc, Francis Kramarz, and Sandra Nevoux, "When Short-Time Work Works," Institute of Labor Economics, July 2018, https://www.iza.org/publications/dp/11673/when-short-time-work-works; and Florentino Felgueroso and Marcel Jansen, *Una valoración de los ERTE para hacer frente a la crisis del COVID-19 en base a la evidencia empírica y desde una perspectiva comparada* [*An Assessment of ERTEs to Fight the COVID-19 Crisis According to Empirical Evidence and Under a Comparative Perspective*], Fundación de Estudios de Economía Aplicada, June 2020, https://documentos.fedea.net/pubs/fpp/2020/05/FPP2020-06.pdf.

9

Policies to Preserve Worker-Firm Links During the Pandemic: Lessons from the UK's Coronavirus Job Retention Scheme

JONATHAN CRIBB AND PAUL JOHNSON

Each country's experience of the COVID-19 pandemic and the policy response to it has been slightly different. Among all the choices the United Kingdom's government made regarding economic policy during the pandemic, a key one was creating the Coronavirus Job Retention Scheme, better known in the UK as "the furlough scheme." This was not the only government scheme aimed at mitigating unemployment and protecting people's incomes during the pandemic, but it was the most high profile. We want to examine the furlough scheme's key judgment that it was important to keep their employees in their jobs, even if they were not working. This option was preferred to having employers make redundant millions of employees and having the state support them through an out-of-work benefit system.

This chapter aims to set out the key details regarding the UK's furlough scheme and the other accompanying policies the UK government used during the pandemic to support employees and businesses. This includes details of how the program changed over time to reflect the pandemic's changing situation and how the program's support was scaled back over the summer of 2021. In addition, we present analysis from survey and administrative data sources to assess how the furlough scheme has affected the labor market as a whole, different industries, and different types of people. Finally, we discuss some potential implications of the furlough scheme for the future.

We show that the furlough scheme, which was set up quickly at the start of the pandemic, supported at its peak 30 percent of UK employees' incomes (8.9 million people) and has cost around £70 billion during the pandemic. It was extended six times in total. The final extension came in March 2021, which announced the final closure of the scheme at the end of September 2021. There have been other important features of the scheme, such as introducing the ability to be "flexibly furloughed" while working fewer hours than usual, and there have been significant increases in the cost to employers of furloughing people, particularly as the scheme has wound down.

While it is near impossible to know how many job losses would have occurred without the scheme, the UK has experienced relatively modest falls in employment (which includes furloughed people) and rises in unemployment during the pandemic—considerably smaller than during the Great Recession, even though the fall in gross domestic product (GDP) has been much larger. Despite a spike in redundancies in late summer and autumn of 2020 (as the cost of furloughing people rose), the reemployment rates of redundant workers, particularly younger and more educated people, have also been significantly higher than during the Great Recession.

Although some increases in unemployment are forecast for the end of 2021 as the furlough scheme ends, unemployment is not a primary concern in the medium run in the UK. Surveys of employers carried out by Office for National Statistics as the scheme ended suggested that 71 percent of those still furloughed in September 2021 returned to work at or above usual hours in October, after the scheme closed, and only 3 percent of them had been made permanently redundant.[1]

With the likelihood of elevated unemployment retreating, the furlough scheme can, in many ways, be judged a success. Instead of unemployment, the greater cause of concern in the UK labor market in autumn 2021 is a large number of unfilled vacancies, particularly in a few sectors such as hospitality and heavy goods vehicle driving. While much of this is likely to be driven by other factors (including a reduced number of EU workers because of the pandemic and the UK leaving the European Union), the closure of the furlough scheme was still an important step to allow for labor to be reallocated to new uses in the aftermath of the pandemic.

The COVID-19 Pandemic in the UK

For readers not familiar with the UK's pandemic experience, it is worth setting out some basic facts about the pandemic's course and the government's response to it.

- With the number of cases and people in hospital growing rapidly, on March 16, 2020, Prime Minister Boris Johnson requested that people stop "non-essential contact with others" and "stop all unnecessary travel." March 23 was the first lockdown, in which people were given "a very simple instruction—you must stay at home." Only essential workers were able to travel to work to perform their jobs. Registered deaths from COVID-19 peaked at over 1,000 per day in early April and then fell rapidly.[2]
- As the lockdown was eased in the summer of 2020, most people had few restrictions. Throughout the autumn, the government had a tiered system of restrictions, in which restrictions were greater in areas of higher COVID-19 prevalence.
- However, cases and deaths continued to rise through the autumn to around 400 deaths per day by the end of October, leading to a one-month second lockdown in November.
- The UK medicines regulator approved the Pfizer and AstraZeneca vaccines in December 2020, with the successful rollout (starting with health care workers and the elderly) accelerating in January 2021. A 12-week gap between doses was introduced in February.
- As the more transmissible Kent variant (subsequently named alpha) spread through the UK in December, the government announced a third national lockdown on January 4, 2021. Deaths per day peaked at around 1,400 in mid-January, after which they fell rapidly.
- Lockdown restrictions were lifted gradually between early March (when schools reopened) and mid-July (when almost all domestic restrictions were lifted).
- The delta variant, combined with lifted restrictions, has led to another wave in COVID-19 infections during the late summer and autumn, though deaths per day averaged 100–150 between late August and early November. This is thanks to almost 88 percent of people age 12 and over being vaccinated by early November, with near-universal coverage among the older population. Booster vaccinations started in early October 2021.

The Coronavirus Job Retention Scheme

The UK Chancellor of the Exchequer Rishi Sunak announced the creation of the Coronavirus Job Retention Scheme (i.e., the furlough scheme) on March 20, 2020, just before the first full lockdown. This was a policy unlike any other in modern British history in terms of its scale and the speed with which it was devised and because it provided such a high rate of earnings replacement for people who would likely otherwise have been made unemployed.

The key policy decision was that the government would pay employers to furlough their employees, covering 80 percent of pre-pandemic pay up to a cap of £2,500 per month (around $3,250 or €3,000, based on pre-pandemic exchange rates). This meant that the government would provide 80 percent of pay for anyone earning up to £37,500—around the 75th percentile of pre-pandemic annual pay. Pre-pandemic pay was measured as usual pay plus overtime (not including any bonuses, noncash pay, or employer pension contributions) and was based on the pay period that ended on or before March 19, 2020. In practice, this means that for most employees (who are paid monthly), it was based on pay in February 2020. Firms could not reduce furlough pay below 80 percent of this level. Furloughed employees were always allowed to search for work and be employed by another employer or undertake self-employment while furloughed.

Employers could choose to furlough their employees without consultation, but employees could also request to be furloughed (for example, so they could look after children or because they were clinically vulnerable to COVID-19), though these requests did not have to be granted.

Initially, employers did not face any direct financial cost of furloughing their employees. This meant that there were relatively few redundancies at the beginning of the pandemic, but employers could use the furlough scheme for some employees while making others redundant, if they wished.

Her Majesty's (HM) Revenue and Customs operated the furlough scheme by providing payments to employers, which would then distribute the payments to their furloughed employees through their normal payroll systems. Employers would have to make a claim for their furloughed employees between six and 14 days before the end of the pay period (usually the end of the month) to make sure employers received the funds in time to distribute them to their furloughed employees.

Furloughed employees were taxed on their furlough pay as if it were normal earned income; employees had income tax and National Insurance withheld as usual through the government's Pay-as-You-Earn tax system. Only private-sector employers were allowed to furlough employees. The chancellor backdated the scheme to March 1 and said the scheme would run until the end of May 2020, though he explicitly said he would extend it if necessary.

Table 1 shows that the furlough scheme was indeed extended multiple times—six times extending the end date of the scheme plus additional announcements that changed the terms of the scheme. Figure 1 shows that, at its peak in May 2020, 8.9 million jobs were on furlough, around 30 percent of the 29 million payrolled employees in the UK in February 2020 (or 38 percent of private-sector employees).

As restrictions were lifted, the number on furlough fell to around 2.5 million but rose again in the second lockdown (in November) and third lockdown (in January) to reach five million in mid-January 2021. The scheme finally ended on September 31, 2021. The gross cost of the furlough scheme to the government has been enormous, totaling £70 billion[3]—just over 3 percent of 2019 GDP (albeit spent over 19 months).

There have been big differences in how the furlough scheme has supported different industries and types of workers. Figure 2 shows the proportion of employees furloughed in June and October 2020, near the peak (June) and the trough (October) of furloughing that year. With hotels and restaurants closed, 73 percent of workers in accommodation and food services were furloughed in June 2020. Construction was also a shut-down sector (though not in the later lockdowns), with 58 percent furloughed. Jobs in education (9 percent) and finance and insurance (7 percent) were much less affected. Even during October 2020, 22 percent of workers in accommodation and food services were furloughed.

The differences by age were also stark in the first lockdown, with 43 percent of employees age 18–24 furloughed, compared to 26 percent for 45- to 54-year-olds. There was a U-shaped curve by age, however, with 31 percent of employees age 65 and over furloughed. This curve, though much less pronounced, was still evident in October 2020. In June 2020,

Table 1. Timeline of Announcements About the UK's Furlough Scheme

Announcement Date	Details
March 20, 2020	Furlough scheme introduced, to end May 2020 and backdated to March 1, 2020
April 17, 2020	Furlough extended until the end of June 2020
May 12, 2020	Furlough extended until the end of October 2020 Flexible furlough plus some employer contributions from August 2020
July 1, 2020	Start of flexible furlough brought forward to July from August 2020
September 24, 2020	Announcement that the furlough is to be replaced with the Job Support Scheme from November 2020 to April 2021
October 9, 2020	Job Support Scheme expanded to businesses forced to close by local restrictions
October 22, 2020	Increased generosity of Job Support Scheme is announced
October 31, 2020	Furlough scheme extended to the end of December 2020 Job Support Scheme, which was scheduled to start on November 1, postponed (and eventually scrapped)
November 5, 2020	Furlough scheme extended to the end of March 2021
December 17, 2020	Furlough extended until the end of April 2021
March 3, 2021	Furlough extended until the end of September 2021 Increased employer contributions are required from July 2021

Note: Bolded dates signify dates that the furlough scheme was introduced or extended.
Source: Her Majesty's Treasury and Rishi Sunak, "The Chancellor Rishi Sunak Provides an Updated Statement on Coronavirus," March 20, 2020, https://www.gov.uk/government/speeches/the-chancellor-rishi-sunak-provides-an-updated-statement-on-coronavirus; Her Majesty's Treasury, "Chancellor Extends Furlough Scheme to End of June," April 17 2020, https://www.gov.uk/government/news/chancellor-extends-furlough-scheme-to-end-of-june; Her Majesty's Treasury, "Chancellor Extends Furlough Scheme Until October," May 12, 2020, https://www.gov.uk/government/news/chancellor-extends-furlough-scheme-until-october; Her Majesty's Treasury, "Flexible Furlough Scheme Starts Today," July 1, 2020, https://www.gov.uk/government/news/flexible-furlough-scheme-starts-today; Her Majesty's Treasury and Rishi Sunak, "Chancellor Outlines Winter Economy Plan," September 24, 2020, https://www.gov.uk/government/news/chancellor-outlines-winter-economy-plan; Her Majesty's Treasury and Rishi Sunak, "Job Support Scheme Expanded to Firms Required to Close Due to Covid Restrictions," October 9, 2020, https://www.gov.uk/government/news/job-support-scheme-expanded-to-firms-required-to-close-due-to-covid-restrictions; Her Majesty's Treasury, "Plan for Jobs: Chancellor Increases Financial Support for Businesses and Workers," October 22, 2020, https://www.gov.uk/government/news/plan-for-jobs-chancellor-increases-financial-support-for-businesses-and-workers; Her Majesty's Treasury and Rishi Sunak, "Furlough Scheme Extended and Further Economic Support Announced," October 31, 2020, https://www.gov.uk/government/news/furlough-scheme-extended-and-further-economic-support-announced; Her Majesty's Treasury and Rishi Sunak, "Chancellor Statement to the House—Furlough Extension," November 5, 2020, https://www.gov.uk/government/speeches/chancellor-statement-to-the-house-furlough-extension; Her Majesty's Treasury, "Chancellor Extends Furlough and Loan Schemes," December 17, 2020, https://www.gov.uk/government/news/chancellor-extends-furlough-and-loan-schemes; and Her Majesty's Treasury and Rishi Sunak, "Budget Speech 2021," March 3, 2021, https://www.gov.uk/government/speeches/budget-speech-2021.

Figure 1. Number of Employments Furloughed, March 2020–September 2021

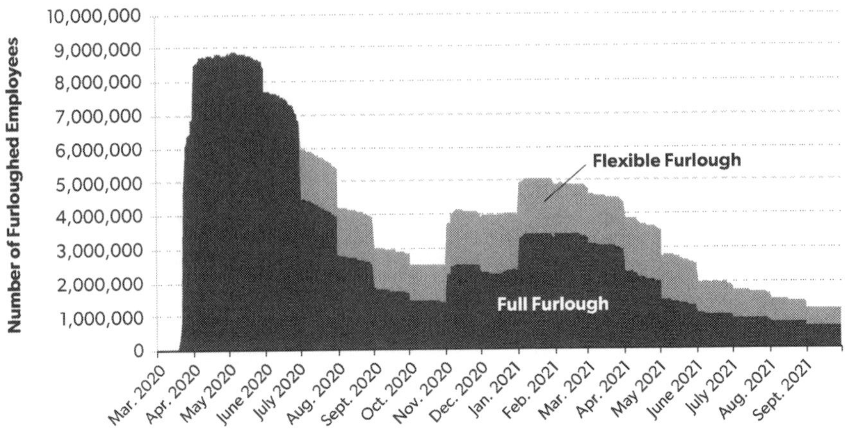

Source: Her Majesty's Revenue and Customs, "Coronavirus Job Retention Scheme Statistics: 29 July 2021," December 16, 2021, https://www.gov.uk/government/statistics/coronavirus-job-retention-scheme-statistics-16-december-2021/coronavirus-job-retention-scheme-statistics-16-december-2021.

male employees were slightly more likely to be furloughed than were female employees (32 percent vs. 27 percent), though this difference was not apparent in October.

It is worth describing a number of the changes to the scheme that occurred during its lifetime.

Flexible Furlough. Originally planned for August 2020 but brought forward by a month to July 2020, the flexible furlough scheme allowed employees to work for their employer for some of their usual hours but not all of them. This could be done if the employer had some work for the employee but not enough for them to undertake their usual hours or to allow employees to combine their work with childcare responsibilities, particularly in January and February 2021, when schools were closed.

Under this scheme, employees were paid as normal for the hours they worked, but in addition, the usual hours of work they did not work were covered by the furlough scheme (i.e., the government covered 80 percent of the pay for the unworked hours). As shown in Figure 1, when first introduced in July 2020, 1.5 million jobs were on flexible furlough (25 percent of the

Figure 2. Proportion of Employees Furloughed by June 30, 2020, and on October 31, 2020, by Sex, Age, and Industry

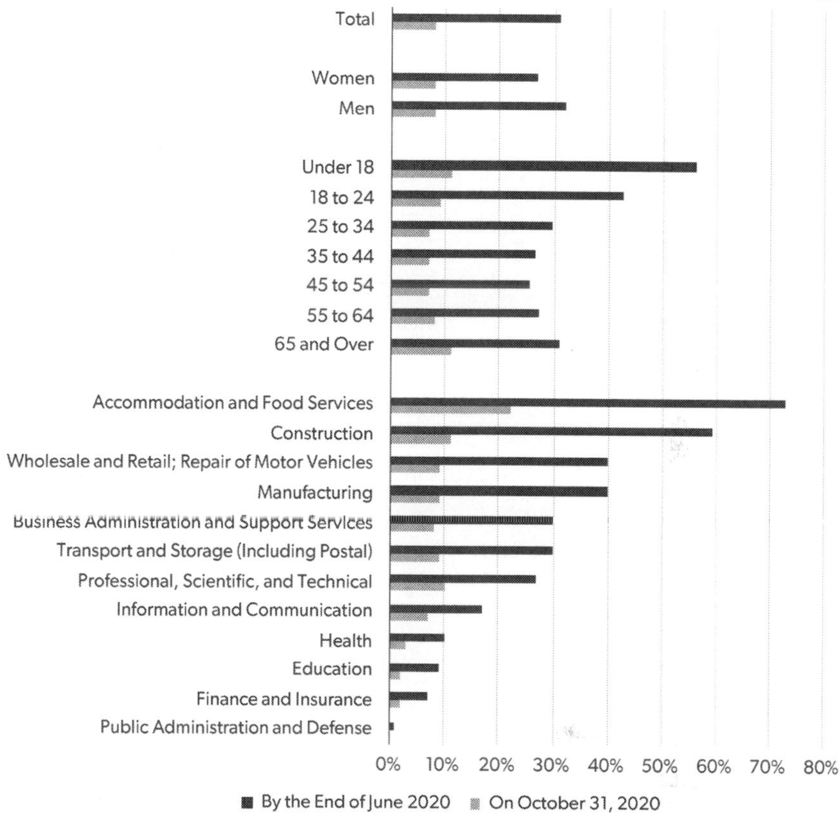

Note: October data include flexible furlough (which was not available in spring 2020).
Source: Authors' calculations using Her Majesty's Revenue and Customs, "Coronavirus Job Retention Scheme Statistics: August 2020," August 21, 2020, https://www.gov.uk/government/statistics/coronavirus-job-retention-scheme-statistics-august-2020; and Her Majesty's Revenue and Customs, "Coronavirus Job Retention Scheme Statistics: December 2020," July 29, 2021, https://www.gov.uk/government/statistics/coronavirus-job-retention-scheme-statistics-december-2020.

six million). As public health restrictions have eased, the *fraction* of all furloughed people that are flexibly furloughed has risen. At the end of September 2021, 500,000 people were on flexible furlough (44 percent of the total).

Employer Contributions. Initially, there was no direct cost (other than the administrative cost) of keeping an employee fully furloughed. On May

12, 2020, it was announced that from August 2020, employers would have to pay the employer's National Insurance contributions (NIC) on employees' pay and the employer pension contributions. As shown in Table 2, this increased the cost of keeping an employee furloughed, for example, up to £110 per month for a full-time minimum wage worker, £231 per month for someone on pre-pandemic median pay, and £412 per month for someone at the 75th percentile of pre-pandemic pay.

In the government's budget in March 2021, alongside the extension to September 2021, the chancellor announced that the scheme would be wound down in part by increasing the minimum employer contributions for hours not worked (on top of pension and NIC costs). In July 2021, employers had to pay 10 percent of salary (so the government would cover 70 percent), and in August and September 2021, employers had to cover 20 percent of salary (with the government covering 60 percent). This meant the monthly cost of fully furloughing an employee on median pay rose to £439 in July and £646 in August and September.

In addition to the government increasing employer contributions and ending the scheme in September 2021, firms reopening for business as restrictions were lifted meant that the scheme naturally wound down in part, as employers could "un-furlough" and request their employees return to work. This preserved link between employees and employers has undoubtedly helped many firms and employees return to normal working more quickly than otherwise.

Indeed, between the end of March 2021 (just after the announcement about the final extension of the scheme) and the end of August 2021, 1.6 million workers left the furlough scheme. Most of those were brought back to work, as from April to August there were around only 170,000 redundancies. Although 1.1 million workers were still on the furlough scheme as it ended, surveys of employers carried out by the Office for National Statistics at the time suggested that 71 percent of those still furloughed in September 2021 returned to work at or above usual hours in October and only 3 percent of them had been made permanently redundant.[4]

Job Support Scheme. The Job Support Scheme was announced in September 2020 and was intended to replace the furlough scheme between November 2020 and April 2021. Employees would receive support through

Table 2. Direct Employer Cost of Keeping an Employee on Furlough, March 2020–September 2021

	Monthly Cost of a Fully Furloughed Employee on Different Levels of Pay		
	£16,200 (35 Hours per Week on Minimum Wage)	£24,900 (Median)	£37,800 (75th Percentile)
March–July 2020	£0	£0	£0
August 2020–June 2021	£110	£231	£412
July 2021	£245	£439	£727
August–September 2021	£380	£646	£1,042

Note: Calculations are based on the 2021–22 tax and automatic enrollment system. We assumed the minimum employer pension contributions of 3 percent of qualifying pay. Median and 75th percentile earnings are based on 2019 Annual Survey of Hours and Earnings annual pay. Minimum wage is that for people over 25 years old, since April 2021.

Source: Authors' calculations using UK Office for National Statistics, "All Data Related to Employee Earnings in the UK: 2019," https://www.ons.gov.uk/employmentandlabourmarket/peopleinwork/earningsandworkinghours/bulletins/annualsurveyofhoursandearnings/2019/relateddata; and Pensions Regulator, "Earnings Thresholds," https://www.thepensionsregulator.gov.uk/en/employers/new-employers/im-an-employer-who-has-to-provide-a-pension/declare-your-compliance/ongoing-duties-for-employers-/earnings-thresholds. See Her Majesty's Revenue and Customs, "Rates and Thresholds for Employers 2021 to 2022," September 17, 2021, https://www.gov.uk/guidance/rates-and-thresholds-for-employers-2021-to-2022.

the Job Support Scheme only if they were working at least one-third of their usual hours. Employees would be paid as normal for the hours they worked. For those hours not worked (up to two-thirds of normal hours), the employer would pay half, and the government would pay the other half (up to a cap).

Despite the rebrand, this would essentially have ended the full furlough scheme but kept a revised version of the flexible furlough scheme—one that provided similar levels of income protection to employees[5] but that had a higher employer cost than the flexible furlough scheme. The proposed scheme was expanded and made more generous to employers even before it was introduced, but, in the face of a second and then third lockdown, it was never in fact introduced. The initial furlough scheme, which was supposed to wind down as lockdowns eased, was ultimately extended to September 2021.

Number and Timing of Extensions. The extensions of the furlough scheme at some points helped create certainty for businesses and at other points created uncertainty. In mid-May 2020, seven weeks before it was due to expire, the scheme was extended to the end of October. Amazingly, the furlough scheme was extended again on October 31, only a day before it was due to be replaced by the Job Support Scheme. There were also further extensions in November and December 2020 (to the ends of March and April, respectively) and a final extension in early March to the end of September 2021. The fact that the successful vaccination program has limited deaths and hospitalizations despite significant numbers of infections from the delta variant (particularly among the younger population) during the summer and autumn of 2021 means that the chancellor has been able to stick to his final extension.

Some people are likely to have been made redundant in the expectation of the scheme ending in November 2020 (the proposed end date for more than five months, abandoned only at the last minute). That said, this was not widespread enough to materially affect unemployment, which was at 5.0 percent, 5.1 percent, and 5.2 percent in September, October, and November 2020, respectively. The last-minute nature of the policy change led to considerable criticism at the time, and it looks as though HM Treasury in particular learned from this experience, providing considerably more long-term certainty and consistency later in the pandemic.

Other Policies Designed to Support Businesses and Workers

While the furlough scheme is the largest and most well-known of the policies designed to preserve worker-firm links in the UK during the pandemic, it is not the only scheme. In this section, we briefly touch on other important policies.

Self-Employment Income Support Scheme. Self-employed workers were not eligible for the furlough scheme. Instead, on March 26, 2020, the chancellor announced the Self-Employment Income Support Scheme, which provided support to self-employed workers who lost income due to the pandemic. It provided grants worth 80 percent of pre-pandemic profits for eligible workers, up to a cap of £7,500 per quarter. Applications had to be made every quarter. The scheme was extended to the end of September 2021.

According to the House of Commons Library, the cost of the first four (out of five) quarterly payments was around £25 billion, supporting 2.8 million people.[6] As set out by Jonathan Cribb, Isaac Delestre, and Paul Johnson, the scheme was generous to those who could claim it, particularly in the early stages, when take-up was estimated to be over three-quarters of all potentially eligible self-employed workers.[7] Any loss of income could trigger payment of the full amount, and little or no evidence of loss was required.

However, large numbers of self-employed people were ineligible: 1.3 million self-employed did not qualify because less than half of their pre-pandemic income came from self-employment. Others did not qualify because they had pre-pandemic self-employment income of more than £50,000 or because they were newly self-employed and did not have a tax record of self-employment income from the previous year.

The motivation for the scheme was largely to provide income protection to the self-employed that mirrored the furlough scheme. Largely for administrative reasons, it was less well targeted, overcompensating many and under-compensating some.

Loans and Grants to Businesses. In addition to the direct support to employers to cover labor costs of furloughed workers, government-backed loans to businesses were introduced, and grants were made available. The idea was not to allow temporary restrictions on trading to cause otherwise profitable firms to close, especially as massively reduced incomes would cause severe cash flow problems. By keeping businesses trading, the government also aimed (among other things) to preserve firm-worker links.

There were two main sets of loan schemes. Bounce Back Loans were aimed at small businesses. They were 100 percent backed by the government up to £50,000, with no interest for up to 18 months. The scheme ran to March 31, 2021. There were also Coronavirus Business Interruption Loans, which were 80 percent backed by the government for much larger amounts (up to £50 million for the largest businesses). They were interest-free for 12 months, and the scheme ended on March 31.

Together, these schemes disbursed £79 billion, 60 percent of which was through the Bounce Back Loans.[8] There have been particular concerns about fraud on the Bounce Back Loan scheme due to the 100 percent government guarantee, with a potential government cost of the scheme of £19 billion—as estimated by the government's Office for Budget Responsibility—due to defaults on the loans.[9]

In addition to the loans, the government has provided over £22 billion of support for businesses through grants and waivers for taxes on businesses' properties, which were targeted at the retail, hospitality, and leisure sectors. On average, these totaled £22,000 per eligible business.[10]

Other Policies. In addition to these schemes, a Job Retention Bonus was announced in July 2020. The plan was to pay employers £1,000 per employee who had previously been furloughed but who remained continuously employed between the (planned) end of the furlough scheme in October 2020 and January 2021. It was never implemented, as the furlough scheme was extended.

Finally, a range of policies increased the generosity of the existing UK means-tested benefit system for working-age people, called Universal Credit (UC). UC is provided to low-income families whether they are in or out of work (though the means test means entitlements are generally higher for out-of-work families). There was an increase of £20 per week in the basic amount of UC; there were increases in benefits for self-employed people with very low earnings (due to the suspension of a feature known as the Minimum Income Floor) and increases to the payments made to low-income renters of private-sector accommodation.

These did not act to support links between firms and workers but instead sought to provide increased financial support for poorer households. Notably, given the way UC is structured, these changes increased benefit entitlement for low-income families that are both in and out of work. The £20-a-week increase was withdrawn at the end of September 2021.

Figure 3. Real GDP in the UK and Total Employment 2007–21, Indexed to 100 in 2019

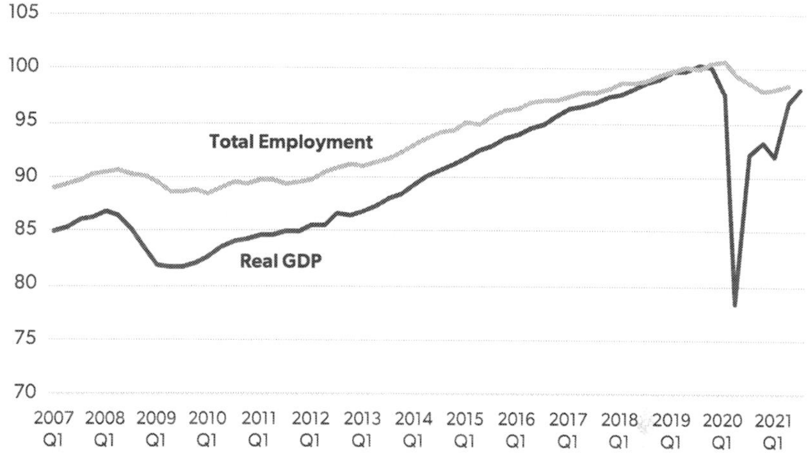

Source: UK Office for National Statistics, Gross Domestic Product Index: CVM: Seasonally Adjusted, https://www.ons.gov.uk/economy/grossdomesticproductgdp/timeseries/ybez/qna; and UK Office for National Statistics, Number of People in Employment (Aged 16 and over, Seasonally Adjusted), https://www.ons.gov.uk/employmentandlabourmarket/peopleinwork/employmentandemployeetypes/timeseries/mgrz/lms.

Effects of Government Support on the Labor Market During the Pandemic

Figure 1 shows that during the initial lockdown in May 2020, 8.9 million (30 percent) employees were furloughed. It is hard to know how many of these employees would have lost their jobs without the furlough scheme, but a large number could have reasonably done so.

As Figures 3 and 4 show, the rate of job loss was low given what happened to national income. Figure 3 shows that real GDP fell by 22 percent between the end of 2019 and quarter two of 2020 (during the first lockdown), much more than the Great Recession's 7 percent peak-to-trough fall in GDP. GDP partially recovered before falling again during the winter of 2020–21 and then making a recovery as the economy reopened in the spring. By quarter three of 2021, estimates suggested that GDP was 1.8 percent below its 2019 level. In comparison, Figure 3 shows that there was

Figure 4. UK Employment and Unemployment Rates, 2007–21

Note: Employment and unemployment rates are of those age 16 and over. Months refer to three-month averages starting that month.
Source: UK Office for National Statistics, A01: Summary of Labour Market Statistics, December 14, 2021, https://www.ons.gov.uk/employmentandlabourmarket/peopleinwork/employmentandemployeetypes/datasets/summaryoflabourmarketstatistics.

comparatively little change in total employment (which includes those who are furloughed as employed).

Figure 4 shows the changes in UK employment and unemployment rates in more detail. The employment rate of those age 16 and over fell by 1.6 percentage points, from 61.7 percent in January–March 2020 to 60.1 percent in January–March 2021. In January–March 2021, it started to recover, reaching 60.5 percent by June–August 2021. This compares to a 2.5 percentage point fall in the employment rate between 2008 and 2011. The rise in unemployment has been even more muted, rising from 4.0 percent in early 2020 to 5.2 percent in late 2020 and falling back to 4.5 percent in summer 2021.

Even with the end of the furlough scheme in September 2021, a survey of independent forecasters expects unemployment to rise slightly, on average, to just 5.0 percent by the end of 2021, compared to a peak of 8.5 percent in 2011.[11] The forecasts for unemployment at the end of 2021 have fallen steadily throughout 2021, with greater confidence from the private sector; public-sector bodies, such as the Bank of England; and the government's forecaster (i.e., the Office for Budget Responsibility) that the end of the furlough scheme will not lead to large rises in unemployment. As mentioned earlier, Office for National Statistics surveys suggest that few of those who remained on furlough in September 2021 lost their jobs.

The muted rise in unemployment is largely down to the relatively small fall in employment, though it is also due in part to a rise in economic inactivity, which rose from 35.9 percent of the 16-and-over population pre-pandemic to 36.7 percent in summer 2021. Switching to economic activity after job loss has been more common for older workers who have lost their jobs, and younger people have increasingly decided to stay in full-time education rather than enter the labor market.[12]

Jonathan Cribb et al. provide another way of seeing the effects of the furlough scheme, looking at the fraction of people who were not working any hours per week during the pandemic.[13] The fraction of the working-age population that had a job (as an employee or self-employed) but did not work any hours during the spring of 2020 rose by 9 percentage points, or 3.5 million people. The changes in the fraction of people who were inactive and unemployed were modest in comparison.

This rise in the fraction of people who report not working any hours per week, including in the first lockdown, in the Labour Force Survey (as shown in Figure 5), is considerably smaller than the number of people furloughed (as shown in Figure 1). Cribb et al. set out several reasons for this, including some measurement differences.[14] Most interestingly, though, some people may have continued to work at least a few hours a week even when they were furloughed. Indeed, a survey of furloughed people in the UK conducted by Abi Adams-Prassl et al. found that two-thirds of furloughed employees continued to work at least one hour per week during the first lockdown.[15]

Although the furlough scheme has helped the UK avoid large-scale rises in unemployment and employment, there was a spike in redundancies in summer and autumn 2020, as seen in Figure 6. This spike started in August 2020, at the point that employers started having to pay to keep employees furloughed (as shown in Table 2). However, the rise in redundancies was short-lived, dropping dramatically in the first quarter of 2021. Overall,

Figure 5. Share of People Not Working During the Pandemic

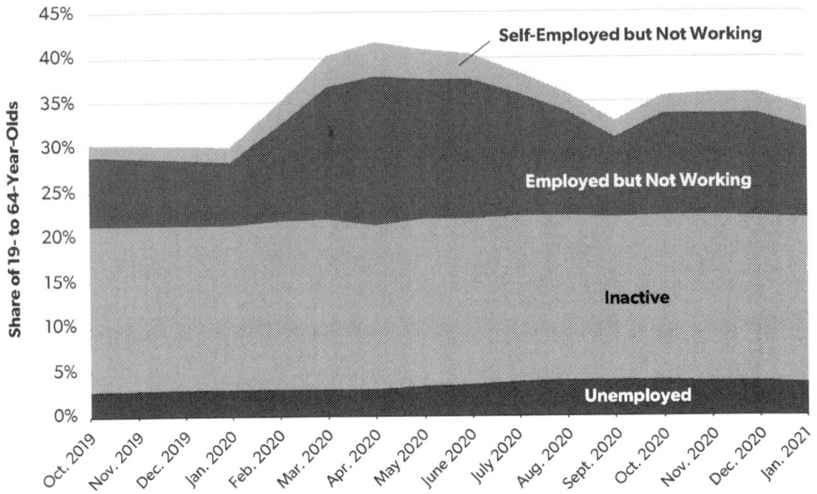

Note: This includes people age 19–64 and shows the forward-looking three-month moving average.
Source: Jonathan Cribb et al., *Living Standards, Poverty and Inequality in the UK: 2021: IFS Report R194*, Institute for Fiscal Studies, July 2021, Figure 3.1, https://ifs.org.uk/uploads/R194-Living-standards-poverty-and-inequality-in-the-UK-2021.pdf.

225,000 people per quarter have been made redundant during the pandemic, compared to 140,000 people per quarter in the year before the pandemic.

Interestingly, Jonathan Cribb and Adam Salisbury use longitudinal data to show that the reemployment rates of redundant workers six months after losing their job are higher than during the Great Recession (58 percent reemployed rather than 51 percent), although this is lower than the pre-pandemic period (66 percent).[16] Younger, more educated redundant workers (and those outside London) have seen reemployment rates hold up much better than have older workers, less educated workers, and those in London.

Although job losses could rise in the autumn as the furlough scheme ends, unemployment is not the most pressing labor market issue in the UK. The most pressing issue, as of late summer 2021, appears to be the large number of unfilled vacancies. Figure 7 shows the number of vacancies as measured by the Office for National Statistics Vacancy survey since 2019. In the third quarter of 2021, the number of vacancies stood at a record

Figure 6. Redundancy Rate per Thousand Employees, 2007–21

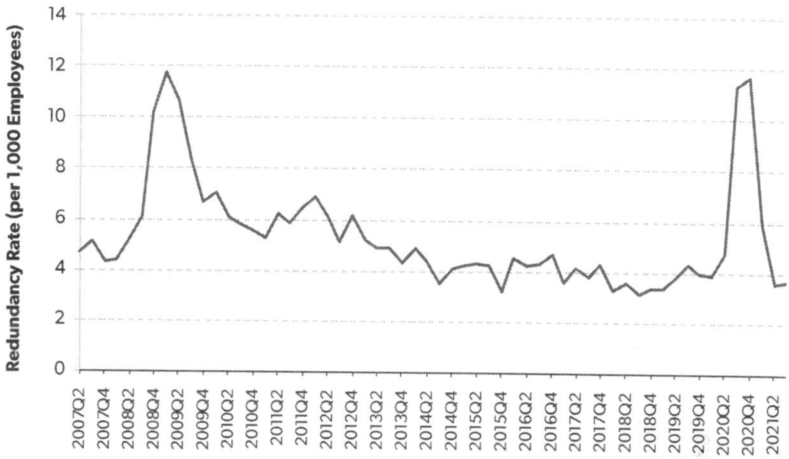

Source: Jonathan Cribb and Adam Salisbury, *Employment and the End of the Furlough Scheme: IFS Green Budget Chapter 9*, Institute for Fiscal Studies, October 2021, https://ifs.org.uk/uploads/9-Employment-and-the-end-of-the-furlough-scheme-.pdf. The latest data point (2021Q3), representing data from June to August 2021, is from Labour Force Survey data. See UK Office for National Statistics, LFS: ILO Redundancy Rate: UK: All: SA, December 14, 2021, https://www.ons.gov.uk/employmentandlabourmarket/peoplenotinwork/redundancies/timeseries/beir/lms.

Figure 7. Number of Vacancies in the UK, Thousands

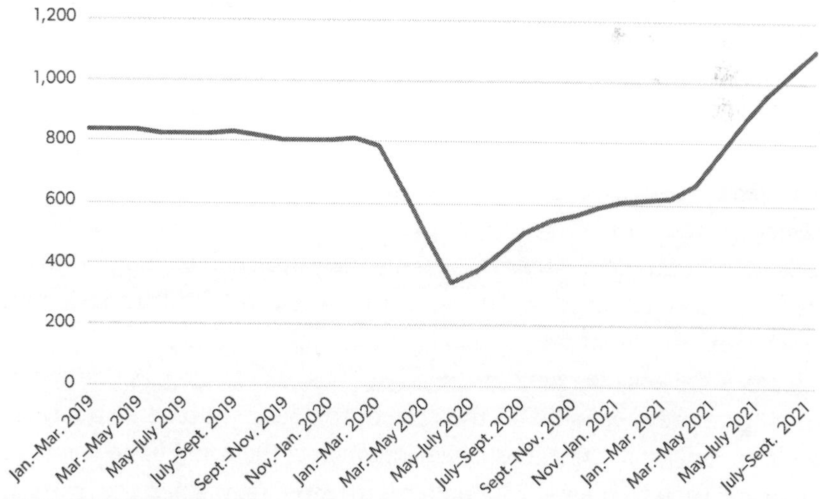

Source: UK Office for National Statistics, VACS01: Vacancies and Unemployment, December 14, 2021, https://www.ons.gov.uk/employmentandlabourmarket/peoplenotinwork/unemployment/datasets/vacanciesandunemploymentvacs01.

high of 1.1 million, 36 percent higher than the three months before the pandemic (December 2020–February 2021).[17] Online vacancy data show that the high levels of vacancies are particularly concentrated in transport (particularly heavy-good vehicles) and hospitality, among other industries.

Various evidence suggests that the ending of the furlough scheme in September is not materially reducing these vacancy rates. Records of online job vacancies did not fall between the end of September and mid-November 2021, and relatively few people seem to have been made redundant following the end of the furlough scheme. Other potential reasons for the high vacancy rates include significantly reduced numbers of workers from the European Union due to a combination of the pandemic and Brexit and certain occupations becoming much less attractive to work in (again, potentially due to the pandemic).

Discussion and Conclusion

Looking back on the support the British government provided to the labor market—and on the furlough scheme as a whole—several things stand out.

First, the scheme overall can be judged as a success in terms of preserving the link between workers and firms. While there have been some redundancies, there have not been large increases in unemployment or falls in employment, particularly considering how large the fall in GDP was in spring 2020. In summer 2021, the number of unfilled vacancies was high and could have been ameliorated in part by an earlier ending to the furlough scheme. But it is not clear that this issue (rather than, for example, reduced numbers of workers from the EU) is the *key* driver of the higher levels of vacancies. In addition, it is unlikely that the furlough scheme could have been removed before the end of most public health restrictions in England (on July 19, 2021).

Second, the key judgment at the start of the pandemic was that it was better (or more acceptable to the public) for the government to pay for people to remain in their jobs rather than allow them to be made unemployed and then to support unemployed workers with (a potentially more generous) welfare system. The benefit of this has been to maintain the link between workers and firms. However, the scheme has existed for far longer than was originally planned—19 months. This length of time makes it hard to assess the value of maintaining these employer-employee matches. It is much more likely to be worth maintaining worker-firm matches when people are unable to work for their employers for a couple of months.

Given that during the last quarter of 2021 there was not any indication of rises in unemployment, and there is therefore likely to be fairly little labor market scarring related to unemployment, this would appear to vindicate the policy. The government's forecaster—the Office for Budget Responsibility—judged that in October 2021, the potential output of the economy has likely been reduced by 2 percentage points due to the pandemic. This is lower than was considered in March 2021, and only a small fraction of this (0.4 percentage points) is due to higher unemployment or lower labor force participation. (The rest is due to capital shallowing, lower total factor productivity, and lower population resulting from emigration.) That said, the cost was extremely high—over 3 percent of GDP from the furlough scheme and well over 5 percent of national income, if all support schemes are included.[18]

Finally, furlough provided a high level of the earnings replacement compared to that provided by the UK benefit system, which provides little insurance—especially to higher earners or those living in middle-to-high-income families when they experience job loss. Instead, it focuses benefit spending on families (particularly those with children) with relatively low incomes. Unlike the furlough scheme, no account is taken of previous earnings. Unemployed workers who have significant savings or a partner with a high salary are only eligible for a Jobseekers' Allowance worth around £325 per month for six months, compared to the maximum of £2,500 per month under the furlough scheme.[19]

Of course, the counterpart to the low level of insurance provided for many redundant workers is that they generally have strong work incentives to find a new job. For those who lose their jobs when the furlough scheme ends, the (much lower) amount of government support they receive could be a significant shock. The experience of 2020 and 2021 also raises the question of whether a UK government will introduce, or reintroduce, significant elements of contributory benefits (rather than means-tested benefits) that have slowly been removed from the welfare system since World War II.[20]

Perhaps the most pressing issue, though, is the treatment of the self-employed by the welfare state. Over 18 months, it proved impossible to design a system of support for the self-employed that was anywhere near as well targeted as that for employees—leaving many with far too much compensation and many with far too little.

Notes

1. UK Office for National Statistics, "Coronavirus (COVID-19) Latest Insights: Work," November 11, 2021, https://www.ons.gov.uk/peoplepopulationandcommunity/healthandsocialcare/conditionsanddiseases/articles/coronavirusCOVID19latestinsights/work.

2. UK Prime Minister's Office, "Prime Minister's Statement on Coronavirus (COVID-19): 16 March 2020," March 16, 2020, https://www.gov.uk/government/speeches/pm-statement-on-coronavirus-16-march-2020; and UK Prime Minister's Office, "Prime Minister's Statement on Coronavirus (COVID-19): 23 March 2020," March 23, 2020, https://www.gov.uk/government/speeches/pm-address-to-the-nation-on-coronavirus-23-march-2020.

3. Her Majesty's Revenue and Customs, "Coronavirus Job Retention Scheme Statistics: 29 July 2021," December 16, 2021, https://www.gov.uk/government/statistics/coronavirus-job-retention-scheme-statistics-16-december-2021/coronavirus-job-retention-scheme-statistics-16-december-2021.

4. UK Office for National Statistics, "Coronavirus (COVID-19) Latest Insights."

5. As shown by Torsten Bell et al., "The Winter (Economy Plan) Is Coming," Resolution Foundation, September 25, 2020, https://www.resolutionfoundation.org/publications/the-winter-economy-plan-is-coming.

6. Antony Seely, *Coronavirus: Self Employment Income Support Scheme: Briefing Number 8879*, UK House of Commons Library, November 1, 2021, https://researchbriefings.files.parliament.uk/documents/CBP-8879/CBP-8879.pdf.

7. Jonathan Cribb, Isaac Delestre, and Paul Johnson, "Who Is Excluded from the Government's Self Employment Income Support Scheme and What Could the Government Do About It?," Institute for Fiscal Studies, January 27, 2021, https://ifs.org.uk/publications/15276; and UK National Audit Office, *Implementing Employment Support Schemes in Response to the COVID-19 Pandemic*, October 23, 2020, https://www.nao.org.uk/report/implementing-employment-support-schemes-in-response-to-the-COVID-19-pandemic.

8. Steve Browning, *Coronavirus: Business Loans Schemes: Briefing Number 8906*, UK House of Commons Library, November 4, 2021, https://researchbriefings.files.parliament.uk/documents/CBP-8906/CBP-8906.pdf.

9. UK Office for Budget Responsibility, *Economic and Fiscal Outlook—November 2020*, November 2020, https://obr.uk/efo/economic-and-fiscal-outlook-november-2020.

10. Kate Ogden and David Phillips, *COVID-19 Support Through the Business Rates System: How Does the Pattern of Support Vary Across England?*, Institute for Fiscal Studies, June 2020, https://ifs.org.uk/uploads/BN293-COVID-19-support-through-the-business-rates-system.pdf.

11. Her Majesty's Treasury, *Forecasts for the UK Economy: A Comparison of Independent Forecasts*, October 2021, https://www.gov.uk/government/statistics/forecasts-for-the-uk-economy-october-2021.

12. Jonathan Cribb and Adam Salisbury, *Employment and the End of the Furlough Scheme: IFS Green Budget Chapter 9*, Institute for Fiscal Studies, October 2021, https://ifs.org.uk/uploads/9-Employment-and-the-end-of-the-furlough-scheme-.pdf.

13. Jonathan Cribb et al., *Living Standards, Poverty and Inequality in the UK: 2021*, Institute for Fiscal Studies, July 2021, https://ifs.org.uk/uploads/R194-Living-standards-poverty-and-inequality-in-the-UK-2021.pdf.

14. Cribb et al., *Living Standards, Poverty and Inequality in the UK.*

15. Abi Adams-Prassl et al., "Furloughing," *Fiscal Studies* 41, no. 3 (September 2020): 591–622, https://doi.org/10.1111/1475-5890.12242.

16. Cribb and Salisbury, *Employment and the End of the Furlough Scheme.*

17. UK Office for National Statistics, VACS01: Vacancies and Unemployment, December 14, 2021, https://www.ons.gov.uk/employmentandlabourmarket/peoplenotinwork/unemployment/datasets/vacanciesandunemploymentvacs01.

18. UK Office for Budget Responsibility, *Economic and Fiscal Outlook*, October 2021, https://obr.uk/efo/economic-and-fiscal-outlook-october-2021.

19. Jonathan Cribb and Tom Waters, "A Shock to Come at the End of Furlough?," Institute for Fiscal Studies, June 30, 2021, https://ifs.org.uk/publications/15501.

20. Andrew Hood and Paul Johnson, "70th Anniversary of the Beveridge Report: Where Now for Welfare?," Institute for Fiscal Studies, December 3, 2012, https://election2017.ifs.org.uk/publications/6475.

10

How Was the US Government Able to Borrow So Much During the COVID-19 Pandemic?

RICARDO REIS

Between the start and end of 2020, the United States federal government increased its indebtedness by a staggering $4.5 trillion. In 2021, a further $1.9 trillion was added to that number. This led gross government debt to peak at 135 percent of US gross domestic product (GDP) in the middle of 2020. Although inflation lowered the debt-to-GDP ratio to 123 percent by the end of 2021, these levels are still well above the indebtedness at the end of the Civil War or the World Wars.

How was this possible? How could the government borrow so much, especially when there are no plans to fix the hole in Social Security or deal with the ever-rising costs of health care? Where were the "bond vigilantes" that previous Democratic administrations complained about for putting the brakes on any spending plan? Why have the interest rates at which the government can borrow fallen rather than shot up during this period? Was the government simply lucky during this time, and is it actually about to face troubles in rolling over this debt, forcing a decade of austerity over Americans? Or is there no limit to how much the government can borrow, and has the 2020 experience proven that it is so?

This chapter provides some answers to these questions. It is divided into four parts. First, it presents the long-run trends over the past 20 years that have allowed the government to borrow more. While the 2020 increase in debt was sharp, the underlying features that allowed it to happen were visible during the previous two decades. Second, it examines what was special about the COVID-19 pandemic that made it easier for the government to borrow. The lockdown policies, together with the Federal Reserve's actions, played a central role. Third, it discusses why there is a limit to how much the government can borrow and what determines that limit. Finally, it asks what could lead that limit to tighten in the future and how policies could mitigate the risk of a debt crisis.

The 21st-Century Rise in Public Debt

From the Civil War until around 1960, the path of US government debt followed a clear pattern. Sometimes, the government would have exceptional expenses, with wars being their most extreme version. Those expenses were sudden and unexpected, but they lasted a short time and were paid for by borrowing. Then, for the decade (or more) that followed, the government would run primary surpluses, collecting more in tax revenues than it spent on purchases and transfers while rolling over the public debt. This allowed it to pay the debt gradually but steadily. Plotting public debt over time revealed sharp increases followed by steady declines. Over a few decades, the debt would remain approximately stable.[1]

The buyer of a government bond faces two risks. First, the state might choose to default on its commitment. Second, the value of the currency in which the payment will be made might fall.

The classic management of public debt, with large but short-lived deficits followed by persistent surpluses, ensured that default was unlikely. After all, the government committed to generate the surpluses that backed the debt, and it could easily point to the surpluses it ran before as proof of that commitment. In turn, the gold standard ensured that while inflation could be volatile, it was not persistent. A bondholder's payment would vary year to year, but the real value of payments to those holding debt for many years was fairly stable. The US government had little trouble borrowing, and the limits to public debt were ultimately determined by the limits to the primary surpluses the government could run.

Around the late 1960s, the nature of US government spending changed and, as a result, so did the profile of debt over time—and the risks for bondholders. The changes probably started with the Great Society programs of Lyndon B. Johnson, which increased public involvement in saving for retirement, alleviating poverty, and paying for health services. The government budget became increasingly dominated by steady expenses that could not be reverted quickly.

Figure 1. Public Debt as a Percentage of GDP

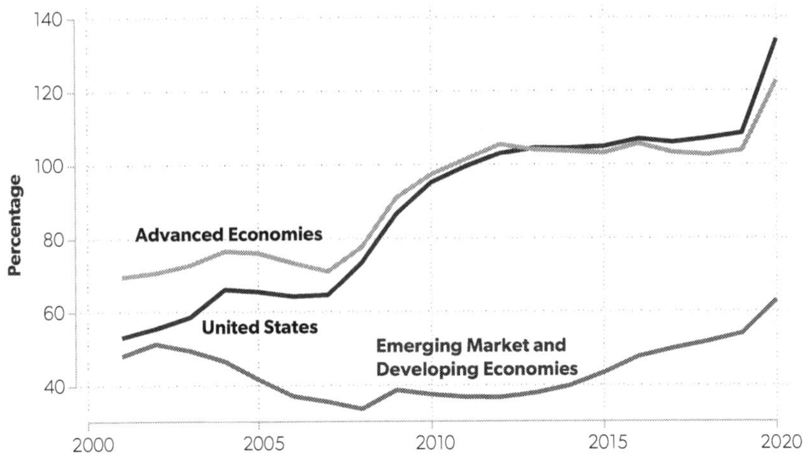

Note: The groups of advanced economies and emerging and developing economies include 40 and 156 economies, respectively.
Source: The data come from the International Monetary Fund's World Economic Outlook dataset for 2001–20. See International Monetary Fund, "World Economic and Financial Surveys: World Economic Outlook Database—WEO Groups and Aggregates Information," October 2021, https://www.imf.org/external/pubs/ft/weo/2021/02/weodata/groups.htm.

Whereas before, in the overall government budget, the major items were government purchases of goods and services often associated with defense and infrastructure, now government transfers to households had gradually become the dominant item. In the 1970s, the Great Inflation marked a break from the past as well. It persisted for many years, and when it was brought down in the 1980s, the increase in the price level was not reversed.

Finally, in the 1980s, a third change materialized. During Ronald Reagan's presidency, public deficits were high mostly due to tax costs, not military spending. Moreover, the increase in the resulting public debt led only to modest public surpluses almost a decade later, during the Clinton administration, and those did not last long.[2]

As a result, at the start of this century, the dynamics of debt were different than in the past. Deficits were steady and growing. Debt kept rising steadily. Public borrowing jumped after a recession, as it did in 2001, or after a financial crisis, as it did in 2007–09. But it did not decline steadily in

Figure 2. International Monetary Fund Forecasts for Public Debt as a Percentage of GDP

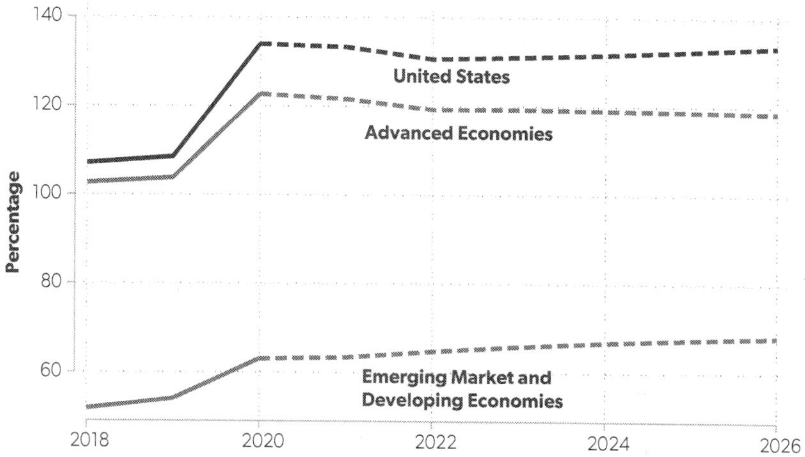

Source: The data come from the International Monetary Fund's World Economic Outlook dataset for 2001–20. See International Monetary Fund, "World Economic and Financial Surveys: World Economic Outlook Database—WEO Groups and Aggregates Information," October 2021, https://www.imf.org/external/pubs/ft/weo/2021/02/weodata/groups.htm.

the following years, as it had before. Forecasts of deficits for the next many decades became the norm. Failed attempts to reform Social Security, and the trend of increasing health care prices, made it unlikely that the government could cut spending on social transfers.

This phenomenon was not exclusive to the United States. In many other advanced economies, while with different timings, similar changes took place. Figure 1 shows the path of debt for the United States and the group of advanced economies. Public debt almost always grew, sometimes suddenly and sometimes steadily.

Gone are the days when the public debt would steadily fall between crises. Nowadays, in quiet times, debt is stable or slightly grows, and in crises it jumps. The jump of 2020 is noticeable in size, but it confirms the pattern of the past 20 years.

Figure 2 shows the International Monetary Fund's forecasts for the evolution of public debt for the same two groups plus the United States over the next five years. These are forecasts conditional on no new shocks—that is, no wars, pandemics, recessions, or other motives for debt to jump. They take the benign view that the next five years will be the calm after the COVID-19 storm. All forecasts are imperfect, and these depend so much on political developments that they are particularly inaccurate. However, they are useful because they show the pattern of debt expected according to the fiscal regime that has prevailed over the past two decades.

Strikingly, the forecasts are for public debt to barely fall, even though it is starting from record levels. If anything, these forecasts are more optimistic than those that come from the Congressional Budget Office and the fiscal councils in the different advanced economies. Almost no country has announced any measure that would lead their public debt to fall. On the contrary, both in the European Union and the United States, current discussions revolve around which new spending programs should be adopted. In short, the old classic debt pattern is gone.[3]

The Unusual Features of Public Borrowing During the Pandemic

There are three important economic justifications for why public debt should rise in recessions.[4] The first is sometimes called the principle of tax smoothing. Tax rates over income, consumption, and investment are distortionary in that they discourage those activities. In a recession, when economic activity is already reduced, the government should not be discouraging it further. Therefore, tax rates should be kept relatively constant. Yet, as the tax base to which those rates apply has shrunk (after all, that is the definition of a recession), tax revenues will fall. Likewise, transfers are distortionary. By keeping their formulas fixed, more people become eligible for unemployment benefits, food stamps, and other social programs, so the total amount spent increases during recessions. With lower tax revenues and higher transfer payments, the deficit will rise during a recession—and with it the public debt.

The second reason is often associated with John Maynard Keynes and is sometimes called countercyclical stabilization. In a recession, resources are often idle, since the productive capacity of the economy is above what the aggregate demand for goods and services may be. By running a deficit, the government is either raising the disposable income of people (via cutting their taxes or raising their transfers), which raises their demand for consumption goods, or increasing its own demand for goods and services through government purchases. This demand is met with production, using those idle resources and stimulating the economy. Government deficits can help reduce the amplitude of the recession and speed up the recovery.

A third reason is the provision of social insurance, often called the work of the automatic stabilizers. For many reasons, many people are not adequately insured against idiosyncratic losses of income. Recessions are times when the risk of losing one's job or having a pay cut are higher. Fearful of these risks, households will react to the start of a recession by raising their savings—to increase their nest egg and brace for the storm with some funds if these risks materialize. However, this contraction in spending amplifies the recession by lowering the demand for goods and services. If the government provides an effective safety net, then during a recession it can provide social assistance, and it can give people the liquid means to remain connected to the labor force. This may effectively ensure that the recession is short and not amplified by individuals' fears. These automatic stabilizers, such as unemployment insurance and poverty payments, imply deficits during recessions.

The contraction in economic activity in the first half of 2020 was the sharpest in US history. As the COVID-19 virus spread, people self-isolated, and governments imposed lockdowns. The result of a massive withdrawal of labor input from production was an unavoidable massive reduction in output. Locked at home, people spent less, produced less, and traded less with each other. With an unprecedentedly large recession, it is therefore no surprise that the deficit was especially large—and justifiably so.

All three of the conventional forces driving deficits were at work and enhanced by the features of the pandemic recession. First, since lockdowns were expected to be temporary, businesses closed their doors and households stayed at home while hoping to resume in full force after a few months. Investments were delayed and projects rescheduled, leading to a sharper contraction in the spring of 2022, as economic agents expected a strong recovery that fall. Raising taxes in the spring would have deepened the recession by encouraging firms and households to put off work and production even more.

Second, the lack of demand for goods and services left many businesses without sales, even when they could have continued producing. By providing transfers to those businesses or even buying some of their services, the government kept them afloat. This had the combined motivation of ensuring that some of their idle resources were used and that their productive capacity was preserved for when the economy would reopen.

Third, uncertainty at the start of the pandemic was large. The savings rate out of disposable income rose sharply. Providing a safety net was especially important to prevent even further declines in spending, and the need for support was especially acute for households in which income abruptly fell to zero.

At the same time, this does not explain why governments were able to borrow so much. It only explains why they would have wished to borrow this much. An alternative way to put the question is: How did the governments find so many investors willing to lend to them, and why did the interest rate that they were charged not rise during 2020?

Figure 3 places this challenge more starkly, by plotting across countries the increase in the public deficit due to the pandemic against the level of the public debt before the pandemic. One might expect that the larger a country's debt, the less it would be able to borrow after a large shock. In other words, if there is a limit to fiscal capacity, then those closer to that limit should be unable or unwilling to spend as much.

Yet, as the figure shows, the opposite was true in the data. The relation is weakly positive between the two variables. This pattern is present both across and within groups of countries at different stages of economic development.

To understand why this was possible, focus on the United States. A great share of the public spending went to transfers to households and firms. Following the trends discussed in the previous section, government spending is dominated by transfer payments not just overall but especially during recessions. The businesses and households that received these transfers had their doors shut to protect their health. Some received checks from the government and used those to replace their lost earnings and keep out of poverty. Many instead deposited this extra income in the bank. These banks in turn deposited these new deposits at the Federal Reserve, as

Figure 3. Response to COVID-19 Pandemic

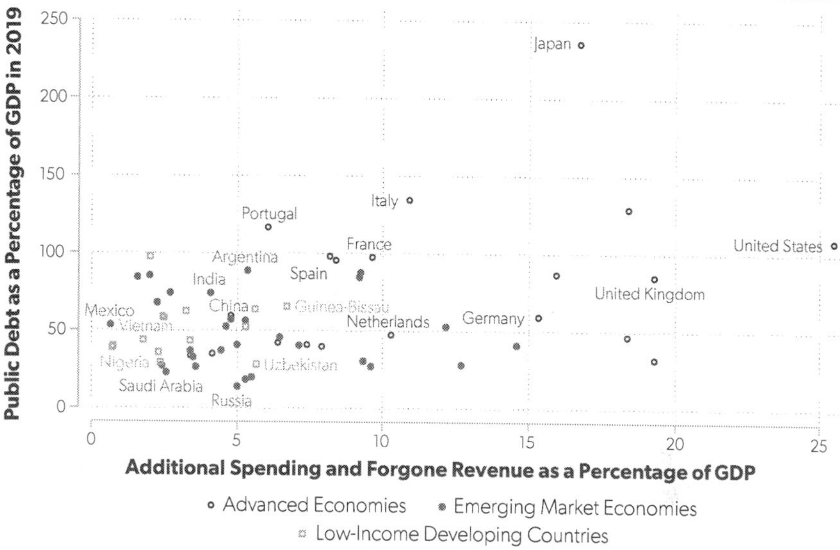

Source: For public debt, see International Monetary Fund, "World Economic and Financial Surveys: World Economic Outlook Database—WEO Groups and Aggregates Information," October 2021, https://www.imf.org/external/pubs/ft/weo/2021/02/weodata/groups.htm. For spending and forgone revenue, see International Monetary Fund, Fiscal Monitor Database of Country Fiscal Measures in Response to the COVID-19 Pandemic, October 2021, https://www.imf.org/en/Topics/imf-and-covid19/Fiscal-Policies-Database-in-Response-to-COVID-19.

there were few investment projects worthy of a loan. The Federal Reserve bought the government debt.[5]

Therefore, indirectly, the main buyer of all the newly issued government bonds was the Federal Reserve. But rather than printing currency, the central bank was borrowing from households and firms the extra savings that the government transfers had allowed them. The measure of the ease with which the US federal government could borrow is a measure of the poor targeting of its transfer payments. Because so many transfers went to firms and households that did not need them, but also that were locked at home and could not spend them, they were handed back to the government through the purchase of government bonds.

In an idealized, hypothetical world, imagine that before the year ended in 2020, the government were to levy an extraordinary tax on these same households and firms and use it to repay all the debt that resulted from the pandemic. From the perspective of the households, the tax would be paid with the saved transfer from a few months earlier. From the perspective of the government, the debt would have been back close to where it started.

Instead, by the end of 2020, the government debt was high, as were private savings. These started being spent gradually, fueling the quick recovery in 2021 but leaving behind the public debt. If the balances of savings proceed to normalize, then the pressure on the price of the outstanding government bonds will be felt. Whatever fiscal limits and pressure on interest rates there might be, they may not be felt until 2022 and beyond. But are there such limits, and if so, what are they?

Is There a Limit on Public Borrowing?

The laws of accounting dictate that the government could pay for public debt in two ways. The first would be to have surpluses by collecting more in tax revenues than the amount it spent on purchases and transfers. As described earlier, this was the dominant way for many decades.

The second is to pay a poor return on that debt to lenders. At one extreme example, if that return is –100 percent, then the lender gets nothing in return for holding the debt. This might more accurately be called a total default on debt. In this case, debt is exclusively paid by defaulting on the promises made to the bondholders.

At the other extreme, say that the debt's return to its investors is exactly the same as they would get by alternatively investing in the capital stock of the private economy. In that case, to roll over public debt over time, the government would be paying the bondholders the same as they get on their alternative investments. At some point in the future, the bondholders will require repayment, and at that point, only surpluses can provide that payment. Therefore, in this case, surpluses exclusively pay for the debt, whether in the present or future.

Between these two extremes, though, there exists another source of revenues for sustaining the debt. This has been called the fiscal revenue from public borrowing—or debt revenue for short. If bondholders receive a return from holding public debt below what they could get from private investment, then they are incurring an opportunity cost from lending to the government. That cost is a gain to the government. The simplest way for the government to realize that gain would be to borrow and invest in the private economy. But even if this is not realized directly in this way, the gains from borrowing at a low return are realized indirectly later because the size of the surpluses that will be needed in the future are now smaller.

The size of this debt revenue is given by the difference between the return on private investment (call it *m*, for market return, or marginal product of capital) and the return on public debt (call it *r*) times the stock of the public debt that is being rolled over into the future. The United States had the enviable position of having positive debt revenue for most of the past century. The condition $r < m$ has on average held over decades and has allowed the US to sustain a positive amount of public debt, even though on average it has run a small deficit.[6]

In the past 20 years, though, this gap has increased significantly. Figure 4 illustrates this by plotting *m*, *r*, and the growth rate of the economy, often called *g*. The return on private investments has been relatively constant, but the return from lending to the government has fallen significantly. Thus, the gap between *m* and *r* that drives the debt revenue term has risen substantially. In 2020, the gap was approximately 7 percent, which, given a public debt of approximately 130 percent of GDP, implies a debt revenue term of 9 percent of GDP. This was unusually large, but on average since the start of the century, the debt revenue has been about 4 percent of GDP per year, larger than any surplus that the United States had run in a long time.

The present value of these two revenue flows to the government—the primary surplus and the debt revenue—is then what sustains public debt. If the debt rose above this limit, then the government would be forced to default. The laws of accounting would still hold because a default would reduce the return to bondholders. In the case of default, the fall in return would not come despite no default, as happened for centuries in the United States, but directly because of the default. However, being able to have *r* less than *m*, so bondholders are voluntarily willing to be paid little absent default, is the key to having a sustainable public debt.

But what explains why *r* is less than *m* in the first place? Why would private investors be willing to lend to the government at a lower return than they could get by lending to firms or investing directly in the stock markets—or in their own projects? Even when the private sector produces financial assets that, on account of the counterparties involved and the collateral in place, seem to mimic almost exactly the payoffs from a bond issued by the Treasury, the Treasury bond pays a lower interest rate. Economists have come up with different reasons for why this might be so.[7]

First, government debt is especially safe relative to almost any alternative investment. The United States federal government has never defaulted on its debt obligations, unlike almost any private borrower. Especially after the financial crisis of 2007–09, the desire for safety in investment may have risen, explaining also why the return on government bonds fell, as investors were happy to hold this safe investment even if at a lower return.

Moreover, even if, on aggregate, the private sector as a whole could invest in the capital stock of the economy without any risk of default, the returns to this investment would be volatile depending on the state of productivity or on sales in a given year. The government instead sells bonds with returns that depend only on inflation, effectively shifting the risk that comes from fluctuations in tax revenues and spending to taxpayers in the future. (Of course, perhaps the safety of US public bonds is no longer assured if the US is reaching the limits of its debt capacity, but financial markets often miss large changes in regime.)

Second, government bonds are also especially liquid—easy to sell for currency if its holder needs to satisfy some spending emergency. Because the government is the largest individual borrower in the economy, the bonds that it issues end up being widely held and traded by different agents in the private sector. The government debt market is designed to enhance this liquidity, as the US Treasury only issues debt in a few maturities and only rarely introduces any new form of borrowing. Therefore, the bonds that are traded are homogenous, maximizing the scale of the individual market for each.

This liquidity is self-reinforcing: As people expect to be able to sell public bonds easily, they are more willing to hold them, and a thick market for public bonds emerges. After the global financial crisis, with the realization that some private bonds that seemed liquid could become hard to sell in

Figure 4. ***m*, *r*, and *g* for the US**

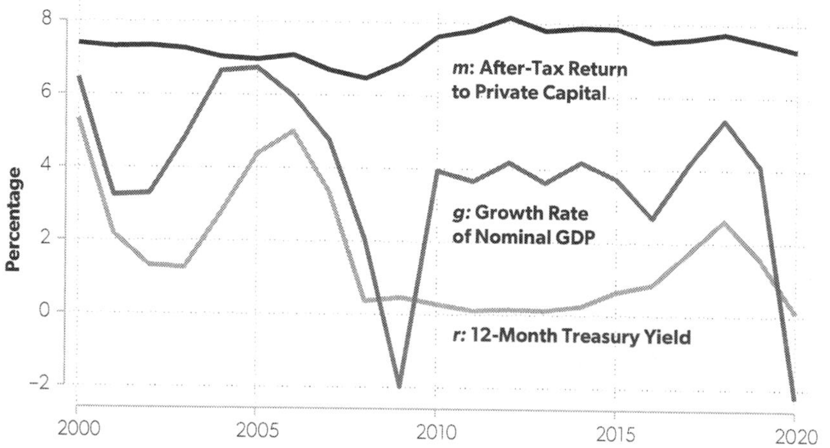

Note: Dividing capital income by the private capital stock and subtracting corporate taxes and two-thirds of proprietors' income account for their labor income.
Source: Data on nominal GDP for the US come from International Monetary Fund, World Economic Outlook Database, October 2021, https://www.imf.org/en/Publications/WEO/weo-database/2021/October. Data for the 12-month Treasury yield come from Federal Reserve Bank of St. Louis, Market Yield on U.S. Treasury Securities at 1-Year Constant Maturity, Quoted on an Investment Basis, https://fred.stlouisfed.org/series/DGS1. Data for *m* come from US Department of Commerce, Bureau of Economic Analysis, National Income and Product Accounts, Table 1.10, https://apps.bea.gov/iTable/iTable.cfm?reqid=19&step=3&isuri=1&select_all_years=0&nipa_table_list=51&series=a&first_year=1929&last_year=2021&scale=-9&categories=survey&thetable; and US Department of Commerce, Bureau of Economic Analysis, Fixed Assets Accounts Tables, Table 6.1, https://apps.bea.gov/iTable/iTable.cfm?reqid=10&step=3&isuri=1&table_list=41&series=q&first_year=1925&allyears=0&tabledisplay=&scale=-99&last_year=2020.

a crisis, the desire for liquidity services provided by public debt may have risen, explaining the data in Figure 4.

Third, government bonds are widely used as collateral in financial transactions. Many financial institutions hold government bonds as a by-product of buying and selling other assets. The government plays a key role in shaping this demand through its design and enforcement of financial regulations. These often require banks to hold a significant amount of government bonds against their short-term liabilities. The tightening of these regulations after the global financial crisis also broadly coincides with the fall in the required return on government bonds visible in Figure 4.

Fourth, the increase in global savings of the past two decades has benefited especially the demand for US government bonds. That increase in the supply of savings is the result of several structural changes in the world economy. The aging of the population in advanced economies has meant that a large cohort of middle-aged households is saving for retirement. These households put a part of their savings into US public bonds to diversify their investments and are attracted by the bonds' safety and liquidity. The fast growth of emerging market economies together with the slow development of their financial markets has led private agents in those economies to put their savings abroad, again benefiting the demand for US public bonds.

The increasing dominance of the US dollar in international transactions also creates a demand for US public bonds, as foreign firms want to hold some savings denominated in US dollars to make payments to their suppliers. Finally, the increase in inequality has come with an increase in savings for two separate reasons. First, richer households tend to save more. Second, with inequality comes higher individual uncertainty that triggers a desire to save more in a safe asset, such as US government bonds.

In summary, the US government's ability to borrow so much is tightly linked to the rising demand for the services that the resulting government bonds provide. Across the world, banks, firms, and households have sought the safety, liquidity, and convenience of US government bonds for decades—and increasingly so since the turn of the century. This has raised the limit on borrowing continuously. Moreover, as the large transfers to households and firms during 2020 were in part saved, these extra savings further increased the demand for public bonds.

Therefore, even as the government was raising the supply of public debt during the pandemic, the demand for it was rising as well. The US stayed well within the limit of fiscal capacity, able to borrow without an increase in interest rates.

These trends may have given the impression that there is no such limit. But that limit exists, and public policies that do not acknowledge it and what drives it can put the sustainability of the public debt into question. I turn to these policies next.

What Public Policies Could Precipitate, or Prevent, a Debt Crisis in the United States?

An important danger to the sustainability of public debt as of the start of 2022 is the risk of persistent inflation. Relative to their private counterparts, public bonds are mostly affected by the risk of inflation devaluing the dollars that they will later pay. Some of the gap between m and r, and the associated debt revenues the US government has benefited from, has been the result of the small-to-zero premium against inflation risk.

The past 20 years have also been one of the most successful periods in maintaining price stability, with inflation averaging close to 2 percent per year from the start of 2000 until the end of 2019. Investors in US bonds have not required extra compensation against the risk of inflation because the Federal Reserve has been so successful at its task.

Yet inflation rose in the United States throughout 2021, reaching 7 percent by the end of the year, fueled by unusual expansionary policy by the Federal Reserve. At the same time, surveys reveal a great deal of uncertainty about whether this inflation will persist into the next few years. Compounding this uncertainty, the temptation to have inflation rise as an alternative to raising or cutting spending is of course higher at a time when public debt is so high.

Even if the feared inflation may come only in a distant horizon, it quickly results in a devaluation of the US dollar relative to other currencies. This depreciation imposes a loss on foreign investors even before the expected inflation materializes. All combined, the fear of inflation reduces the specialness of government bonds because it makes them less safe. Even if inflation reduces the real value of the debt at first, it also persistently lowers the debt revenue term. Inflation therefore lowers the debt limit and could become a triggering factor behind a debt crisis in the United States.

To sustain public debt, an important policy step would be to uphold and respect the independence of the Federal Reserve from pressure by the government toward inflating away the debt. Further, if the Federal Reserve continues to show difficulties in keeping inflation under control, US policymakers may consider revising its mandate to put a greater weight on inflation control.[8]

A second policy concern is with the liquidity of US government bonds. In March 2020, it was unexpectedly difficult to sell them. The financial institutions that intermediate their trade were hampered by restrictive regulations adopted during the financial crisis, which constrained their actions at the height of the pandemic.

Moreover, while global crises have traditionally come with capital flows toward US government bonds in search of safe harbor, the pandemic recession was special, as countries needed to sell those government bonds to pay for the health emergency in their borders. As a result, for a few days, interest rates on US government bonds spiked, and for a few hours, the liquidity of the market was compromised as prospective sellers were unable to execute those sales.[9]

At the time, the Federal Reserve intervened swiftly, buying the government bonds for sale and lending to the financial intermediaries in that market. This aggressive intervention was crucial to reinforce the liquidity of US government bonds. Investors were assured that even if the private liquidity in this market were threatened, the Federal Reserve would come to the rescue and inject public liquidity in its place.

At the same time, as a result of these interventions, the Federal Reserve now owns more government bonds as a share of GDP than it has ever had in its history. As concerns for inflation may require it to reduce the size of this balance sheet, it will have to find private buyers for those bonds, testing the liquidity of the market.

Reforms to the way in which the market for government bonds works should be high on the priorities for financial reform to reduce the risk of a new liquidity freeze. Likewise, reinforcing the US government's commitment to honor its debts to foreigners is especially important at a time when restrictions to foreign trade are rising and there may be legitimate fears that capital controls are on the way.

Third, understanding that public debt is sustained today by debt revenues should lead to some fiscal caution. While these revenues have been large and growing for 20 years, because they depend on investors being attracted by the services of US public debt, they are also potentially unstable. As the experience of most countries can testify, perceptions of safety, liquidity, and convenience as collateral can diminish relatively quickly. With their disappearance, the debt revenue also disappears, as interest rates on government debt spike.

The way to ensure this does not trigger a debt crisis is to have a clear fiscal framework and the flexibility to turn the course of fiscal policy, generating primary surpluses on short notice. The ability to do so assures investors that fears about the solvency of the US government will be proven wrong. If debt revenues fall, the surplus will rise to ensure that debt stays within the fiscal capacity.

There has long been a perception that the US could fully execute such a reversal if needed, for instance, by introducing a value-added tax or temporarily cutting some defense spending. Whether that perception is still valid can reasonably be questioned. This matters because the perception that the United States could implement austerity contributes to it not ever having to do so.

Conclusion

The steady decline in the real return on government bonds over the past 20 years created new fiscal space for the government to borrow. Because the gap between the return on public bonds and the return on private capital investments widened, the US government started collecting a sizable debt revenue by effectively "selling" the special services that the bonds were providing to their holders. Whether those services were due to the safety, liquidity, or collateral ability of the government debt, they increased in value and so created fiscal capacity. The US government took advantage of this new capacity by having debt rise after the 2001 recession and the 2007–09 financial crisis and stabilize at new plateaus.

When the pandemic recession arrived, the US government ran large deficits. Because a large part of the extra spending was in transfers to households and firms that chose to save them, the demand for government bonds and their special services increased even more. The pandemic expanded fiscal capacity (even if temporarily) while using some of it through the higher public debt. As that expansion in capacity recedes, whether the current public debt will hit the fiscal capacity limit is an open and crucial question. To safeguard against the possibility of a debt crisis, the government would be wise to reinforce its commitment to price stability, fix the flaws in the public debt market that may endanger its liquidity, and develop the fiscal flexibility that allows it to use surpluses to back the debt in a crisis.

There were many merits—and some flaws—to the speedy and large government intervention during 2020. Fortunately, lack of fiscal capacity was not one of the problems the government had to deal with. But this should not be taken for granted. Ensuring the debt's sustainability is especially important over the next decade to slowly pay off what was left over from these extraordinary times.

Notes

1. For the global history of public debt over this period, see Barry Eichengreen et al., *In Defense of Public Debt* (Oxford, UK: Oxford University Press, 2021), https://global.oup.com/academic/product/in-defense-of-public-debt-9780197577899. For its history in the United States, see George J. Hall and Thomas J. Sargent, "Debt and Taxes in Eight U.S. Wars and Two Insurrections," in *The Handbook of Historical Economics*, ed. Alberto Bisin and Giovanni Federico (Cambridge, MA: Academic Press, 2021), 825–80.

2. To learn more about attempts to explain this change, see Pierre Yared, "Rising Government Debt: Causes and Solutions for a Decades-Old Trend," *Journal of Economic Perspectives* 33, no. 2 (Spring 2019): 115–40, https://www.aeaweb.org/articles?id=10.1257/jep.33.2.115.

3. See Olivier Blanchard, "Public Debt and Low Interest Rates," *American Economic Review* 109, no. 4 (April 2019): 1197–229, https://www.aeaweb.org/articles?id=10.1257/aer.109.4.1197; and Neil R. Mehrotra and Dmitriy Sergeyev, "Debt Sustainability in a Low Interest Rate World," *Journal of Monetary Economics* 124 (November 2021): S1–S18, https://www.sciencedirect.com/science/article/abs/pii/S0304393221000945.

4. For a survey, see S. Ali Abbas, Alex Pienkowski, and Kenneth Rogoff, *Sovereign Debt: A Guide for Economists and Practitioners* (Oxford, UK: Oxford University Press, 2019), https://oxford.universitypressscholarship.com/view/10.1093/oso/9780198850823.001.0001/oso-9780198850823.

5. See David Autor et al., "The $800 Billion Paycheck Protection Program: Where Did the Money Go and Why Did It Go There?" (working paper, National Bureau of Economic Research, Cambridge, MA, January 2022), https://www.nber.org/papers/w29669; Jonathan Parker et al., "Household Spending Responses to the Economic Impact Payments of 2020: Evidence from the Consumer Expenditure Survey" (working paper, National Bureau of Economic Research, Cambridge, MA, January 2022), https://www.nber.org/papers/w29648; and Raj Chetty et al., "The Economic Impacts of COVID-19: Evidence from a New Public Dataset Built Using Private Sector Data" (working paper,

National Bureau of Economic Research, Cambridge, MA, November 2020), https://www.nber.org/papers/w27431.

6. See Ricardo Reis, "The Constraint on Public Debt When r < g but g < m," Centre for Economic Policy Research, March 2021, https://cepr.org/active/publications/discussion_papers/dp.php?dpno=15950#.

7. For more on these reasons and a survey of the literature behind them, see Ricardo Reis, "The Fiscal Revenue from Public Borrowing," *Journal of Economic Perspectives,* forthcoming.

8. See Ricardo Reis, "Steady Prices, Sustainable Debt," *Finance and Development* (March 2022): 17–19, https://www.imf.org/en/Publications/fandd/issues/2022/03/Steady-prices-sustainable-debt-Reis.

9. See Annette Vissing-Jorgensen, "The Treasury Market in Spring 2020 and the Response of the Federal Reserve" (working paper, National Bureau of Economic Research, Cambridge, MA, August 2021), https://www.nber.org/papers/w29128.

About the Authors

Roel Beetsma is professor of macroeconomics and dean of the faculty of economics and business at the University of Amsterdam and visiting professor at the Copenhagen Business School. He is also a member of the European Fiscal Board, the Centre for Economic Policy Research, and CESifo (Munich). He sits on the supervisory boards of a pension fund and a wealth management company. He has been a consultant for the European Central Bank, the European Commission, and the International Monetary Fund. His scientific work focuses on budgetary policy and pension economics. His research has been published in many academic journals, such as the *American Economic Review*, the *Journal of Economic Literature*, and the *Economic Journal*.

Jeff Borland is Truby Williams Professor of Economics at the University of Melbourne. He received a PhD from Yale University and a bachelor's degree (honors in economics and history) from the University of Melbourne. His main research interests are the operation of the Australian labor market and program and policy design and evaluation.

Russell Cooper is professor of economics at the European University Institute. He received a PhD from the University of Pennsylvania in 1982 and has held positions at Yale University, the University of Iowa, Boston University, the University of Texas at Austin, and the Pennsylvania State University. Cooper is a National Bureau of Economic Research faculty research associate and a fellow of the Econometric Society.

Miles Corak is a professor of economics with the Department of Economics and the Stone Center on Socio-Economic Inequality at the Graduate Center of the City University of New York.

Jonathan Cribb is an associate director at the Institute for Fiscal Studies. His research focuses on the impacts of government policies on labor markets and retirement savings. He received a PhD in economics from University College London.

Raymond Gradus is professor of public economics and administration at the School of Business and Economics at the Vrije Universiteit Amsterdam. He is also a fellow of Tinbergen Institute and chairman of the Committees for Financial Supervision of the Dutch Antilles. He was affiliated with the Dutch Ministries of Finance and Economic Affairs, and he served as the director of finance at the Dutch Ministry of Social Affairs and Employment. His research interests are public administration, local government, environmental policy, and social security. He has published in many academic journals, such as *International Public Management Journal*, *Public Administration*, *Ecological Economics*, and *Oxford Economic Papers*.

Jennifer Hunt is a professor of economics at Rutgers University. Previously, she held positions at McGill University, the University of Montreal, and Yale University and in the US Departments of Labor and Treasury. She received a PhD from Harvard University and a bachelor's degree from the Massachusetts Institute of Technology.

Xavier Jaravel is associate professor of economics at the London School of Economics and Political Science. He holds a PhD from Harvard University. His research studies inclusive growth, innovation, international trade, and inequality; his work has also generated important insights in applied econometrics, including event studies and shift-share designs. His research has led to international recognition, including the 2021 Award for the best French economist under 40. In the RePEc/IDEAS ranking for top young economists, he is ranked 10th worldwide. In 2021–22, he was chief economist at the Inspection Générale des Finances at the French Finance Ministry.

Juan F. Jimeno is an adviser at the Bank of Spain, a professor at the University of Alcalá, and a research associate at CEMFI, the Center for Economic and Policy Research, and the Institute of Labor Economics. He holds a PhD in economics from the Massachusetts Institute of Technology.

Paul Johnson is director of the Institute for Fiscal Studies and a visiting professor in the department of economics at University College London. Previously he has worked at Her Majesty's Treasury, the Department for Education, and the Financial Services Authority. Between 2004 and 2007, he was deputy head of the UK's Government Economic Service.

Tom Krebs is a professor of economics at the University of Mannheim, the academic director at the Forum New Economy, and a member of the German Minimum Wage Commission. He has been a visiting professor at the German Ministry of Finance and an economic consultant to the International Monetary Fund, World Bank, and Federal Reserve Bank of Minneapolis.

Ricardo Reis is the A. W. Phillips Professor of Economics at the London School of Economics. He received the 2021 Jahnsson Award for best economist in Europe under the age of 45, was elected to the Econometric Society in 2019, and received the 2016 Bernacer Prize. He is an academic consultant to the Federal Reserve Bank of Richmond, the Riksbank, and the Bank of England. He received a PhD from Harvard University.

Ian M. Schmutte is an associate professor in the department of economics at the University of Georgia and a fellow of the Global Labor Organization and the Labor Dynamics Institute. He has worked with the US Census Bureau's Longitudinal Employer-Household Dynamics and Center for Enterprise Dissemination programs. His research in labor economics covers a wide set of topics, with a focus on how regulations and social institutions affect earnings and job mobility. Schmutte also studies data privacy, focusing on methods to protect respondent confidentiality while maintaining accuracy in official statistics.

Immo Schott is associate professor of economics at the University of Montreal. He received a PhD from the European University Institute.

Michael R. Strain is the director of Economic Policy Studies and Arthur F. Burns Scholar in Political Economy at the American Enterprise Institute. He is a research fellow with the Institute of Labor Economics in Bonn, a research affiliate with the Institute for Research on Poverty at the University of Wisconsin–Madison, and an elected member of the National Academy of Social Insurance.

Stan Veuger is a senior fellow in economic policy studies at the American Enterprise Institute. He is also the editor of AEI Economic Perspectives, as well as a fellow at the IE School of Global and Public Affairs and at Tilburg University.

The American Enterprise Institute for Public Policy Research

AEI is a nonpartisan, nonprofit research and educational organization. The work of our scholars and staff advances ideas rooted in our commitment to expanding individual liberty, increasing opportunity, and strengthening freedom.

The Institute engages in research; publishes books, papers, studies, and short-form commentary; and conducts seminars and conferences. AEI's research activities are carried out under four major departments: Domestic Policy Studies, Economic Policy Studies, Foreign and Defense Policy Studies, and Social, Cultural, and Constitutional Studies. The resident scholars and fellows listed in these pages are part of a network that also includes nonresident scholars at top universities.

The views expressed in AEI publications are those of the authors; AEI does not take institutional positions on any issues.

RESEARCH STAFF

SAMUEL J. ABRAMS
Nonresident Senior Fellow

BETH AKERS
Senior Fellow

J. JOEL ALICEA
Nonresident Fellow

JOSEPH ANTOS
Senior Fellow; Wilson H. Taylor Scholar in Health Care and Retirement Policy

LEON ARON
Senior Fellow

KIRSTEN AXELSEN
Nonresident Fellow

JOHN P. BAILEY
Nonresident Senior Fellow

CLAUDE BARFIELD
Senior Fellow

MICHAEL BARONE
Senior Fellow Emeritus

ROBERT J. BARRO
Nonresident Senior Fellow

MICHAEL BECKLEY
Nonresident Senior Fellow

ERIC J. BELASCO
Nonresident Senior Fellow

ANDREW G. BIGGS
Senior Fellow

MASON M. BISHOP
Nonresident Fellow

JASON BLESSING
Jeane Kirkpatrick Visiting Research Fellow

DAN BLUMENTHAL
Senior Fellow

KARLYN BOWMAN
Distinguished Senior Fellow Emeritus

HAL BRANDS
Senior Fellow

ELISABETH BRAW
Senior Fellow

ALEX BRILL
Senior Fellow

ARTHUR C. BROOKS
President Emeritus

RICHARD BURKHAUSER
Nonresident Senior Fellow

JAMES C. CAPRETTA
Senior Fellow; Milton Friedman Chair

TIMOTHY P. CARNEY
Senior Fellow

AMITABH CHANDRA
Nonresident Fellow

LYNNE V. CHENEY
Distinguished Senior Fellow

JAMES W. COLEMAN
Nonresident Senior Fellow

MATTHEW CONTINETTI
Senior Fellow; Patrick and Charlene Neal Chair in American Prosperity

ZACK COOPER
Senior Fellow

JAY COST
Gerald R. Ford Nonresident Senior Fellow

DANIEL A. COX
Senior Fellow

SADANAND DHUME
Senior Fellow

GISELLE DONNELLY
Senior Fellow

MICHAEL BRENDAN DOUGHERTY
Nonresident Fellow

ROSS DOUTHAT
Nonresident Fellow

COLIN DUECK
Nonresident Senior Fellow

MACKENZIE EAGLEN
Senior Fellow

NICHOLAS EBERSTADT
Henry Wendt Chair in Political Economy

MAX EDEN
Research Fellow

JEFFREY EISENACH
Nonresident Senior Fellow

EMILY ESTELLE
Research Fellow

ANDREW FERGUSON
Nonresident Fellow

JESÚS FERNÁNDEZ-VILLAVERDE
John H. Makin Visiting Scholar

JOHN G. FERRARI
Nonresident Senior Fellow

JOHN C. FORTIER
Senior Fellow

AARON FRIEDBERG
Nonresident Senior Fellow

JOSEPH B. FULLER
Nonresident Senior Fellow

SCOTT GANZ
Research Fellow

R. RICHARD GEDDES
Nonresident Senior Fellow

ROBERT P. GEORGE
Nonresident Senior Fellow

JOSEPH W. GLAUBER
Nonresident Senior Fellow

JONAH GOLDBERG
Senior Fellow; Asness Chair in Applied Liberty

BARRY K. GOODWIN
Nonresident Senior Fellow

SCOTT GOTTLIEB, MD
Senior Fellow

PHIL GRAMM
Nonresident Senior Fellow

WILLIAM C. GREENWALT
Nonresident Senior Fellow

SHEENA CHESTNUT GREITENS
Jeane Kirkpatrick Visiting Fellow

JIM HARPER
Nonresident Senior Fellow

WILLIAM HAUN
Nonresident Fellow

FREDERICK M. HESS
Senior Fellow; Director, Education Policy Studies

BRONWYN HOWELL
Nonresident Senior Fellow

R. GLENN HUBBARD
Nonresident Senior Fellow

HOWARD HUSOCK
Senior Fellow

BENEDIC N. IPPOLITO
Senior Fellow

MARK JAMISON
Nonresident Senior Fellow

FREDERICK W. KAGAN
Senior Fellow; Director, Critical Threats Project

STEVEN B. KAMIN
Senior Fellow

LEON R. KASS, MD
Senior Fellow Emeritus

JOSHUA T. KATZ
Senior Fellow

KLON KITCHEN
Senior Fellow

KEVIN R. KOSAR
Senior Fellow

ROBERT KULICK
Visiting Fellow

PAUL H. KUPIEC
Senior Fellow

DESMOND LACHMAN
Senior Fellow

DANIEL LYONS
Nonresident Senior Fellow

NAT MALKUS
Senior Fellow; Deputy Director, Education Policy Studies